Preventing Lethal Violence in New Orleans,

A Great American City

Preventing Lethal Violence in New Orleans,

A Great American City

Edited By
Lydia Voigt, Dee Wood Harper,
and William E. Thornton Jr.

University of Louisiana at Lafayette Press
2015

ISBN 13 (paper): 978-1-935754-69-5

http://ulpress.org
University of Louisiana at Lafayette Press
P.O. Box 40831
Lafayette, LA 70504-0831

Printed in the U.S.A. on acid-free paper.

Library of Congress Cataloging-in-Publication Data

Preventing lethal violence in New Orleans, a great American city /
edited by Lydia Voigt, Dee Wood Harper, and William E. Thornton.
    pages cm
  ISBN 978-1-935754-69-5 (alk. paper)
  1. Murder--Louisiana--New Orleans. 2. Violence--Louisiana--New
Orleans. I. Voigt, Lydia. II. Harper, Dee Wood. III. Thornton, William E.
  HV6534.N45P74 2015
  364.409763'35--dc23
                    2015017226

Cover images © Cheryl Gerber. Used by permission of the photographer.

Contents

Foreword

New Orleans is deeply etched in the minds of many Americans. Katrina is one reason, of course. The devastation that was unleashed and the horrific challenges that the city endured will not soon be forgotten. Indeed, ten years on the scars are still visible and the struggle to rebuild continues. But New Orleans resonates for many other reasons as well. Its music, history, food, culture, nightlife, and jazz, to name a few, are unique. Visiting this vibrant city almost feels like being in another country.

There is another aspect of New Orleans, however, that is quintessentially American. Typically bypassed by the tourists and often neglected in the media, violence remains one of the city's biggest challenges. For years, going back well before Katrina, New Orleans has suffered one of the highest homicide rates in the United States. Even as violence has declined nationally and in the city in recent years, New Orleans has stubbornly clung to its position in the upper echelon of American violence. In 2014 for example, New Orleans ranked in the top ten with a homicide rate nearly 42 per 100,000 residents.

Historically, cities with a violence problem have often looked the other way. As long as the violence was contained in certain areas and tourists or the economy were largely untouched, it was business as usual. Things are different now and for the better. New Orleans has acknowledged its challenges and has embarked on serious renewal and reform efforts at multiple levels of governance. A major part of this effort took place in the fall of 2012 at the conference "Preventing Lethal Violence in New Orleans," held on the campus of Loyola University New Orleans. A broad spectrum of participants came together, including scholars, politicians, nonprofit organizations, police leaders, and concerned citizens. The goal was to better understand the problem of violence and design effective solutions.

The book before you, *Preventing Lethal Violence in New Orleans*, presents the major fruits of that conference. As the editors Lydia Voigt, Dee Wood Harper, and William E. Thornton Jr. highlight in the preface, the book is historically grounded but also aimed to make life better, with special attention devoted to innovative research evidence on the most promising programs relevant to New Orleans. Several chapters provide the history of the city and its violence problem (including gun, domestic, and gang violence), along with underlying structural and cultural causes. Other chapters describe various intervention approaches including public health, community, and police endeavors. By shedding new light on both problems and solutions, the citizens of New Orleans and scholars of criminology are in the debt of the book's contributors.

Robert Sampson
Henry Ford II Professor of Social Sciences
Harvard University
Cambridge, MA
October 2015

Acknowledgments

First, we would like to express our appreciation to President Kevin Wm. Wildes, S.J., Ph.D., at Loyola University New Orleans for his vision of bringing national experts and practitioners to campus to engage in discussions and share best practices that may be applied in addressing violence in New Orleans, as well as for his encouragement throughout the project and support for the two-day conference, "Preventing Lethal Violence in New Orleans," held on campus in October 2012. We would also like to thank other members of the Office of the President, particularly Gail Howard, executive assistant to the president, for her help with all arrangements related to the event. In addition, we would like to offer a special word of thanks to Dr. Marc Manganaro, provost and vice president of Academic Affairs, for his introductory comments and the support of the Office of the Provost. Our thanks also go to members of the Office of Institutional Advancement, including Terry Fisher, former associate vice president for marketing, for her guidance and expertise in marketing all aspects of the conference.

We are, of course, especially grateful for the contributions of our guest speakers and invited participants. First, we thank our guest speakers on the opening day of the conference, including: Robert Sampson, Henry Ford II Professor of Social Sciences at Harvard University; David Kennedy, Director of the Center for Crime Prevention and Control and Professor at John Jay College of Criminal Justice; Karen DeSalvo, New Orleans Health Commissioner and C. Thorpe Ray Endowed Chair of Internal Medicine at Tulane University; Nikki Jones, associate professor of sociology, University of California, Santa Barbara; and Ronal W. Serpas, former superintendent of the New Orleans Police Department, and current professor of practice, Department of Criminology and Justice, Loyola University New Orleans.

Our invited participants and contributors, some of whom are featured in this volume, deserve special acknowledgment and a world of thanks. The participants and contributors include: Jeffery Adler, professor of history and criminology and Distinguished Teaching Scholar, University of Florida; Sara Bacon, behavioral scientist for the Centers for Disease Control, Washington, D.C.; Lin Huff-Corzine, professor of sociology, University of Central Florida; Jay Corzine, professor of sociology, University of Central Florida; Sean Goodison, senior research associate at Police Executive Research Forum, Washington, D.C.; David Hemenway, professor of health policy and director of the Harvard Injury Control Research Center, Harvard University; Peter Iadicola, professor and chair, Department of Sociology and Anthropology, Indiana University-Purdue University; Wendy C. Regoeczi, associate professor of criminology, Criminology Research Center, Department of Sociology, Cleveland State University; Rae Taylor, associate professor of sociology, Loyola University New Orleans; Marc Riedel, professor of sociology, Southeastern Louisiana University and emeritus professor at Southern Illinois University; John G. Boulahanis, associate professor, Department of Sociology and Criminal Justice, Southeastern Louisiana University; and John Penny, professor of sociology, Southern University of New Orleans.

Our guest participants presented overwhelming evidence of positive long-term and enduring effects of broad-based community development and neighborhood interventions, not only offering important solutions to violence, but also renewing hope.

Lydia Voigt, Joseph H. Fichter, S.J., Distinguished Professor of Social Sciences

Dee Wood Harper, emeritus professor of sociology, criminology, and justice

William E. Thornton Jr., professor of sociology, criminology, and justice

Loyola University New Orleans
2015

Introduction to Book

Lydia Voigt, Dee W. Harper, and
William E. Thornton Jr.

New Orleans has the dubious distinction of possessing one of the highest per capita murder rates in the United States, and from all indicators, gun violence and murder continues unabated in the city despite significant reductions in recent years, especially 2012 and 2013. For example, the murder rate for 2014 stands at 42 per 100,000 population. In addition, Louisiana has some of the harshest sentencing laws in the country, even compared to Texas, which fuels a high incarceration rate. In fact, Louisiana imprisons more of its people than any of its U.S. counterparts. Louisiana has an incarceration rate of 867 per 100,000 followed by Mississippi with a rate of 686. Moreover, the incarceration rate for the city's African American population is over 1,700 per 100,000. In New Orleans, "doing time" in prison has become a way of life in many neighborhoods and literally destroys families and entire communities. In many inner city families, almost all males in the family have served time and most residents have a friend or relative in prison. Many young males come to perceive future incarcerations as an accepted fate, and this trend has only increased in recent years, especially in the post-Katrina years.

In response to seemingly unprecedented violence in New Orleans, key city leaders as well as other public and private community groups and a virtual plethora of crime experts have come up with various violence prevention and control programs. Many of these efforts, all well intended, focus on the criminal justice system, especially the police and judiciary, while others address neighborhood and community efficacy as expressed by the growth of informal groups and advocacy organizations stressing any number of things, including faith-based programs, youth recreational programs, job and work force development, and the role that parents play in building strong families. Although the coordination of these efforts is by no means unified, one thing is clear: many citizens agree with Mayor Mitch Landrieu's statement that there is a "culture of death and violence in the city of New Orleans" and that in order to solve the situation, the "entire community needs to be engaged," not just the New Orleans Police Department. In Landrieu's State of the City Address on May 22, 2012, he recapped his administration's efforts at thwarting violence by building public trust in the NOPD, creating a team of federal law enforcement specialists to prosecute drug kingpins, making teenagers aware of the consequences of criminal behavior, improving job and housing opportunities for ex-offenders, and providing community conflict-resolution and trauma-counseling services, instituting preventive efforts related to gang-related homicide, and having every streetlight in the city working by year's end. Clearly, these efforts suggest that a broader-based solution as well as innovative thinking backed by research from other cities that have historically experienced violent crime and found solutions is necessary.

Under the auspices of the President's Office at Loyola University New Orleans, the Department of Criminal Justice sponsored a two-day conference in October 2012 on the problem of lethal violence in New Orleans with a special emphasis on research related to innovative practices and programs that may be brought to bear on the problem.

The president of Loyola, Reverend Kevin Wildes, S. J., who is keenly aware of the problem of crime in New Orleans especially through his service on the Civil Service Commission, which monitors the New Orleans Police Department, called upon the Criminal Justice Department faculty to organize and host a conference including roundtable discussions and presentations of invited papers on successful and proven strategies to prevent violence with special emphasis on addressing the culture of violence in urban environments, including considering issues and solutions related to social inequality and social justice, strengthening community infrastructure and efficacy, developing community and criminal justice partnerships, incorporating community restorative processes, increasing alternative sentencing, and expanding public health efforts at violence prevention.

This book, inspired by the conference on Preventing Lethal Violence in New Orleans held in October 2012, offers a sample of the presentations and roundtable discussions related to the historical and cultural uniqueness of New Orleans and its record of homicides over the years—with special attention given to innovative research evidence on the most promising programs that may be applied to New Orleans by addressing the problem of interpersonal lethal violence, its distribution across the city, epidemiological patterns and structural etiology, and ways to ameliorate it through community efforts.

In "New Orleans Homicide in Historical Perspective," Jeffrey Adler provides a context for the current homicide problem in New Orleans by offering a fascinating historical perspective suggesting that the city's modern murder crisis has deep roots extending back at least one hundred years. He reports, for example, that in 1925, New Orleans's homicide rate was double that of Chicago, three times that of Washington, D.C., six times that of New York City, more than a dozen times that of Boston, and nearly forty times that of Canada's largest cities. Adler notes, "In short, for over a century, New Orleanians, far more than their counterparts in other American cities and towns, have resolved interpersonal disputes with deadly violence."

In "New Orleans Neighborhood Patterns of Homicide and Key Structural and Cultural Linkages—1940 to 2013," Lydia Voigt, Dee W. Harper, and William E. Thornton provide an overview of homicide trends and patterns in New Orleans spanning seven decades. They show that while homicides in the city vary across time and space, some patterns in relation to structural and cultural linkages associated with demographic, ecological, and geographical distributions of homicides have remained relatively similar (i.e., zones with high murder rates have relatively long histories of high rates, even though populations have fluctuated with regard to number and composition). Some neighborhoods seem to be completely immune to lethal violence while others are saturated almost to the point of ceasing to exist or function in any meaningful way as neighborhoods. Short of retaliatory murder, informal means of social control do not seem to exist in these high-murder neighborhoods.

In "The Chain of Violence and the Lessons for New Orleans," Peter Iadicola examines the chain of violence (i.e., structural, institutional, and interpersonal violence) and its ramifications for the development of strategies to mitigate violence in New Orleans. While interpersonal violence such as retaliatory homicide is the type of violence most people think of, he argues that structural and institutional forms of violence, which are accomplished through policies and laws that are enforced informally and formally and that serve to reinforce the hierarchical order of society, affecting both the extension and denial of civil and basic human rights of individuals, must be addressed in order to realize long-term reductions in lethal violence. Iadicola notes that Hurricane Katrina exposed the scourge of structural and institutional forms of violence that had previously been occurring on a daily basis in New Orleans due to the deep rooted problems of inequality and concentrated poverty.

In "The Public Health Approach to Violence Prevention," David Hemenway compares the public health perspective/response to the criminal justice perspective/response on violence. He notes that while the criminal justice perspective treats violence as a threat to community order, the public health perspective views violence as a threat to community health. For instance, victims often appear to receive minimal attention by the criminal justice system (interest is mainly in their role as potential witnesses in the prosecution process); whereas the public health approach not only directs attention to victims through development of assistance programs, but also focuses on victims through efforts to organize them to act socially and politically to reduce violence levels within their communities. Moreover, while criminal justice responses to violence concentrate on apprehension and punishment of perpetrators of violence, public health responses primarily emphasize prevention and changing the environment that promotes violence. Hemenway provides many examples of the public health approach in action, with illustrations from Boston and the Harvard Youth Violence Prevention Center. He discusses how such an approach may be applied to the problem of gun violence in New Orleans, focusing on gun policies as a way of reducing rates of violent death including homicide, suicide, and unintentional gun deaths.

In "Criminal Homicide and Firearms in New Orleans," Sean Goodison examines gun-related homicides in the city and makes suggestions for efforts on the part of the police to reduce gun violence. These things include: (1) directed police patrols in gun hot spots, (2) traffic stops within gun hot spots as a form of incapacitation and recovery of firearms, (3) "pulling levers," specialized targeted delivery of multiple criminal justice organizations such as the "Ceasefire" program, and (4) various gun regulation measures.

In "Intimate Partner Homicide in New Orleans," Rae Taylor provides commentary on the structure and organizational responses to intimate partner homicide (IPH). She finds that compared to other forms of homicide, IPH is relatively low. When it does occur, it appears to be in areas marked by moderate racial isolation and concentrated poverty while other types of homicide such as drug and revenge/retaliatory murder occur in extreme racial isolation and extreme concentrated poverty. Taylor indicates that the status of victim services in New Orleans can best be described as "in transition" and there is a definite lack of emergency shelters for domestic violence victims and their children.

In "Life and Death in the Big Easy: Homicide and Lethality in Twenty-First-Century New Orleans," Jay Corzine, Lin Huff-Corzine, Aaron Poole, James McCutcheon, and Sarah Ann Sacra apply the concept of lethality (i.e., that only a small percentage of violent encounters that could result in a death actually have a fatal outcome) to contemporary New Orleans to determine if it can provide increased understanding of its homicide problem. They find that New Orleans's homicide problem is linked to an unusually high lethality rate that has characterized the city for at least the past two decades. The researchers suggest that the city should focus on three things to reduce lethality: (1) gun use in assaults and robberies, (2) the disorganization of the illegal drug trade, and (3) the provision of emergency medical services for violent crime victims.

In "The Importance of Communication, Coordination, and Context in Reducing Lethal Violence," Wendy C. Regoeczi argues that law enforcement can play a key role in reducing and preventing lethal violence in New Orleans. She suggests that critical elements for developing successful strategies include: (1) the importance of understanding and tracking changes in the situational context of homicide and (2) the development of strategies to improve communication and coordination within and outside the criminal justice system. The benefit of police-researcher partnerships for producing effective crime reduction strategies are also reviewed in the chapter.

In "The Future of Lethal Violence Abatement in New Orleans," Ronal W. Serpas discusses the reformation of the New Orleans

Police Department and its efforts to control homicide and other types of violent crime since he was appointed Superintendent of the NOPD in 2010 by Mayor Mitch Landrieu. He addresses past problems in the NOPD and several innovations implemented since he took over the department, including: (1) A sixty-five point plan to reform the department; (2) the use of multi-agency gang units; (3) social network analysis; and (4) the use of citizen satisfaction surveys in informing strategies to improve police and citizen collaboration. Serpas discusses the terms and conditions of the Federal Consent Decree that resulted from the Department of Justice investigation in 2011 and notes that the reformation of the NOPD will understandably take many years. He reports, however, that the significant reduction of murders in New Orleans in 2013 and the continuation of murder reduction in 2014 suggest that changes made in the NOPD, as well as other efforts such as *NOLA for Life*, a city-wide murder reduction strategy initiated in 2012, give a positive indication that New Orleans can turn around its lethal violence problem.

1   New Orleans Homicide in Historical Perspective

Jeffery Adler

Lethal violence sears daily life in early twenty-first-century New Orleans, terrifying many residents, dominating local news, and cementing the city's reputation for violent crime. Recent Federal Bureau of Investigation data confirm the worst fears of New Orleanians: the city suffers from the highest homicide rate in the nation. Overall, New Orleanians do not necessarily commit more crime than other Americans, but the city stands alone in the rate at which its residents die from criminal violence. While the level of homicide in the United States remained flat during the opening decade of the twenty-first century, New Orleans's homicide rate spiked, more than doubling between 2000 and 2007. The local rate dipped by 46 percent between its 2007 high-water mark and the end of the decade, though even in 2010 New Orleanians died from homicide at nearly ten times the national level (Wellford et al., 2011: pp. 2-4).

A series of blistering natural disasters, social crises, and institutional problems has contributed to New Orleans's homicide rate. The New Federalism of the 1980s, for instance, constricted the flow of federal support for local government at the same time that massive "white flight" transferred wealth to the suburbs and concentrated poverty in the city. Moreover, the crack epidemic of the 1980s and 1990s sharply increased drug-related violence in New Orleans, accelerating the flow of middle-class residents, resources, and jobs out of the city. Hurricane Katrina brought unimaginable devastation to an urban center already enduring high rates of poverty and violent crime, and recent, gruesome, highly publicized incidents of police brutality eroded public faith in law enforcement.

Some New Orleanians, particularly young African American men, suffer from especially high homicide rates, reflecting this toxic mixture of mounting social problems and vexing institutional chal-

1

lenges. Many residents have become reluctant to turn to the police and to the legal system to resolve disputes. Such a loss of confidence in law enforcers and public institutions, in combination with high levels of gun possession and a quick resort of violence, has fueled this deadly spiral of violence and helped to transform minor, trivial disputes into lethal confrontations.

New Orleans's homicide problem, however, is not a recent development, although the social and institutional challenges of the last quarter-century have added significantly to rates of violent crime. A historical perspective suggests that the city's modern murder crisis has deep roots, extending back at least a hundred years. A century before Hurricane Katrina struck, eight decades before crack first appeared on American streets, and six decades before white flight and its related political backlash exacerbated local poverty, New Orleans was already one of the most violent urban centers in the United States, with homicide rates towering above the national average. While Memphis reigned as the murder capital of the United States for most of the early twentieth century, New Orleans usually followed close behind. In the opening decade of the last century, for example, New Orleans was the fourth most violent American urban center, trailing only Memphis, Charleston, and Savannah (*Literary Digest*, October 19, 1912). During the 1910s and 1920s, the city ranked between third and sixth nationally in lethal violence (*Spectator*, December 20, 1917; April 1, 1926). In 1925, New Orleans's homicide rate was double that of Chicago (at the height of Al Capone's power), three times that of Washington, D.C., six times that of New York City, more than a dozen times that of Boston, and nearly forty times Canada's homicide rate (*Spectator*, April 1, 1926). Criminal violence claimed twice as many people in New Orleans during this period as in all of England, even though the latter had a population almost one hundred times the former (*New Orleans Item*, March 28, 1926). In short, for over a century, New Orleanians, far more than their counterparts in other American cities and towns, have resolved interpersonal disputes with deadly violence. Thus, recent events, and the resulting explosion in crime, did not create New Orleans's homicide problem as much as they added to the city's long-established record of deadly violence—and made the Louisiana urban center the national leader in violent death.

*   *   *

Although violent crime rates have fluctuated over time (see figure 1), recent decades have been especially homicidal, and violence in modern New Orleans dwarfs that of a century ago. Over the period from 1900 to 2010, the city's homicide rate was nearly quadruple the national rate ("Homicide Reports"; Uniform Crime Report, 1932-2010). It ebbed in 1957, at 7.9 homicides per 100,000 residents, which was roughly double the national average, and peaked in 1994, with a rate of 86, which was nearly ten times the national mean. Between 1985 and 2010, New Orleans's homicide rate averaged 55—nearly eight times the national level. By comparison, during the 1921-1945 period, the local homicide rate ranged from a low of 11.3 (in 1940) to a high of 30.3 (in 1925) or more than triple the national figure. New Orleans's mean homicide rate for this era was 17.7.[1] Also highlighting the magnitude of the recent spike, the ten most murderous years in the city since the period when Theodore Roosevelt occupied the White House were all clustered after 1990, even though homicide rates nationally plunged during the 1990s and remained steady (and low) during the opening decade of this century.

The recent surge in homicide notwithstanding, New Orleans's ranking for lethal violence was similar in the early twentieth century, hovering among the most violent urban centers in the nation, and homicide in today's city is, in many ways, remarkably similar

---

1. The quantitative data for the early twentieth century was drawn from a statistical analysis of the New Orleans Police Department's "Homicide Reports," supplemented with newspaper accounts, legal records, homicide witness interview transcripts, and other sources. The "Homicide Reports" include detailed records of every homicide reported to the police and provide demographic information on the victim and offender, a description of the crime scene, and a summary of the crime itself. The records are remarkably complete; the annual tallies, for example, are nearly identical to homicide totals in the FBI's *Uniform Crime Reports*. Some annual volumes of the homicide reports, however, have been lost, and thus this analysis covers the period from 1921 through 1945 but omits the missing years of 1932-34, 1936-1937, 1940, and 1944. Aggregate data on the missing years has been pieced together using other sources, though the case-level dataset, with 1,543 homicides, does not include the missing years. Moreover, every homicide was traced into three New Orleans newspapers as well as a range of other original sources. Sources such as these police case files are extremely rare and are seldom extant for eras before the closing decades of the twentieth century, typically limiting the depth of historical research on crime. The surviving New Orleans records, however, contain the detailed data to support a fine-grained quantitative analysis of homicide for the 1921-45 period.

Figure 1: U.S. and New Orleans Homicide Rates, 1900-2000

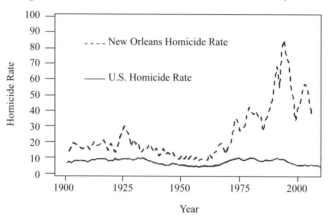

to deadly conflict between the end of World War I and the end of World War II. Regional factors account for some of this continuity. A century ago, as is the case today, homicide rates were particularly high in the Deep South, and the most violent cities were clustered in this region. Moreover, the basic character of lethal violence in early twentieth-century New Orleans resembled homicide in Memphis, Atlanta, Birmingham, and other southern urban centers, as it does today (Barnhart, 1932; Durrett and Stromquest, 1924). Many of the social and institutional forces that contribute to lethal violence in early twenty-first-century New Orleans, in short, can be traced to the early twentieth-century city.

In both periods, lethal violence in New Orleans disproportionately affected African American residents. According to a recent study, in 2009, 92 percent of New Orleans homicide victims and 97 percent of offenders were African American (Wellford et al., 2009: pp. 11, 16). By comparison, between 1921 and 1945, African American residents accounted for 71 percent of local homicide victims and 67 percent of offenders, and the mean African American homicide rate was 44 per 100,000—more than five times the white rate (see figure 2). But in early twentieth-century New Orleans, African American residents comprised only 29 percent of the city's population, whereas nearly two-thirds of early twenty-first-century New Orleanians are African American. Thus, the degree of disproportionality is similar in the two periods.

Figure 2: African American and White Homicide Rates, 1921-1945

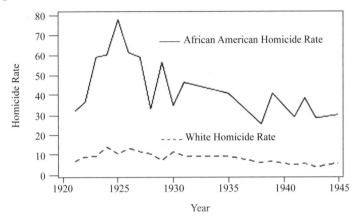

Moreover, in both eras, lethal violence rarely crossed racial lines. Although some of the most unsettling, highly publicized murders in the two periods were inter-racial killings, intra-racial conflicts generated the lion's share of lethal violence. During the late twentieth century, 87 percent of African American male homicide victims died at the hands of African American killers, while the figure for the 1921-1945 period was also 87 percent (Lowry, 1988: 1133).

The relationship between social class and violence defies simple explanation, though economic factors have likely contributed to social disorganization and interpersonal conflict. The concentration of homicide in the city's African American community, in both eras, appears to be linked to high levels of poverty and unemployment. During the early twentieth century, African American New Orleanians constituted the poorest segment of the city's population, and African American killers were especially poor; between 1921 and 1945, 85 percent of African American offenders and 88 percent of African American victims were either unemployed or held the lowest-paying jobs in the local labor market.

Deadly fighting was an overwhelmingly masculine activity during both periods, and men comprised the vast majority of New Orleans homicide offenders and victims. In 2009, men committed 95 percent of New Orleans homicides and constituted 87 percent of the victims of lethal violence. (Wellford et al., 2011: pp. 11, 16). The basic pattern was similar early in the last century, when men made up 80 percent of killers and 77 percent of victims.

Age patterns were also similar for the two eras. In early twenty-first-century New Orleans, the median age for killers is 23 and for their victims is 27 (Wellford et al., 2011: pp. 11, 15). In early twentieth-century New Orleans, killers were slightly older than they are today, with a median age of 29, and the median age of victims was 28. But the figures are, in fact, roughly comparable; a century ago, children matured later, reflecting poorer nutrition and health, and left home and struck out on their own later than is the case now.

Trends in weapon use have changed only modestly over time. In early twenty-first-century New Orleans, guns are the weapon of choice. Nearly 90 percent of recent homicides have been committed with firearms and 78 percent with handguns (Wellford et al., 2011: p. 8). Law enforcers and policy makers consistently express alarm at the easy availability of cheap handguns. While the proportion of homicides committed with firearms was lower early in the last century, guns, and revolvers in particular, were the overwhelming weapon of choice of killers then as well. Nearly two-thirds of victims died from gunshot wounds between 1921 and 1945, and long before law breakers, law makers, and law enforcers had heard the phrase "Saturday-night special," New Orleans killers relied on inexpensive handguns. For over one hundred years, local reformers and government officials have noted the link between the proliferation of guns in the city and homicide (*New Orleans Times-Picayune*, May 25, 1923). Fluctuations in gun violence also accounted for much of the variation in the city's early twentieth-century homicide rate (see figure 3); spikes in local homicide correlated with increased gun violence, while drops in the city's homicide rate mirrored decreased gun violence.

The motives for killing have also changed surprisingly little since the age of silent films, flappers, and speakeasies. A 2011 analysis of New Orleans homicide noted the "ordinariness" of lethal violence in the city; most deadly encounters grow out of prosaic conflicts (Wellford et al., 2011: pp. 22). Nearly eight decades earlier, C. C. Dejoie, a prominent African American newspaper publisher had characterized the city's "high rate of homicide" in nearly identical terms. "These lives," he explained, "have been taken usually in arguments about trivial things" and for "inconsequential reasons" (*Louisiana Weekly*, December 12, 1942). Just as Mardi Gras is not the

Figure 3: New Orleans Homicide Rate and Firearm Homicide Rate

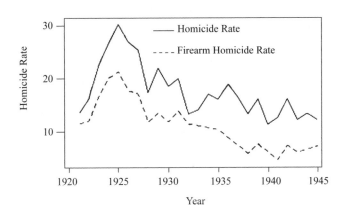

wellspring for homicide in modern New Orleans, neither Storyville during the opening decades of the last century nor rum-running during Prohibition accounted for a significant share of local blood-letting, and the city's violence is not, and was not, confined to the French Quarter or concentrated during Carnival. Rather, as Dejoie noted, murder was bound up in the rhythms and routines of everyday life in the early twentieth-century city. And, as today, the local homicide rate was so alarming because deadly violence typically began with commonplace, unexceptional disagreements.

In other ways as well, early twentieth-century murder seems eerily similar to its modern counterpart, despite the far-reaching social changes that have unfolded since Huey Long ruled Louisiana. Between 1921 and 1945, 34 percent of homicide victims died at the hands of acquaintances and 10 percent at the hand of strangers, compared with 40 percent and 14 percent, respectively, in modern New Orleans (Wellford et al., 2011: pp. 14). Similarly, decades before residents had air conditioning and well before most New Orleanians had indoor plumbing, 29 percent of homicides occurred in personal residences. The figure for the early twenty-first century is 32 percent (Wellford et al., 2011: pp. 7-8).

But homicide has changed over the last century, and there are some significant differences between early twentieth-century lethal violence and its modern counterpart. Most important, family life was more violent in the early twentieth century, erupting at a higher rate and accounting for a significantly larger proportion of New

Orleans homicides. Domestic conflict generated nearly a fourth of local homicides between 1921 and 1945, compared with a twentieth of New Orleans homicides in 2009 (Wellford et al., 2011: p. 14). Most of this difference is in spousal murder, which produced 17 percent of local homicides during the early period but only 3 percent today. Closely related, women, especially African American women, killed far more often in the early twentieth century, typically dispatching their abusive husbands — or common-law partners (Adler, 2010). From 1921 until 1945, New Orleans women committed 19 percent of local homicides, whereas the modern figure is less than 5 percent; women committed one-fourth of African American homicides during this era (Wellford, 2011: p. 16).

Homicide trends were not static between the end of World War I and the end of World War II. Rather, they changed significantly, though in counter-intuitive ways. Although recent studies by criminologists have concluded that poverty fuels violence, particularly in the African American community, New Orleans homicide spiked during the early 1920s, a period of great prosperity, and plummeted during the Great Depression, when the economy crumbled and unemployment soared. These shifts occurred among both white and African American residents, who killed at high rates when the economy boomed and at low rates when it collapsed.[2]

The distinctive features of early twentieth-century homicide notwithstanding, the broad-based similarities between the eras prove to be more striking than the differences. In both periods, New Orleans ranked among the most violent cities in the nation. Furthermore, killers, as well as their victims, were overwhelmingly African American, men, young, and poor in both eras, and the offenders typically relied on firearms, especially handguns. Finally, disputes over mundane, ordinary matters accounted for the majority of early twentieth-century and early twenty-first-century homicides and often occurred between acquaintances. Hence, the recent surge in violence followed trends that emerged nearly a century earlier.

In short, the quick, deadly resort to violence to resolve prosaic disagreements in modern New Orleans is the product of decades of historical circumstances, particularly for African American resi-

---

2. At first glance, this appears to suggest that relative deprivation accounted for the changing trends, but New Orleans's homicide rate began falling during the late 1920s (see figure 1), when the local economy remained robust.

dents. During the early twentieth century, for example, street justice and violent self help to resolve mundane disputes were already
well established. The roots of the modern crisis, therefore, can be
found in practices that appeared and became entrenched during
the first half of the last century.

A complex blend of early twentieth-century ecological and institutional factors simultaneously increased African American vulnerability to violence and encouraged the violent self-help responses that produced homicide. In myriad ways, racial discrimination in
the age of Jim Crow engrained these practices, for African American
New Orleanians faced constant threats from white residents eager
to preserve the region's fragile racial order. But the realities of daily
life in an early twentieth-century southern city also reinforced the
conditions and pressures that triggered violent conflict.

Overt acts of racial violence were unusual events in New
Orleans, accounting for less than 1 percent of homicides between
1921 and 1945, though such violence cast a wide shadow. Just before he shot and killed two men on a street car in 1925, for example,
Frank DeRocha, a twenty-three-year-old blacksmith, announced
"I just feel like killing me a nigger tonight" (*New Orleans Times-
Picayune*, November 18, 1925). White residents often defended
such behavior; all-white juries routinely acquitted the defendants;
and African American residents recognized that this kind of violence posed an omnipresent threat in early twentieth-century New
Orleans. Very much like lynchings during this era, acts of egre-
gious racial intimidation conveyed a clear and pernicious message far beyond their frequency (*Louisiana Weekly*, May 31, 1941).
A local African American newspaper repeatedly warned residents
to be on guard against acts of racial terrorism and even suggested
that African Americans need to be prepared to defend themselves
should the need arise (*Louisiana Weekly*, March 15, 1930; April 23,
1933).

More prosaic experiences, however, also made daily life unstable and dangerous for early twentieth-century African American
New Orleanians, and institutional practices encouraged African
American residents to resolve disputes informally and often with
violence. Crime infected African American neighborhoods during
this period, but legal institutions provided these residents with little protection.

The New Orleans Police Department, in particular, failed to serve early twentieth-century African American city residents. The city had no African American police officers from the end of Reconstruction until 1950 (Moore, 2010: 31). Moreover, during this era the all-white police department defined its core mission as preserving the racial hierarchy believed to be the bulwark against social disorder (Fichter, 1964: pp. 32-33; Myrdal, 1944: p. 535; Johnson, 1943: p. 72; Adler, 2012). In 1924, for instance, Police Superintendent Guy Molony explicitly attributed New Orleans's high homicide rate to the city's "negro problem." (*New Orleans Item*, July 6, 1924) Molony added that "if it were not for the colored murders, New Orleans and the entire South would have an excellent record." Similarly, a 1925 grand jury report lamented "the total disregard that many negroes have acquired for life and law" (*New Orleans Item*, March 3, 1925). Again and again, police officials argued that New Orleans suffered from a high homicide rate "because of the negro" (*New Orleans Times-Picayune*, October 24, 1924; *New Orleans Times-Picayune*, October 11, 1930).

Thus, according to many white residents, especially police and municipal officials, African Americans — and African American crime — posed the greatest threat to social order during the early twentieth century. Police officials believed that African Americans were "naturally" volatile and violent and that this aggressive behavior jeopardized social stability when it bled across racial lines (*New Orleans Times-Picayune*, December 25, 1925; Adler, 2012: p. 516). Therefore local law enforcers principally sought to protect white New Orleanians from African American residents. Nor was this an unusual interpretation of the crime statistics of the era; early twentieth-century social scientists and other experts concurred, providing academic corroboration and justification for popular assumptions and police attitudes toward African American residents and crime (Hoffman, 1926: p. 23; Brearley, 1932: pp. 111-16; Dollard, 1937: p. 269; Muhammad, 2010).

As a consequence, New Orleans policemen devoted scant attention to black-on-black violence or to crime in African American neighborhoods, which they viewed as inevitable and unmanageable. Rather, municipal officials focused police protection on either white residential sections or business areas, leaving African American sections of the city under-patrolled (Smith, 1946: pp.

8-9). When law enforcers responded to African American intra-racial violence, they were often casual and indifferent ("Homicide Reports," January 30, 1936). In a 1925 editorial, the *New Orleans Item* (November 16, 1925) expressed concern with this view, lamenting the practice of routinely dismissing African American intra-racial crime with the attitude "It's only another negro fight and not important." Witnesses to homicides between African Americans sometimes reported that patrolmen seemed uninterested in investigating the crimes. "It is commonly known in the underworld," a local African American newspaper (*Louisiana Weekly*, April 13, 1929) complained, "that when one Negro violates the law by harming another of his group little or nothing will be done." Simply put, New Orleans policemen under-reacted to such crime.

For white residents, city officials, and local law enforcers, black-on-white crime, however, was another matter altogether and had to be addressed quickly and decisively. Writing in 1931, an African American newspaper publisher (*Louisiana Weekly*, April 18, 1931) observed that "when Negroes kill Negroes, they are not punished," but when they attacked white residents, "behold how great a matter a little fire kindleth." Police officials responded frantically and hysterically to black-on-white violence, fearing that the innate volatility of African American residents, no longer contained within households and segregated neighborhoods, made every white New Orleanian vulnerable and endangered social stability. Although whites killed African Americans more than twice as often as African Americans killed whites in New Orleans between 1921 and 1945, the former provoked little police reaction, while the latter produced immediate, indiscriminate roundups and dragnets. On August 18, 1943, for example, a white woman, peering out her window late at night, observed a white man, later identified as Peter Sansone, a fifty-three-year-old shipyard worker, "lying on the sidewalk" and "a man who appeared to be a colored man" walking further down the street ("Homicide Reports," August 18, 1943). James Purcell, the acting police superintendent, quickly "ordered the arrest of all Negroes found prowling around the streets late at night" (*New Orleans Times-Picayune*, August 19, 1943). The police arrested, detained, interrogated, and fingerprinted nearly a thousand men (*Louisiana Weekly*, September 4, 1943). Those with guns or knives were "charged with carrying dangerous weapons," while "those out of employment and unable to give a satisfactory explanation for their presence on the street at a late hour" were "charged with vagrancy and held for investigation" (*New Orleans Times-Picayune*, August 19, 1943). Nor was this an isolated reaction to black-on-white crime. A similar roundup in 1932 following the murder of a white grocer yielded nine hundred African American prisoners, all of whom were photographed, fingerprinted, and questioned, while a 1933 dragnet produced 540 arrests (*Louisiana Weekly*, April 2, 1932; September 30, 1933).

If early twenty-first-century police brutality is the horrifying exception, in early twentieth-century New Orleans such treatment was routine and publicly defended, further undermining African American confidence in local law enforcers. Repeatedly, policemen beat, kicked, and even sodomized prisoners, particularly African American men suspected of attacking white New Orleanians (*Louisiana Weekly*, May 30, 1931; February 11, 1939; November 8, 1941; June 6, 1942; Moore, 1990: p. 67). African American residents knew all too well that precinct-house interrogations often ended with visits to Charity Hospital. More frightening still, many suspects were "taken for rides" and assured that, unless they confessed, they would never return. Many prisoners described being offered the choice of confessing or going on "a one-way ride to Metairie" or a "one-way ride to City Park" (*Louisiana Weekly*, January 13, 1934; *New Orleans Times-Picayune*, November 19, 1941). In 1939 the American Civil Liberties Union (Moore, 1990: p. 59) ranked New Orleans as one of the three worst cities in the nation for civil liberty violations, and a year later the *Louisiana Weekly* (February 3, 1940) charged that "At least once a week some poor unfortunate Negro is 'gone over' by our sadistically inclined police department."

Local law enforcers did not deny that they engaged in such "severe questioning" tactics. To the contrary, police superintendents boasted about their aggressive approach to crime fighting, particularly to solve black-on-white violence. In 1923 Superintendent of Police Guy R. Molony celebrated the department's use of the "modern, up-to-date 'third-degree.'" (*New Orleans Item*, July 18, 1923) In 1939 Chief of Detectives John J. Grosch (*New Orleans Times-Picayune*, June 1, 1939) went further, telling the local Rotary Club "if it were not for the 'third degree' methods by which I have forced legal admissions in cases where I had every reason to be sure of the guilt,

New Orleans would today be delivered over to organized rackets and brutal crime as New York, Chicago and other cities." Grosch threatened to resign if municipal officials curtailed such an effective crime-fighting tool. A year later, Harold Lee, a Newcomb College philosophy professor and social activist, concluded "that the Negro had no rights that the police felt obliged to protect" (Moore, 1990: p. 65).

When African American suspects, terrified by the prospect of riding to the precinct station, being interrogated with "third-degree methods," or going for a "one-way ride," were not compliant, local policemen responded with deadly force. In 1932, an African American writer (*Louisiana Weekly*, May 14, 1932) argued that "the least resistance offered by colored prisoners results in death for the latter. Policemen," he added, "cannot take unarmed civilians to jail without murdering them." Louisiana criminal law defined "self-defense" loosely during this period, and law enforcers enjoyed particularly wide latitude in employing deadly force. New Orleans policemen took full advantage of the self-defense provisions in the criminal code and killed an average of five suspects per year during this period, nearly two-thirds of whom were African American (Adler, 2012: pp. 505, 514). In an era when the city had one of the highest homicides rates in the nation, nearly 5 percent of all victims of lethal violence died at the hands of the local police. In some instances, local law enforcers killed wantonly in acts of clear racial domination.

More often, however, policemen killed African American residents who "resisted arrest." Typically, patrolmen attempted to apprehend the suspect for questioning or on suspicion of loitering, vagrancy, or drunkenness. Some suspects proved to be non-compliant, tussled with patrolmen, and were shot and killed in the process. Other suspects fled, an act of defiance that infuriated local law enforcers, who demanded submission from African American residents and viewed non-compliant behavior as a prelude to violent resistance. In the ensuing chase, according to New Orleans policemen, the fleeing suspect reached for his pocket—the so-called "hip-pocket move" (*New Orleans Times-Picayune*, June 18, 1939; Vyhnanek, 1998: p. 31; Adler, 2012). Insisting that he believed that the suspect was drawing a weapon, the officer lawfully employed deadly force, although nearly two-thirds of the fleeing suspects who made such furtive movements proved to be unarmed. One outraged 1930s white observer concluded that local policemen "did not think any more of shooting a 'nigger' than a dog" (Moore, 1990: p. 67). "It is not to be wondered at," an African American journalist (*Louisiana Weekly*, May 20, 1939) explained in 1939, "that the average Negro boy or man runs when approached by either uniformed or plainclothed officers, for all of us unfortunately have a thorough knowledge of the brutal treatment accorded those of our group who fall into the toils of the law for any reason whatsoever."

For both police and African American residents, the prophesy of a violent encounter was self-fulfilling. Policemen confronting resistance responded with force, and African American New Orleanians, fearing police brutality, often either fled or attempted to resist arrest, accelerating the cycle of violence, encouraging policemen to employ greater force, and making residents unwilling to trust local law enforcers. On the one hand, such mutual fear and mistrust generated high levels of lethal shootings by police officers, while, on the other hand, this acrimony left African American New Orleans increasingly reluctant to enlist the police to resolve disputes and therefore more likely to rely on self-help solutions.

Early twentieth-century courts also offered little protection to African American New Orleanians, failed to provide alternatives to street justice, and therefore left these residents to fend for themselves. District attorneys, judges, and jurors mirrored local policemen in their treatment of crimes involving African American residents, responding to intra-racial violence with liberal doses of leniency, indifference, and resignation. White and African American observers, municipal and police officials, and even parish district attorneys conceded that the courts under-reacted to black-on-black violent crime. In 1924, for example, Police Superintendent Molony (*New Orleans Item*, July 6, 1924) complained that "we are just too lenient with them [African Americans]. It is almost impossible to get a jury who will convict a negro for killing another negro." An African American newspaper editor (*Louisiana Weekly*, February 10, 1940) offered a more trenchant explanation for this curious phenomenon, writing "the attitude of the law is that when a Negro kills another, he is doing the country a favor." Other commentators suggested that white district attorneys, judges, and jurors believed that African American residents lacked the capacity for sufficient forethought to commit murder. "The majority of the killings of Negroes," one writer (*Louisiana Weekly*, June 26, 1943) suggested, "are spur-of-the moment types of slayings, and bereft of the pre-meditation motive without which there can be no verdict of mur-der." When African Americans were convicted for intra-racial kill-ings, they were frequently sentenced to prison terms of a year or two for manslaughter.

District attorneys, judges, and jurors proved to be even more le-nient and forgiving when white residents killed African American New Orleanians. Indictments and convictions were rare for such homicides, regardless of the circumstances. One white suspect, for example, crowed that he had "nothing to worry about over the kill-ing of a 'nigger'" (*Louisiana Weekly*, January 6, 1934). Likewise, two members of a 1942 grand jury investigating a homicide remarked "this was just a case of policemen shooting a 'nigger' and 'that was all right'" (Moore, 1990: p. 68).

A very different Orleans Parish criminal-justice system appeared when African American residents were charged with killing local whites. Many white New Orleanians feared that African American residents were becoming emboldened and uncontrollable, and thus individual acts of black-on-white violence seemed to foretell a po-tential collapse of the racial order. The notoriously corrupt and in-efficient police instantly became aggressive crime fighters, and the normally languid courts became harsh and draconian. The com-plete absence of African American residents from juries facilitated such a transformation, for these New Orleanians were not deemed eligible for criminal-court juries between 1888 and 1935, when the U.S. Supreme Court ruled that African American residents could not be excluded from such service (*Louisiana Weekly*, August 3, 1935; *New Orleans Times-Picayune*, November 5, 1935; *Powell v. Alabama*). Parish officials, however, managed to keep African American New Orleanians off criminal court juries for another decade, providing still more evidence that the police and courts did not protect these residents (*Pierre v. Louisiana*; *Baton Rouge Advocate*, February 26, 1944).

Early twentieth-century African American New Orleanians, in short, viewed the courthouse, like the police precinct station, and the parish jail as sites where white residents enforced a brutal system of oppression and racial control (*Louisiana Weekly*, May 20,

1939; May 31, 1941). While criminal-justice officials and law enforcers would have challenged the term "oppression," they would have agreed that local legal institutions were core mechanisms of racial control, insisting that preserving the city's racial order safeguarded social stability. It is hardly surprising that African American crime victims refrained from turning to the criminal-justice system for redress, that African American suspects did not submit to police demands, and that the legal system did little to discourage or control crime in African American neighborhoods during the first half of the twentieth century.

The political system also failed to provide protection for African American New Orleanians. In the age of Jim Crow, African American residents wielded little political influence. The city's 1940 population included 149,034 African Americans, only four hundred of whom were registered voters (Hirsch, 1992: p. 273). In northern cities, immigrants often wielded considerable political muscle at the ward or precinct level, as aldermen, beholden to neighborhood voters in the heyday of the political machine, pressured the municipal police to serve local voters and intervened when constituents appeared in court (Johnson, 1979: pp. 172-74). But no such patronage system operated for African American New Orleanians; public officials served only white residents. As a consequence, political institutions proved to be no more responsive to African American residents than were legal institutions.

Ecological factors interacted with this institutional failure and transformed trivial disputes into homicides. Crime abounded in New Orleans's African American neighborhoods during the early twentieth century. In part, this reflected the poverty of the residents. In part, it flowed from the vice industries that city officials concentrated and tolerated in the sections of New Orleans where African American residents lived, for brothels and gambling halls generated crime and attracted rough visitors (Louisiana Weekly, August 31, 1940). These forces, in combination, left African American New Orleanians living in a violent world and shorn of legal protection.

Not surprisingly, many African American residents, largely unprotected by the police and the courts and living in crime-ridden neighborhoods, recognized their vulnerability and learned, over time, to rely on a fluid mix of informal responses to crime and violence, ranging from seeking the advice of religious leaders to resorting to violent self-help. According to late 1930s ethnographers, many African American New Orleanians taught their children toughness and aggressive self-defense as core survival tools (Davis and Dollard, 1940: pp. 50, 270). While some residents struggled to avoid the streets and the social contexts most likely to be dangerous, others carried weapons for protection (Schultz, 1962: p. 481).[3] Men routinely tucked handguns and dirks into their trousers, while an African American woman might place a small knife or an ice pick "in her bosom" ("Homicide Reports," December 23, 1930; *Louisiana Weekly*, October 14, 1939).

Such self-help fed on itself. The proliferation of weapons left unarmed residents vulnerable and encouraged them to consider carrying pistols and knives, if only to ward off threats. New Orleans police officers knew well that African American residents often carried weapons, and hence local law enforcers were especially quick to rely on their service revolvers when they encountered African American suspects. And, most important, the pistols and ice picks carried for protection in neighborhoods where residents had little access to the police were most often used during minor disputes with friends, spouses, and acquaintances. Thus, disagreements over card games or household finances rapidly escalated, particularly as the participants recognized that the friend or acquaintance with whom they were bickering was also likely to have a weapon.

In yet another way, ecological and institutional forces collided to increase the death toll from such disputes. In early twentieth-century New Orleans, the treatable wounds of African American residents often produced lethal injuries. Most local hospitals did not admit African American patients during this era, and the city's Charity Hospital maintained a limit on the number of "negro beds" (*New Orleans Times-Picayune*, June 5, 1927). If the institution did not have an empty bed allotted for an African American patient, then the injured party was turned away. The racial ideology of the period also influenced the conduct of white physicians at Charity Hospital, some of whom refused to treat fatally injured African American residents, insisting that the wounds were minor (*Louisiana Weekly*, November 23, 1929). According to one ob-

3. For studies that explore self-help, extra-legal mechanisms of social control, and responses to the loss of faith in state institutions, see Schultz (1962); Black (1983); Tyler (2006); Edwards (2009). For an analysis of the impact of the "loss of legitimacy," see LaFree (1998).

server (*Louisiana Weekly*, December 3, 1932), "the doors of Charity Hospital have been slammed shut in the face of Negro patients who have been dying on their feet." Likewise, African American gunshot victims were frequently unable to secure ambulance service to Charity Hospital ("Homicide Reports," January 5, 1926; January 10, 1943). Put differently, institutional racism directly increased the death toll from violent disputes involving African American New Orleanians, buoying the local homicide rate, increasing residents' vulnerability, and, no doubt, encouraging some to respond even more aggressively in mundane disputes.

*   *   *

For African American residents, in particular, decades and decades of reliance on street justice and self-help practices helped to make New Orleans one of the most violent cities in the nation long before the crises of the late twentieth century and the early twenty-first century. The habit of carrying weapons—and drawing them during trivial disputes—need not have been culturally reproduced.[4] Daily experience from living in violence-filled neighborhoods and without access to police protection and legal redress reinforced self-reliance and the aggressive self-help that underscored it. Institutional racism receded slowly over the course of the twentieth century, but new crises emerged just as the criminal justice system abandoned the remnants of Jim Crow. When crack appeared, when white flight accelerated and exacerbated inequality, when the New Federalism of the 1980s reduced support for municipal government, when Katrina hit, and when well-publicized episodes of police brutality contributed to the challenges endured by American American residents, the city's homicide rate soared, and New Orleans became the murder capital of the nation. But the

4. Since the publication of Marvin Wolfgang's *Patterns in Criminal Homicide* (1958), scholars have fiercely debated the theory that a "subculture of violence" accounted in elevated levels of homicide in African American communities. Wolfgang's explanation generated so much controversy because, according to its critics, it implied that some forms of violence became normative and culturally engrained. Thus, the theory's detractors argued, Wolfgang asserted that African American culture contributed to inner-city violence. I am suggesting that ecological pressures, rather than cultural tradition, encouraged African American residents to carry handguns and ice picks, some of which were used to resolve petty disagreements.

roots of this crisis extended deep into the city's past, when racial conflict and overt discrimination were routine and accepted, forcing African American residents into spatial and social settings suffused with the potential for violence and hence encouraging them to carry weapons and to respond quickly and violently to everyday forms of conflict. Modern New Orleans's homicide crisis, in short, is the product of at least a century of scorching racial discrimination.

References

Adler, Jeffrey S. (2010). "'Bessie Done Cut Her Old Man': Race, Common-Law Marriage, and Homicide in New Orleans, 1925-1945." *Journal of Social History* 44: 123-43.

———. (2012). "'The Killer Behind the Badge': Race and Police Homicide in New Orleans, 1925-1945." *Law and History Review* 30: 495-531.

Barnhardt, Kenneth E. (1932). "A Study of Homicide." *Birmingham-Southern College Bulletin* 25: 7-38.

Baton Rouge Advocate. (1943).

Black, Donald. (1983). "Crime as Social Control." *American Sociological Review* 48: 34-95.

Brearley, H. C. (1932). *Homicide in the United States*. Chapel Hill: University of North Carolina Press.

Davis, Allison, and John Dollard. (1940). *Children of Bondage: The Personality Development of Negro Youth in the Urban South*. Washington, D.C.: American Council on Education.

Dollard, John. (1937). *Caste and Class in a Southern Town*. New York: Anchor.

Durrett, J. J., and W. G. Stromquest. (1924). "A Study of Violent Deaths Registered in Atlanta, Birmingham, Memphis and New Orleans for the Years 1921 and 1922." Appendix C: Crime Prevention. Memphis: City of Memphis.

Edwards, Laura F. (2009). *The People and Their Peace: Legal Culture and the Transformation of Inequality in the Post-Revolutionary South*. Chapel Hill: University of North Carolina Press.

Fichter, Joseph. (with the collaboration of Brian Jordan) (1964). "Police Handling of Arrestees: A Research Study of Police Arrests in New Orleans." [Unpublished report] New Orleans: Department of Sociology, Loyola University of the South.

Hirsch, Arnold R. (1992). "Simply a Matter of Black and White: The Transformation of Race and Politics in Twentieth-Century New Orleans." In Arnold R. Hirsch and Joseph Logsdon (Eds.), *Creole New Orleans: Race and Americanization*. Baton Rouge: Louisiana State University Press: 262- 319

Hoffman, Frederick L. (1926). "The Increase in Murder." *Annals of the American Academy of Political and Social Science* 125: 20-29.

"Homicide Reports." (1921-1945). Department of [New Orleans] Police, City of New Orleans, Louisiana Division. City Archives, New Orleans Public Library.

Johnson, Charles et al. (1943). *To Stem This Tide: A Survey of Racial Tension Areas in the United States*. Boston: Pilgrim Press.

Johnson, David R. (1979). *Policing the Urban Underworld: The Impact of Crime on the Development of the American Police, 1800-1887*. Philadelphia: Temple University Press.

LaFree, Gary. (1998). *Losing Legitimacy: Street Crime and the Decline of Social Institutions in America*. Boulder: Westview.

Literary Digest. (1912).

Louisiana Weekly. (1928-1945).

Lowry, Philip W., Susan E. Hassig, Robert A. Gunn, and Joyce B. Mathison. (1988). "Homicide Victims in New Orleans: Recent Trends." *American Journal of Epidemiology* 128: 1130-36.

Muhammad, Khalil Gibran. (2010). *The Condemnation of Blackness: Race, Crime, and the Making of Modern Urban America*. Cambridge, MA: Harvard University Press.

Moore, Leonard N. (2010). *Black Rage in New Orleans: Police Brutality and African American Activism from World War II to Hurricane Katrina*. Baton Rouge: Louisiana State University Press.

Moore, William V. (1990). "Civil Liberties in Louisiana: The Louisiana League for the Preservation of Constitutional Rights." *Louisiana History* 31: 59-81.

Myrdal, Gunnar. (1944). *An American Dilemma: The Negro Problem and Modern Democracy*. Volume 2. New York: Harper & Row.

New Orleans Item. (1920-1945).

New Orleans Times-Picayune. (1920-1945).

Pierre v. Louisiana, 306 U.S. 354. (1939).

Powell v. Alabama, 287 U. S. 45. (1932).

Schultz, Leroy G. (1962). "Why the Negro Carries Weapons." *Journal of the American Academy of Criminal Law, Criminology, and Political Science* 53: 476-83.

Smith, Bruce. (1948). "The New Orleans Police Survey." [Unpublished report] New Orleans: Bureau of Governmental Research. *Spectator* (1917-1937).

Tyler, Tom R. (2006). *Why People Obey the Law.* Princeton: Princeton University Press.

Vyhnanek, Louis. (1998). *Unorganized Crime: New Orleans in the 1920s.* Lafayette, LA: Center for Louisiana Studies.

Uniform Crime Report. (1932-2010). Federal Bureau of Investigation.

Wellford, Charles, Brenda J. Bond, and Sean Goodison. (2011). "Crime in New Orleans: Analyzing Crime Trends and New Orleans' Responses to Crime." Bureau of Justice Assistance Report, U. S. Department of Justice [media.nola.crime_impact/other/BJA Crime in New Orleans Report March 2011.pdf.].

Wolfgang, Marvin E. (1958). *Patterns in Criminal Homicide.* New York: John Wiley and Sons.

2 New Orleans Neighborhood Patterns of Homicide and Key Structural and Cultural Linkages 1940-2013

Lydia Voigt, Dee W. Harper, and
William E. Thornton Jr.

Introduction

New Orleans's high murder rates have been the object of public concern and media attention for much of its history (see chapter 1). For example, William Howard Russell, a well-known English journalist who visited New Orleans in 1861, remarked on the unusually high occurrence of lethal violence and the penchant of citizens for carrying weapons. In his view New Orleans was one of the most violent cities in the United States at that time (Russell, 1863: p. 244). Between 1857 and 1859 approximately 255 criminal homicides were reported for New Orleans resulting in an average annual rate of 35 per 100,000 compared to an annual homicide rate of 3.6 per 100,000 in Philadelphia and 7.5 per 100,000 in Boston for the same timeframe (Rousey, 1996: p. 85). The attorney general at that time complained in the newspaper that an ineffective criminal justice system hampered by the reluctance of witnesses to come forward as well as the unwillingness of citizens to serve on juries had resulted in only a small fraction of murders resolved by conviction (e.g., between 1857-1859 only 21 percent of the murders committed were resolved by conviction on a charge of either murder or manslaughter) (Rousey, 1996: p. 85).

Unfortunately, New Orleans continues to make headlines with its high incidence and rates of homicide. Year after year New Orleans is listed among the top ten cities in the United States — often in first place — with respect to its high rate of homicide, which has led to its reputation as the "murder capital" of the nation. What accounts for this long history of lethal violence? What structural and cultural factors are most important in illuminating the nature of the problem and explaining its persistence over time?

The purpose of this chapter is to provide an overview of homicide trends and patterns in New Orleans spanning over seven decades. Since the distribution of homicides in New Orleans vary across time and space, the focus of this chapter is on neighborhood homicide patterns and the structural and cultural linkages associated with the ecological and geographical distribution of homicides.

We begin with a demographic description of New Orleans and a historical account of the city's homicide rates over the past seven decades. This overview serves to provide the context for more in-depth analyses. Following a brief review of the research literature related to key studies focusing on explanations of concentrated distributions of lethal violence and the structural covariates that are typically hypothesized to be related to the ecological clustering of homicides found across time and space, we share the results of an original study of the structural and cultural covariates associated with the New Orleans neighborhood distribution of homicides from 1996 to 2004. This quantitative analysis employs official police statistics on homicides in New Orleans (disaggregated by police zones, which serve as proxies for neighborhoods) and corresponding census information associated with selected structural covariates as well as qualitative data, including: homicide incident reports; coroner's reports; interviews with neighborhood residents, community leaders, and criminal justice personnel; newspaper accounts; and historical information and facts on neighborhoods with extended histories of lethal violence. Finally, we discuss the post-Katrina homicide patterns as well as future speculations in light of significant social changes brought by reconstruction in the aftermath of the hurricane including significant neighborhood transformations; population shifts; institutional, political and economic changes; and challenges facing the city's law enforcement and criminal justice systems.

Demographic Description of New Orleans and the City's Murder Statistics from 1940 to 2013

New Orleans is one of the oldest and most unique cities in the United States. Founded in 1718, it is located in the subtropical southern region of the U.S. in Louisiana just 125 miles up the Mississippi River from the Gulf of Mexico. It currently occupies 181 square miles. In 1771 the population was estimated at 1,349. The first United States Census in 1810 listed New Orleans with a population of 17,242 (U.S. Census of Population, 2000–2010). In 1960 the population reached its historically highest point at 627,525. Since that time the population has been declining through the 1990s. In 2005 the population was recorded at 483,663 (representing a 25 percent decline since 1990), which represents the equivalent of 2,684 population per square mile. According to the 2000 census the estimated greater metropolitan population (SMA) equals 1,337,726. Mass evacuation following Hurricane Katrina in 2005 resulted in significant population attrition. According to the 2010 census, the population of New Orleans has been estimated to be approximately 343,829, which represents a decline of approximately 130,000 people from the 2000 estimate.

The city is known for its rich history and cultural traditions and for its ethnic and racial diversity. Based on the 2000 census, New Orleans has been considered a minority majority city with a racial/ ethnic composition of: white, 28 percent; African American, 67 percent; Hispanic, 3 percent; and Asian 2 percent. According to the 2010 census the city continues its ethnic and racial diversity with the following distribution: white, 34 percent; African American, 60 percent; Hispanic, 5 percent; and Asian, 3 percent (American Community Survey [ACS] 2007–2011). While the city is recognized for its contributions to the arts, especially for being the birthplace of jazz, and its elaborate celebrations, such as Mardi Gras, it is also known for its openness to deviance and the pursuit of all sorts of pleasures, which is captured in the famous adage: "Let the good times roll!" This has attracted millions of tourists annually, which peaked at an annual estimate of over twenty million visitors prior to the Katrina disaster. The city also represents an important commercial center; it has the largest port (based on tonnage) in the United States.

While the kings and queens of Mardi Gras and their lavish parades and balls and the magnificent mansions along Saint Charles Avenue suggest prosperity and opulence, the city also has an exceptionally high rate of poverty. The income and educational levels are among the lowest in the country. For example, according to Department of Labor statistics and adjusted data based on the 2000 census, the median household income is $27,133; almost a third of the population (30 percent) lives below the Federal Poverty Index. Many will surely recall the images of people stranded during the evacuation of New Orleans in 2005 when Hurricane Katrina was approaching the city. One fifth of the population did not have cars and had no alternative but to go to public refuge centers for safety and protection. The educational level has also been relatively low: adult high school graduates (twenty-five years of age or higher) comprise only 75 percent of the population; college graduates constitute just 26 percent of the adult population. According to the 2010 census some improvements may be noted. For example, the 2010 census shows that of the total population of 343,829, approximately 21 percent of all families live below the Federal Poverty Index; high school graduates currently comprise 84 percent; and college graduates (bachelor's degree or higher) comprise 33 percent of adults over twenty-five years of age (American Community Survey [ACS], 2007–2011).

The legal system in Louisiana including the city of New Orleans is unique. The State of Louisiana is the only state in the United States that operates under the *Napoleonic Code* or Civil Law. The Louisiana Criminal Law, however, is currently defined by the *Federal Model Criminal Code* (MCC) serving as the standard across the United States. Criminal justice in Louisiana as well as New Orleans has historically received mixed reviews. While on the one hand police receive commendations on their handling of immensely large crowds during such events as Mardi Gras, on the other hand, complaints and charges of corruption, discrimination, harshness, and brutality are reoccurring themes.

According to official corrections statistics, the State of Louisiana has registered the highest rate of incarceration among the states in the United States. For example, in 2011 the five states with the highest incarceration rates included: Louisiana (865 per 100,000 population), followed by Mississippi (690 per 100,000), Alabama (650 per 100,000), Texas (632 per 100,000), and Oklahoma (631 per 100,000) (Carson and Sabol, *Prisoners in 2011*, 2012: p. 23; Louisiana Statistical Analysis Center, 2013). By comparison the average rate of incarceration for the U.S. is 700 per 100,000. Orleans Parish, which includes the city of New Orleans, has a significantly higher incarceration rate of over 1,500 per 100,000 compared with all other parishes in Louisiana (La. Department of Corrections, 2014; Austin, Ware, and Ocker, 2011: p. 2; Metropolitan Crime Commission, 2013b).

According to statistics published in *Crime in Louisiana 2011*, the state of Louisiana's rate of murder and non-negligent manslaughter is also the highest in the United States (e.g., 11.8 per 100,000 in 2009, 11.0 in 2010, and 11.2 in 2011) (Louisiana Statistical Analysis Center, 2013: p. 46). New Orleans typically accounts for over half of all of the homicides in the state's annual counts (Ibid., p. 76). It should not come as a surprise that according to results of a poll conducted in 2010 by the Kaiser Foundation, the citizens of New Orleans listed crime as the most serious social problem facing the city (Welford, Bond, and Goodison, 2011: p. 1).

Table 1 (below), displays the volume and rate of homicide and population size corresponding to decennial years 1940 to 1990 and annually from 1990 to 2014 for New Orleans. For comparative purposes table 1 also indicates the national average homicide rates.

While the murder rate for New Orleans ranges from 9 to 86, with an average rate of 51.3 for the entire time period shown (1940-2013), the national murder rate has ranged from 5 to 10 over the decades averaging 6.7 over this time span. In New Orleans the murder rates, even the relatively lower rates, are by national comparison substantially higher (over ten times higher than the national rates). For both the city of New Orleans and the nation as a whole, the first half of the 1990s showed the highest murder rates ever. However, beginning in 1995 the national murder rate began a gradual declining pattern, which has stabilized around 5 per 100,000 annually. In New Orleans the murder rates, while also exhibiting a declining trend, however, demonstrated a great deal of variability over the years.

According to table 1, in New Orleans, the year 1940 indicates the lowest volume of homicides (56 incidents with an associated rate of 11 per 100,000 population). The year 1960, which has the highest population count, registers the second lowest volume of murders (58 incidents) and the lowest murder rate (9 per 100,000 population). For over three decades (1940 through 1960) the murder rate in the city has been comparable to the rates in other major cities with similar population sizes. These three decades, which register relatively low annual murder rates, represent a period of time of population expansion and rising prosperity. After 1960 the population size of New Orleans demonstrates a declining pattern, while the murder rate shows an increasing trend (jumping approximately ten points in 1970 and 1980, and twenty points in 1990).

Table 1: New Orleans Murder Rates
with National Comparisons 1940-2014

Year	Volume of Murders	Population	Murder Rate	National Murder Rate
1940	56	494,537	11	6
1950	65	570,445	11	5
1960	58	627,525	9	5
1970	121	591,502	20	8
1980	218	557,515	39	10
1990	304	496,968	61	9
1991	345	500,781	69	10
1992	279	505,008	55	9
1993	395	496,619	80	10
1994	424	493,990	86	9
1995	363	487,179	75	8
1996	351	488,300	72	7
1997	267	488,509	55	7
1998	230	471,157	49	6
1999	158	465,828	34	6
2000	175	483,663	36	6
2001	213	477,932	45	6
2002	258	472,744	55	6
2003	274	476,761	59	6
2004	264	461,915	57	6
2005	na	455,188	na	6

2006	162	208,548	77	6
2007*	209	288,113	73	6
2008	179	336,664	53	5
2009	174	354,850	49	5
2010	175	343,829	49	5
2011	200	360,341	56	5
2012	193	369,250	54	5
2013	156	**378,715**	42	5
2014	150	377,022	42	5

Source: *UCR 2013 Violent Crimes in U.S.* Washington, D.C.: FBI, 2014; *UCR 2014 Violent Crimes in U.S.* Washington D.C.: FBI, 2015.

    *   Some writers (e.g., VanLandingham (2007) and some of the authors in our book have cited a homicide rate of 94.7 for 2007, which was estimated using a relatively smaller population base (suggested by the Brooking Institute); this estimate, however, has not been used by the UCR.

The decade of the 1970s appears to be a turning point with regard to the dramatic increases in the murder rates in New Orleans, peaking in 1994 (standing at 86 per 100,000 population). This decade also marked the start of a downward pattern of population growth as well as shifts in industry with increases in unemployment. [1]

By 1997 the population level seemed to have stabilized with a corresponding drop in homicide rate (55 per 100,000). From 1997-2004 the homicide rate continued to drop until it normalized around 48.7 per 100,000, which equals the average rate from 1997 to 2004. Immediately following Hurricane Katrina in August of 2005, the population in New Orleans fell dramatically from 455,188 in 2005 to 208,548 in 2006. However, according to the 2010 census estimates, the population in New Orleans has rebounded to nearly 80 percent of its size prior to Katrina. Apart from the two spikes in the murder rate in 2006 and 2007 (77 and 73 per 100,000 population, respectively) following the Katrina disaster, the murder rate from 2000 to 2012 has been relatively stable (with a twelve-year average of 55.8 and a median of 55).

1. Our historical assessment of the time periods also confirms research evidence. See Kelly Frailing and Dee Wood Harper (2010) for a thorough documentation of the underlying socioeconomic trends that drove this decline.

New Orleans Neighborhood
Homicide Rates across Time and Space

The city of New Orleans is divided into eight New Orleans Police Department (NOPD) districts. Each district is headed by a district commander and has its own staff, mailing address, and geographic jurisdiction. Figure 1 (below) depicts the city of New Orleans (Orleans Parish) divided into its eight NOPD districts offering a view of the city's geographic proximity to other metropolitan areas.

Figure 1

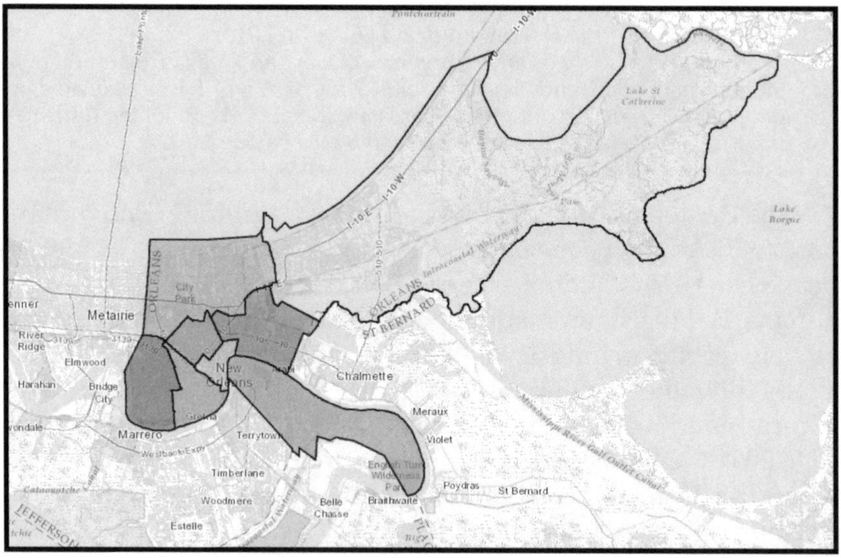

The map below, figure 2, identifies the eight NOPD districts, which include:

District 1: The 1st District covers Tremé and Mid-City.

District 2: The 2nd District covers Uptown and Audubon, incorporating Audubon Park, Audubon Zoo, Tulane University, and Loyola University.

District 3: The 3rd District coverage includes Lakeview, Gentilly, and

Westend, encompassing Dillard University, Southern University of New Orleans, Delgado Community College, University of New Orleans, and City Park.

District 4: The 4th District covers Algiers and English Turn, including the Algiers Ferry Terminal and Mardi Gras World.

District 5: The 5th District covers the 9th Ward and Bywater.

District 6: The 6th District covers the Irish Channel, Central City, and the Garden District.

District 7: The 7th District covers New Orleans East.

District 8: The 8th District covers the French Quarter and Central Business District, including Harrah's Casino, Canal Place, and Bourbon Street.

Figure 2

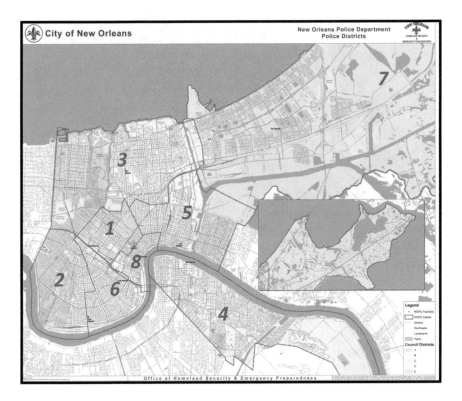

It is important to underscore that while the historical patterns of the spatial spread of homicides in New Orleans has been relatively similar over time, the variation of homicides across neighborhoods is relatively great (Harper, 2007; Harper, Voigt, and Thornton, 2004). In fact, most neighborhoods/areas of the city register relatively few or no murders over the past several decades, while other geographical areas have consistently registered so many murders that average citizens point to these locations and refer to them as killing fields. How can the uneven distribution of murder across time and space be explained? Figure 3 (below) presents a map with a composite depiction of the geographic distribution of homicides across the city of New Orleans for 1960-2000.[2]

Figure 3
1960-2000 Highest Murder Zones

2. Please note: The map above and those following have been created employing the *Arcview* and *SpaceStat* software (Anselin, 1992) using weighted matrices for identifying clustering of homicide and the *Moran Scatterplot Maps* software to illustrate whether homicide rates are distributed randomly across space (Anselin, Cohen, Cook, Gorr, and Tita, 2000; Messner, Anselin, Baller, Hawkins, Deane, and Tolnay, 1999).

Our multi-decade overview of homicide patterns suggests that while there has been relative consistency in the location of the highest distribution of murders in New Orleans for over six decades, these clusters of violent neighborhoods have not been static.

The "hot spots" for murder, which are identified above, have a long standing history for lethal violence. Three of the eight police districts (1st, 5th, and 6th) and within them five zones, have consistently accounted for the highest volume and rate of homicides over the decades. The data also suggests that for large swaths of the city (e.g., 2nd, 3rd, 4th, and 7th police districts) the volume and rate of murder is relatively low (e.g., the rate ranges from 0-2 over the time period).

In order to understand the homicide clusters found in New Orleans over time and space, it is important to consider a neighborhood level analysis and not just a simple cross sectional assessment of the city's demographic or economic indicators. To more fully explain murder requires an examination of the total social context—it's structural, cultural, and historical features (e.g., matching police homicide data for specific areas with demographic, social, and economic characteristics of the areas, which may be gleaned from census track data). For example, Police Zone 6H, which corresponds to census tract 67, may provide a useful case study of demographic and social changes in an area and the corresponding relationship with homicides (see table 2, below).

Based on official police data and matched census track data and historical accounts, Zone 6H was the most populated census track in 1940. However, by 1990 the population declined by 89.4 percent. The murder rate that year was 1,986 per 100,000. It is important to point out that there are thirty-seven murders reported in contiguous census tracts (6I and 6B) with a total population of 4,158 and with 46 percent not in the labor force. It is also interesting to note that 2000 represents the beginning of gentrification in the general area, which accounts for the increase in population.

Table 2: Police Zone 6H (Census tract 67): A Case Study

Year	Annual Volume of Murders	Population Size	% Population Black/White	% Population Not in Labor Force
1940	1	5,687[+]	20/79	34
1950	3	5,636	25/73	33
1960	3	3,681	35/63	34
1970	4	1,862	37/60	43
1980	4	1,149	57/41	44
1990[**]	11[*]	545[++]	48/50	64
2000	5	643[+++]	37/60	43

[+]   The most populous census tract in New Orleans in 1940.
[++] By 1990 population had declined 89.4%.
[+++] Beginning of gentrification.
[*]   Murder rate = 1,986 per 100,000.
[**] 37 murders in 3 contiguous census tracts with a population of 4,158 and 46% not in labor force.

These changes, especially population attrition and high levels of unemployment appear to support William Julius Wilson's (1987) findings related to the development of "truly disadvantaged" neighborhoods. Historical evidence also confirms research results that link growth of drug trade and increasing use of guns in severely disadvantaged neighborhoods of the central city to historic rises in the murder rate from the 1980s through the mid-1990s (see Sheley and Wright, 1995; and Wright and Devine, 1994). Overall, the changes in New Orleans and the corresponding rise in homicide rates seem to support the major findings of the classical social disorganization theory of explaining variations in the rates of crime and violence across neighborhoods.

Key Theoretical Currents and Research Results in the Study of Concentrated Distributions of Homicide across Time and Space

Macro-analysis of ecological and geographic patterns of deviance and crimes with consideration of structural characteristics including historical and cultural features of various locations has received a great deal of attention by social scientists spanning over

180 years.[3] Over the years many researchers have specifically tried to unravel the mystery of reoccurring ecological and geographical clustering of homicides by studying the various spatial and temporal dynamics of nations, regions, cities, neighborhoods, and census blocks (Jones-Webb and Wall, 2008) and their connection with the distribution of homicide rates considering certain historical traditions, cultural norms and values, and structural characteristics.

Taken together, these studies of homicide clustering over time and space have overwhelmingly pointed to the significance of certain places, especially areas with structural characteristics such as high concentrations of poverty and racial and ethnic segregation. Even though some of these basic results have been confirmed over and over, many inconsistencies continue to fuel further investigation. Several distinct lines of approach to the question of the ecological and geographic concentration of homicides are found in the literature. Discussions have mainly focused on (1) the debate over the existence of a culture or subculture of violence and the empirical specification of the most significant cultural factors, and (2) identification of the paths of influence of key structural covariates and the search for relevant intervening variables that come between community structure and lethal violence.

The Culture/ Subculture of Violence Thesis

The "culture of violence" thesis assumes that certain patterns of values and norms characterizing a particular area (such as a nation, region, state, city, or neighborhood) may serve to encourage interpersonal violence or create expectations of violence and even excuse lethal violence under certain circumstances. Often such claims have presumed that this value system persists across racial and ethnic backgrounds and socioeconomic status. This type of macro-analysis generally rests on providing evidence that variations between nations/regions/cities/neighborhoods may be the result

3. See, for example, Guerry 1833; Quetelet, 1835; Park, 1925; Wirth, 1938; Durkheim, 1893/1947, 1897/1951; Simmel, 1950; Merton, 1938; Shaw and McKay, 1942/1969; Hawley, 1950; Newman, 1973; Gibbs and Erickson, 1976; Skogan, 1977, 1990; Cohen and Felson, 1979; Roncek, 1981; Blau and Blau, 1982; Messner, 1983; Sampson, 1987; Sampson and Groves, 1989; Land, McCall, and Cohen, 1990; LaFree, Drass, and O'Day, 1992; Bursik and Grasmick, 1993; Wilson, 1987, 1996; Kubrin and Herting, 2003; Peterson and Krivo, 2005; Hipp, 2007; McCall, Land, and Parker, 2010; and Sampson 2012.

of adherence to values or norms associated with certain historical or cultural traditions that have either a greater or lesser inhibiting force or influencing levels of tolerance for violence.

For instance, the subculture of violence thesis has been applied to community-level analyses and ethnographic studies calling attention to the cultural transference of values and norms that either support violence or at least tolerate violence.[4] For instance, Marvin Wolfgang and Franco Ferracuti in their well-known book, *The Subculture of Violence*, assert that resorting to physical violence appears to be a customary expectation among lower socioeconomic class males and that it is expected and acceptable under circumstances where one's masculinity, reputation, and independence are threatened. They note that both perpetrators and victims of murder are often known to one another and are more likely to have a history of criminal activity preceding lethal events. The authors argue that a community, which holds values that support violence as a routine way of resolving conflict, can expect higher rates of lethal violence.

William Julius Wilson's (1987) conceptualization of the concentration and isolation effects of extreme poverty has inspired a great deal of research seeking to understand association between community cultural and structural factors with concentrations of homicide. Robert Sampson (1993; 2012) claims that community context shapes "cognitive maps" or ecologically structured norms regarding standards and expectations of conduct. These ecologically structured social perceptions influence the probability of violent outcomes. Robert Sampson and Wilson (1995) bringing together structural and cultural variables argue that macro-level socioeconomic conditions that contribute to residential inequality and social isolation ultimately result in the ecological concentration of severely disadvantaged people, which in turn leads to the development of cultural adaptations that are often associated with lack of informal social control and acceptance of violence as a means of resolving conflicts. According to the authors, the concentration of crime and violence in certain areas of American cities is mainly due to concentrated poverty and social isolation and the emergence of patterns of values and norms that adversely affect inner-

---

4. See, for example, Wirth, 1931; Cohen, 1955; Whyte, 1955; Miller, 1958; Cloward and Ohlin, 1960; Wolfgang and Ferracutti, 1967, 1982; Suttles, 1968, 1984; Anderson, 1978, 1999; Wilson, 1987, 1996; Hawkins, 1990, 1997; Sampson, 1993; Pattillo-McCoy, 1999, 2013; and Kubrin and Wadsworth, 2003.

city neighborhoods' capacity for informal social control and social efficacy.

Several ethnographic studies have provided further support for the theory that structurally disadvantaged neighborhoods rely on systems of values and sets of expectations and norms that serve to legitimate or at the very least tolerate violence. For example, Elijah Anderson (1999), in his book *Code of the Streets,* describes the life circumstances and values of the inner-city poor in Philadelphia. Lack of jobs or jobs that pay low living wage, stigma of race, open display of violence associated with drug use and trafficking, and alienation and lack of hope for the future, which typically characterize inner-city environments, place young people at special risk of crime and deviant behavior. Anderson's field study actually identifies two cultural forces running through the neighborhood that shape the residents' value sets and associated patterns of interactions and especially reactions to conflicts:

> *(1)   Decent Values* (referring to middle-class values and mainstream goals) are maintained by working poor families (e.g., they value hard work, education, and self-reliance; they are willing to sacrifice for their children; they are members of faith communities; and they are hopeful of a better future for their children).

> *(2)   Street Values* or "Code of the Streets" (referring to informal rules that organize street order including demands to punish disrespect) are maintained by individuals living in the despair of inner city life who are in opposition to the values of mainstream society (the code demands that disrespect be punished! It is believed that with the right amount of respect a person can avoid "being bothered" in public).

Anderson claims that these two orientations socially organize the community. Their coexistence means that youngsters who are brought up in homes with "decent" values must be able to successfully navigate the demands of the street culture and show respect for the "Code of the Street" culture.

In her book, *Black Picket Fences,* Mary Pattillo (1999; 2013) depicts the advantages and challenges facing black working poor and middle class families who live in spatial proximity and interact at the community level with severely disadvantaged families. Pattillo argues that the "compact geography of the Black Belt does not

suggest a homogeneity of outlook or practice among its residents"
(1999: 209). Both Pattillo and Anderson draw attention to the fact
that the majority of people living in areas of concentrated socioeconomic disadvantage and high levels of crime are law abiding
citizens committed to mainstream norms and values and do not
advocate use of violence. Pattillo concludes that support and empowerment of the often neglected black middle-class would go a
long way to promote mainstream values in poor communities and
help reduce the use of violence.

Neighborhood-level Studies
of Structural Covariates of Homicide

An impressive lineage of researchers dating back to the well-
known research contributions of Clifford Shaw and Henry McK-
ay (1942; 1969) has served to focus criminologists' attention away
from the "kind of people" theories to the "kind of place" theories
of crime. These types of studies have largely emphasized structural
characteristics of an area's socioeconomic status, racial and ethnic
composition, and family structure in predicting geographic clustering of crime, including murder.[5]

Kenneth Land, Patricia McCall, and Lawrence Cohen (1990)
have conducted a review of twenty-one studies with overlapping
structural covariates that are typically hypothesized to be related
to the ecological clustering of homicides. The sample of studies,
which vary by time and unit of analysis (i.e., cities, metropolitan
areas or SMSAs, and states), include the following overlapping covariates: population size, population density, population heteroge-

---

5. See, for example, Blau and Blau, 1982; Sampson and Groves, 1989; Sampson, 1987, 1991, 1993; Harer and Steffensmeier, 1992; Taylor, 1997; Sampson and Raudenbush, 1997; Miles-Doan, 1998; Parker and McCall, 1997; Veysey and Messner, 1999; Titterington, Vollum, and Diamond, 2003; Sun, Triplett, and Gainey, 2004; McCall and Nieuwbeerta, 2007; and Sampson, 2012. The list of structural covariates of homicide has been growing overtime (e.g., indicators include: population distributions taking into account ethnic and racial diversity as well as gender and age distributions; population changes over time (particularly the effects of population mobility and population density); degree of economic inequality; unemployment trends; poverty levels; industrial shifts and polarization of labor; the urban concentration and isolation of the poor and minorities; family structure and family disruption; and degree of collective efficacy/social capital as demonstrated by patterns of community participation and extent of social network systems, effectiveness of informal social controls, and reciprocal levels of support of law and social control organizations/agents.

neity, percent of population age 15-29, percent of male population fifteen years and older, percent divorced, percent of children under the age of eighteen years not living with both parents, median family income, percentage of families living below the official poverty line, the GINI index of family income inequality, percent of unemployment, and a variable indicating southern/non-southern location of cities or metropolitan areas or states.

What is most striking about their findings is that no covariates exhibit consistent statistically significant estimates across all studies. For example, three frequently tested covariates (i.e., population size, population density, and population heterogeneity as indexed by the percent black or white or non-white) fail to exhibit significant positive relationships with homicide rates across studies. Similarly, age structure indices also fail to consistently predict homicide rates (p. 931). The variables measuring a southern culture of violence also prove to be inconsistent predictors. The same can be said of the GINI index of income inequality, even when the percent of poverty is significant. They conclude from their investigation that much of the inconsistency found in the twenty-one studies they have reviewed is mainly attributed to the interference of collinearity[6] (p. 951).

Land, McCall, and Cohen (1990) also perform their own regression model estimations using the same list of overlapping structural covariates allegedly associated with variations in homicide rates. The authors search for significant invariant relationships across time periods and social space is undertaken using large samples, standardized definitions of variables, and an attempt to reduce collinearity among the structural covariates.

In their attempt to diminish collinearity, Land, McCall, and Cohen (1990) identify several structural indexes. For example, their "resource-deprivation/affluence index," appears to have the strongest relationship to homicide rates. This result is consistent across four census periods as well as cities, metropolitan areas, and states.

---

6. Collinearity or multicollinearity refers to a statistical phenomenon in which two or more predictor variables in a multiple regression model are highly correlated, meaning that one can be linearly predicted from the others with a non-trivial degree of accuracy. In this situation the coefficient estimates of the multiple regression may change erratically in response to small changes in the model or the data. Multicollinearity does not reduce the predictive power or reliability of the model as a whole, at least within the sample data themselves; it only affects calculations regarding individual predictors (www.real-statisitcs.com/multiple-regression/collinearity/)

Those areas most deprived have the highest homicide rates, while those most affluent have the lowest rates. The authors claim that these results are consistent with William Julius Wilson's (1987) conclusions related to the concentration and isolation effects of extreme poverty, which account for findings of persistent covariation of the resource-deprivation/affluence index to homicide rates at all levels of analysis (p. 954). Land, McCall, and Cohen's (1990) population-structure index including the percentage-divorced covariate also shows a strong relationship to homicide at all levels of analysis. Finally, age structure as an indicator of homicide appears to be positive only at the state-level of analysis. Regarding the southern subculture of violence thesis, support is only found at the city-level of analysis. For metropolitan areas it is only present in the 1960 dataset suggesting that controls for other variables would probably erase the southern effect.

Over the years numerous studies have specifically addressed the relationship between racial/ethnic segregation and urban homicide particularly looking at differing effects of economic inequality on black and white rates of violence (e.g., Harer and Steffensmeier, 1992; Peterson and Krivo, 1993; Kposowa, Breault, and Harrison, 1995; and Sampson and Wilson, 1995). For instance, Robert Sampson and William Julius Wilson (1995) have conducted a comprehensive review of studies that specifically focus on the relationship between race and criminal violence. They raise concern with a tendency to oversimplify racial and ethnic differences based on either a presumption of a deterministic culture of violence or a set of deterministic social structural influences, especially stemming from relative deprivation. In order to improve understanding of the connection between race/ethnicity and criminal violence, Sampson and Wilson recommend using an integrated structural and cultural approach (i.e., combining key features of Wilson's (1987) structural transformation, Anderson's (1978) cultural adaptation, and Shaw and McKay's (1969) social disorganization).

Ruth Peterson and Lauren Krivo's (2005) review of the post-1995 research literature suggests that structural disadvantage continues to play a critical role across most studies in their review sample in explaining differences in rates of criminal violence for all racial and ethnic groups. They also note that cultural adaptation (e.g., street codes) mainly originate from structural deprivation; however, they note that very few studies adequately measure the "street code" and criminal violence connection (p. 347). While much progress has been made to advance understanding of the complexities related to the ecological concentration of criminal violence in severely disadvantaged neighborhoods, serious methodological questions and gaps in research remain. For example, Peterson and Krivo draw attention to the need to uncover relevant intervening forces that may shed light on the problem (e.g., the effects of criminal justice policies, drug enforcement activities, levels of incarceration, and the effects of community investment and political connections).

Studies of the Distribution of Murder by Motive

Another important issue challenging explanations of variance in rates of murder across space and time, which is independent of the units of analyses, is the nature of the offence itself. It has been claimed that the crime of murder is not one-dimensional and, therefore, may require different explanations for different types of murder (e.g., Parker 1989; Kovandzic, Vieraitis, and Yeisley, 1998; Kubrin, 2003; Kubrin and Weitzer, 2003). However, while disaggregating murder by motive and/or relationship of victim to offender may be theoretically valid, it makes the study of murder, particularly at the neighborhood level, difficult because of the highly skewed nature of the occurrence of murders. Even in neighborhoods with high concentrations of poverty and with the presence of all the other structural and cultural risk factors, murder is still a relatively rare phenomenon. Methodologically, this is only made more complicated by the fact that neighborhoods characterized by severe poverty also represent a highly skewed condition within the context of income distribution. These concerns have motivated Charis Kubrin and Ronald Weitzer (2003) to offer a structural-cultural perspective on specifically *retaliatory* homicide in disadvantaged neighborhoods using statistical and analytical strategies to overcome the problem of measuring and estimating effects of rare phenomena. Their analysis is based on both qualitative and quantitative data. The qualitative data comes from narrative accounts of homicide incidents, which are the source of their cultural information. The quantitative data is derived from the 1990 census data, which provides measures related to the structural correlates, and 1985-1995 police reports, which give the data on the ecological distribution of homicides in St. Louis, Missouri. To address the problems of the highly skewed distribution of the dependent variable, which in this case is the number of homicides (i.e., counts of retaliatory homicides and non-retaliatory homicides), and the high concentration of homicides in specific areas of the city (which is indicated by spatial autocorrelation), the researchers employ the Poisson-based model known as the negative binomial regression and corrective methods of estimating spatial-effects (i.e., the Anselin-Alternative method) to measure the homicide potential (see Anselin et al., 2000).

Kubrin and Weitzer (2003) find three factors (indices) that explain why cultural retaliatory homicides cluster in certain areas of the city: (1) severe economic disadvantage, (2) a neighborhood cultural code reflecting the importance of honor and prestige, the need to address disrespect and save face, and acceptance of using violence for status attainment and personal security, and (3) problematic policing arising from mutual disrespect (i.e., negative police attitudes regarding community inhabitants and in turn the resident's lack of confidence in police ability to address community's crime problems). These three factors combine, resulting in the development of community patterns for resolving disagreements or conflict through informal and often violent means, including retaliatory homicide. Kubrin and Weitzer's description of retaliatory homicide as a type of street justice operating in severely disadvantaged neighborhoods is close to the "crime as social control" phenomenon discussed by Anderson (1999) and Pattillo (1999; 2013) (also see Black, 1983; Parenti, 2000; and Levitov and Harper, 2012).

The Relationship of Incarceration Rates with Murder Rates

Looking at neighborhood incarceration rates as a form of official social control and its effect on murder rates has also interested scholars. For example, Franklin Zimring (2012), in his book entitled *The City That Became Safe: New York's Lessons for Urban Crime and Its Control*, argues that New York City's success in reducing its crime rate, particularly its homicide rate, was not due to increases in its overall incarceration rate. In fact, the opposite seems to be the case (2012: p. 86). Zimring notes: "The modest growth in New York City imprisonment in the first years of the crime drop was about one-third of the national average, and then a substantial decline set in." He continues to argue that "the total incarceration actually occurring in New York City in 2008 was more than 50,000 fewer than would have been consistent with national trends." He concludes: "This huge crime success story took place without even average use of the incapacitation machinery of criminal justice, and alone calls into doubt the status of incapacitation efforts as a necessary condition to large crime declines." If anything, he claims that the real lesson is that New York's lower incarceration rates have been related to significantly lowering the rates of crime including homicide rates (2012: p. 207).

Michelle Alexander (2012), in her book *The New Jim Crow: Mass Incarceration in the Age of Colorblindness*, claims that with the dramatic increase in the disproportionate volume and rate of imprisonment of African Americans and the consequent destruction of African American communities, the U.S. criminal justice system now functions as a contemporary system of social control. By targeting black men through criminal justice policies associated with America's War on Drugs and labeling them as felons, we suddenly have a "legal" form of discrimination in employment, housing, education, and public benefits as well as in denial of the rights to vote and to serve on juries.

The reality of mass incarceration is difficult to dismiss. According to 2012 statistics, the U.S. continues to register the highest incarceration rates in the world since 2002 (International Centre for Prison Studies, 2013). Louisiana stands at the top of the list for highest incarceration rate in the U.S. New Orleans contributes most to the incarceration counts in Louisiana and leads the list of cities with the highest rate in the U. S. (Carson and Sabol, 2012). Alexander (2012) argues that ignoring the disturbing effects of mass incarceration endangers our civil liberties and threatens our nation's fundamental democratic principles.

Structural Covariates and the Patterns of Homicide across Neighborhoods in New Orleans from 1996 to 2004: An In-depth Analysis

Our in-depth analysis of neighborhood patterns of homicide and structural covariates is based on official police data including NOPD annual statistics and a sample of incident reports for 1,975 murders (January 1, 1996-January 1, 2004).[7] To maximize the analysis, this sample only includes homicide cases that have district attorney dispositions and additional data element such as witness information (e.g., reluctance to testify), as well as details regarding cases involving felony drug arrests (e.g., intent to distribute), weapon arrests, and arrests for domestic violence for each zone in the study.

Moreover, census track data for 2000 has been matched to the 107 police zones.[8] The 2000 census, which stands midpoint of the study period, is used to describe the neighborhoods in the four years before and after the census data collection took place with a relatively similar error margin on either side. The following data have been coded for each neighborhood/police zone:

- **Population Size (POP SIZE):** total population of zone.
- **Population Heterogeneity/ Racial Composition (RACIAL COMP):** % African Americans in zone/%white in zone.
- **Population Density (DEN):** % households with 5 or more occupants.
- **Stability (SABIL):** % residing in current household in 1995.
- **High School Education (HS ED):** % 25 years of age and older that have completed high school.
- **Unemployment (UNEMPL):** % unemployed or not in labor force and not in school (15 years of age and over).
- **Family Structure (FAM ST):** % Single-Headed Households with Children
- **Poverty (POV):** % population living below Federal Poverty Index.
- **Public Housing (PUB HU):** zones are classified as containing a public housing development, or being a contiguous neighborhood, or not containing a development or not being contiguous.

7. Our original study included a data set from January 1, 1990, through the first quarter of 2002. The research we use for this chapter has been based on a subsample from 1996 to 2002 to which we added the DA disposition data point as well as homicide data to 2004. The 2000 census data was also used in the analysis.

8. Police zones are used as proxies for neighborhoods. All 107 police zones in the city of New Orleans form the basis of this portion of our study. To match police zones with census tract data in those cases where a police zone is not a unique census tract we apportioned census characteristics based on an average for each data element for each tract. For example, for percent single headed-female household with children, if the police zone includes parts of three census tracts, we take the percent of households for each tract and compute a mean value and assign it to the police zone. As contiguous tracts they are often very similar giving us additional confidence with this methodology.

- **Witness Reluctance (WITNESS)**: number and % of murders in which witnesses who had given statements to the police at the time of arrests subsequently refused to cooperate with the prosecutors.
- **Weapon Arrests (WEAPON)**: total number and % of arrests for illegal gun possession in the zone.
- **Drug Arrests (DRUG)**: total number and % of felony drug arrests in the zone.
- **Domestic Arrests** (DOM ARST): total number and % of arrests for state (felony) domestic violence.
- **Homicides (HOM):** total number of homicides recorded by the police.
- **Murders (MUR)**: total number and % of murders in zones where arrests were made. Other murder-related variables are also created based on police data (i.e., the mean values for each decade) including: the *total number of murders* in zones; *location of murders* (zones where victims were found); *weapon used* (guns, knives, other); *motive for murder* (retaliatory, drug related, argument, domestic, other); and the *sex, age, and race/ethnicity of each victim and perpetrator.*

As noted above, considerable attention over the years has been devoted to scientifically unraveling the complexities surrounding the connection between the concentration of certain structural and cultural features and the ecological concentration of criminal violence or homicide. Most studies irrespective of the unit of analysis (e.g., region, state, SMSA, city, neighborhood, or police zone) usually attempt, through some form of regression analysis, to identify those variables that account for the greatest variance across their units of analysis and with the least amount of multi-collinearity. In order to avoid collinearity, we employ an *i*ndex model[9] suggested by Kenneth Land, Patricia McCall and Lawrence Cohen (1990)

9. Land, Patricia McCall, and Lawrence Cohen (1990) propose an index model with the following formulation: $M=k \ (A+B+C)^i \ (X+Y+Z)^j$. In this case the independent variable is murder (M) and A, B, and C are three independent variables that together comprise an index such as a concentrated poverty index, which could include, for example, such variables as unemployment, percent population living below the poverty line, and percent of adults over 25 years of age not completing high school. The variables *i* and *j* are exponential fit variables. A larger value means that this particular index has a stronger effect on murder (*M*). However, explaining murder rate variance is considerably more complex than a straight linear relationship between a composite index made up of three variables. Thus, a larger number of theoretically relevant variables may go into making up multiple indices. This is the theoretical model that we followed in our study of murder from 1996-2003 in New Orleans.

to perform a principal component analysis in order to simplify the dimensionality of the structural covariate space. Therefore, in addition to conducting an item-by-item analysis of the structural covariates and cultural factors and their relationship to lethal violence, we developed three indices along theoretical lines:

> **(1)   *Neighborhood Structure Index*** (NSI) including population diversity (as measured by % minority population); population density (as measured by % households with five or more persons per household); population stability (as measured by % occupants residing at address five years or more); and family structure (as measured by % single-headed of households with children);

> **(2)   *Concentrated Poverty Index*** (CPI) including poverty level (as measured by % population living below the Federal Poverty Index; unemployment level (as measured by % population fifteen years and older not in school and not in the labor force); education level (as measured by % less than high school education for adults twenty-five years and older);

> **(3)   *Culture of Violence Index*** (CVI) including % felony drug arrests; % weapons arrests; % witness non-cooperation in cases by neighborhood; and calls for service for domestic/intimate/family violence.

We begin with a correlation matrix that shows the statistical association among the variables that are employed in the study. The results are presented in table 3. Every census characteristic of the neighborhoods is highly correlated with variations in the volume of murder at the neighborhood level of analysis. What is particularly striking but not surprising is the relatively high correlations between the violent culture indicators (i.e., drug related arrests, illegal weapon arrests, and witness reluctance) and murder. While the dataset contains information for all 107 police zones and overlapping census tracts in the city, it is again important to note that only three police zones/census tracks account for more than half of all murders over the observational time frame and the majority of police zones/census tracks follow a linear progression and are relatively free of any homicides.

Table 3:
Correlation Matrix Showing the
Association among the Key Variables in the Study

Key Variables	Pop Comp	Fam Str	Den	Stabil	HS Ed	Unem	Pov	Weap	Drug	Witness	Dom Arst	Murders
Pop Comp	1											
Family Str	.626**	1										
Density	.419**	.687**										
Stability	.368**	.323**	320**	1								
HS Edu	.498**	.505**	.310**	.250**	1							
Unempl	.414**	.587**	.493**	.114	.262**	1						
Poverty	.533**	.508**	.432**	.209*	.280**	.470**	1					
Weapons	.245*	.499**	.426**	.144	.318**	.321**	.494**	1				
Drug	.236*	629**	.525**	.149	.445**	.420**	.374**	.720**	1			
Witness	.416**	.501**	.413**	.328**	.369**	.258**	.578**	.608**	.639**	1		
Domestic Arrests	.288**	.264**	.108	.031	.361**	.183	.233*	.256**	.294**	.256**	1	
Murders	.429**	.591**	.479**	.272**	.408**	.373**	.562**	624*	.734**	839**	303**	1

*   Correlation is significant at the 0.05 level (2-tailed)
** Correlation is significant at the 0.01 level (2-tailed)

Further examination using a negative binomial regression model (covering the eight-year span) suggests that the distribution of murder does, generally, vary along theoretically relevant dimensions. For instance, structural variables such as population density and single-headed households play significant roles in explaining murder in high murder zones and are less significant in low murder zones (e.g., Shaw and McKay, 1969; and Sampson and Groves, 1989). Moreover, neighborhood isolation, concentrated poverty, and race are strongly associated with high rates of murder along the lines suggested by Wilson (1987) and Sampson and Wilson (1995).

Overall, neighborhood structural/cultural factors are a great deal more complex than we have first imagined. Not only are city history and context critical, but also neighborhood history and context are important in understanding the structural/cultural dimensions associated with murder. We have found that in

New Orleans in high murder zones there appear to be systems of values and community expectations of violence, which apparently are part of daily routines. For example, we also find that the drug-crime connection, weapons arrests, and witness refusal to testify are significantly linked to variations in murder rates across neighborhoods (e.g., Blumstein, 1995; and Sheley and Wright, 1995).

Below we present a linear regression model depicting the results of the three indices: (1) *Neighborhood Structure Index* (NSI); (2) *Concentrated Poverty Index* (CPI); and (3) *Violent Culture Index* (VCI). As can be seen in table 4, the model accounts for approximately 55 percent of the variance across neighborhoods with most of the variation accounted for by the VCI.

Table 4: Linear Regression Model

Coefficients [a]

Model		Unstandardized Coefficients		Standardized Coefficients
		B	Std. Error	Beta
1	(Constant)	-18.388	2.936	
	CPI	.879	.453	.182
	NSI	1.012	.558	.151
	VCI	2.476	.369	.539

[a] Dependent Variable: murders

54.7% of the variance is explained by the model. What is most significant in this model is the violent culture index (VCI). Neighborhood structure index (NCI) and concentrated poverty index (CPI) contribute relatively little.

A regression path analysis using the same three indices suggests that a strong direct linkage of concentrated poverty to the violent culture index and in turn to variation in murder exists across neighborhoods.

Figure 4: Path Model

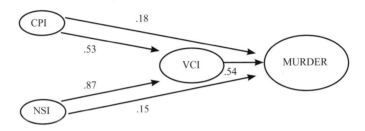

The outcome of this analysis including the path model demonstrates that the *neighborhood structure index* and the variables that make it up contribute little to explaining the variations in murder rate across the city. Particularly noteworthy is the weakness of the association of population stability with murder. While this variable has empirically been connected to homicide predictions particularly in studies with larger aggregations (i.e., cities, SMAs, and regions) and has been shown to be associated with social disorganization, it appears that at the neighborhood level, at least in our research, perhaps the opposite is true. At the neighborhood level a high percent of residents living at the same address for over five years may be a measure of a neighborhood in decline (i.e., negative motility due to large numbers of people *unable* to move) rather than a measure of neighborhood stability where people "choose" to remain. These neighborhoods may have gone through transitional periods with high attrition trends—losing families who have the ability to move out—but at some point those who could have vacated and those who remain are essentially trapped by their inability to leave and are suffering the consequences (see the case study of Police Zone 6H above on page 14).

The "negative motility" or a measure of a stable but trapped resident population may help account for the high levels of distrust of the criminal justice system as measured for example by witness reluctance to testify in murder cases. The inability to leave the neighborhood and the fact of being known to the perpetrators may serve to set the stage for intimidation of witnesses and what has been locally termed as the "silence of violence," which inadvertently may appear to condone and perpetuate violence.

The importance of the relationship between the *concentrated poverty indicators* (CPI) and the *violence culture indicators* (VCI) is strongly established by the evidence. Disadvantaged communities with high levels of murder appear to be characterized by high levels of distrust and disregard for formal mechanisms of social control (reflected in witness refusal to testify) along with the apparent ready availability of weapons, and a willingness to use them, (measured by felony gun arrests in the context of ubiquitous drug trade (reflected in felony drug arrests), and finally the presence of widespread domestic violence (reflected in domestic violence calls for service).

The strong association among drugs, guns, and witness reluctance has led to the exploration of the effect of the disaggregation of murder (by motive) on the model. Results of an analysis of the motive for murder (i.e., domestic, narcotics, and retaliation) and the prosecutor outcomes for each type (i.e., suggesting that cases fail due to the inability to indict because of witness refusal to testify in the case against the accused) are shown in table 5:

Table 5: Indictments vs. Witness Refusal by Motive

Count

Motive	D.A Disposition		
	Indicted	Refused Witness	Total
Domestic	74	6	80
Narcotics	57	71	128
Retaliation	76	68	144
Total	207	145	352

Phi=.378**; p <.001

The table shows a significant relationship between drug and retaliatory murder and witness' reluctance. Comparing drug and retaliatory murder with domestic murder, significant differences in witness reluctance were found.

Domestic homicides rarely have witness issues. In most instances the perpetrator does not even leave the scene of the incident and frequently calls the police to report the crime. Consequently, indictments for these crimes are rarely problematic. On the other hand, in homicides where retaliation and/or drugs are the motives, witness reticence is highly problematic. For example, from 1996 until the end of 2003 there were 1,975 murders recorded in New Orleans. Among the cases where an arrest was made and a witness was identified, the police identified 272 murders that were classified as "retaliatory" or "drug related," of which 133 defendants were indicted. However, in 139 cases (involving retaliation and drug related homicides) where witnesses observed perpetrators committing murders but refused to cooperate with prosecutors to testify, over 50 percent of the perpetrators were back on the streets!

Interviews with police officers suggest that while the homicide division of NOPD has a clearance rate in the 40-45 percent range, they are confident that they know who the killers are in over 80 percent of cases, but lack creditable witnesses to complete the cases. The lack of motivated witnesses to crimes is not a new development in the history of New Orleans; it is cited as a problem in New Orleans by the State of Louisiana's Attorney General as early as 1860 (Rousey, 1996; and Redfield, 2000).

In further analysis, we examine some measures of the relative effectiveness of the criminal justice system (e.g., homicide clearance rates, drug related arrests, arrests associated with illegal weapon possession, and general incarceration rates), and the level of trust in the system held by community members (e.g., witness cooperation in resolving homicide cases). In some neighborhoods the level of trust in the criminal justice system has been eroded to the point of being non-existent as indicated by witness reluctance to testify in murder cases and unlawful gun carrying behavior (measured by arrests for illegal gun possession). Illicit drug activities with neighborhood-based gangs that are armed and wage war on each other and anyone else that might get in their way are characteristic of some of these neighborhoods (e.g., Blumstein 1995; and Sheley and Wright, 1995; Vera Institute, 2007) and contributes to a climate of fear and an understandable lack of motivation to cooperate with the criminal justice system. Sampson and Raudenbush (1997) argue that in such areas individuals may resort to violence as a means of "self-help" because they feel cut off from lawful non-violent means of resolving conflicts; in such environments lethal violence appears to be part of informal social control, which may account for the high concentration of lethal violence in some neighborhoods. This type of "collective efficacy" is often accompanied by collective intimidation or attempts by gangs and drug dealers to promote community-wide non-cooperation with the criminal justice system. Witness intimidation particularly serves to reinforce the perception that cooperation with the criminal justice system is dangerous (Curriden, 1994; Finn and Healey, 1996; and Comparet-Cassani, 2002). Under these circumstances some people may feel that they can commit murder with impunity.

Post-Katrina Homicide Trends — 2006 to Present

New Orleans's unfortunate historical distinction of being the murder and incarceration capital of the United States well preceded the catastrophic consequences following Hurricane Katrina. The breakdown of the criminal justice system along with the collapse of the municipal infrastructure, has served to expose the city's deepest problems that were demonstrated to the world by its inability to respond to the needs of its most vulnerable citizens — the poor, the elderly, and the sick. Crime and violence, long associated with the city's history are also evidenced during every phase of this multi-disaster event we call the "Katrina Disaster" (underscoring the fact that closely following Katrina's strike, there were several levee breaches, a major oil spill, a chemical plant explosion, a breakdown of social order, Hurricane Rita, and over one hundred tornadoes spawned across the region, making this multi-disaster event unprecedented in America's history). The pattern of lethal violence following the Katrina Disaster offers further insights into the nature of the intersection of structural covariates, culture, and violence. The traditional criminal justice system's failure to prevent crime and violence in the past along with its breakdown in the aftermath of the disaster, and its continued challenges in ensuring safety and justice, raises many questions including what alternatives or new vision of justice are possible.

It is worth noting that while the disaster seems to have

brought our attention to some of the worst failings both of a personal and societal nature, it also has inspired some of the best acts of kindness and civic responsibility and neighborhood responses. For example, a strong sense of neighborhood efficacy has developed over many parts of the city, which has been exhibited most notably by post-Katrina neighbors in various communities (rich and poor alike) coming together to help each other rebuild and plan infrastructure improvements. Neighborhoods all around the city have shown high participation rates in annual events such as "night out against crime," which include block parties, often with food and music provided and the presence of district police officers.

Data for this portion of our study comes from official police reports and official population estimates. We also give consideration to several studies: "Crime and Safety in Central City: A Community's Perspective" conducted in 2006 by The Metropolitan Crime Commission (2007); "Proposals for New Orleans' Criminal Justice System: Best Practices to Advance Public Safety and Justice," a report submitted to the Criminal Justice Committee of the New Orleans City Council by the Vera Institute of Justice (2007); Bureau of Justice Assistance, *An Assessment of the New Orleans Police Department Homicide Section: Recommendations for Best Practices*, (2010); Wellford, Bond, and Goodison's *Crime in New Orleans: Analyzing Crime Trends and New Orleans' Responses to Crime* (2011); and *NOLA for Life: A Comprehensive Murder Reduction Strategy* (2012).

We start with an overview of the homicide trends in the post-Katrina era. Even though the population has dramatically been affected by the disaster and the city is substantially smaller in size with the ethnic and racial composition and residential patterns significantly changed (e.g., public housing developments have been dismantled and replaced with less dense multi-income housing and with growth in availability of Section-8 housing across the city of New Orleans and oversight of affordable housing by private property management), the murder rates, with the exception of the two years immediately following the Katrina Disaster, have remained relatively stable in the post-Katrina period. In 2006 the city, with an estimated population of 208,000, registered 162 homicides with a murder rate of 77 per 100,000; and in 2007 the city, with an estimated population of 288,113, registered 209 murders with a murder rate of 73 per 100,000. These two aberrant years represent the highest rates in a seventeen year period. However, the murders concentrated in essentially the same areas that have been identified over and over again in our research. Following 2007, the homicide rate again begins its descending trend with 179 murders in 2008 (rate 53 per 100,000), 174 murders in 2009 (rate 49 per 100,000), and 175 murders in 2010 (rate 49 per 100,000). There is, however, a 13 percent increase in the volume of murders from 2010 to 2011 (199 murders, rate 56 per 100,000); however, thereafter there is a decline in the number of murders with 193 in 2012 (rate 54 per 100,000), and 155 in 2013 (rate 42 per 100,000), a 20 percent drop. The average homicide rate for 2000-2013 is 53.9 and for the last eight post-Katrina years, the average homicide rate is 56.5.

Wellford, Bond, and Goodison (2011) examine homicides in New Orleans in 2009 and 2010 and find that, similar to other cities across the United States, homicides in New Orleans are concentrated geographically. In their study, which examined criminal homicides from April 18, 2009, to May 11, 2010, they find that about 72 percent of the events occurred primarily in Districts 1, 5, 6, and 7 (2011: p. 18). More recent analysis of current years indicates the same findings. For reporting year 2012, districts 1, 5, 6, and 7 resulted in 70 percent of all murders in New Orleans (NOPD spreadsheet, 2013). Wellford et al., reported that the most common "official" motive for murders was drug-related, accounting for about 29 percent of the total, closely followed by homicides committed with firearms in the context of revenge/retaliation killings, followed by arguments and conflicts, 19 percent. Results from 2012 reveal similar findings; however, the percentages are smaller. Narcotics account for about 14 percent of official motives, followed by arguments, 12 percent, and retaliations, 11 percent. (* About 44 percent of "Murder Motives" were reported by the NOPD as ""Unknown" in reporting year 2012). Both victims and perpetrators of homicides tend to be relatively young, African American males who have previous criminal records. Most victims and perpetrators are not employed. This trend continued for the 2012 murders in New Orleans, with 94 percent of victims and about 82 percent of perpetrators being young black males (NOPD spreadsheet, 2013). Wellford et al., find that the connection of homicides with gang involvement in drug markets is apparently less evident in New Orleans now than in the past and also less than in other cities in the United States (p. 22). That finding appears to still be the case at least through the reporting year 2013 based on official NOPD statistics although recent arrests of gang members for the commission of violent crimes including non-lethal shootings have been reported in 2014.

Reasons for the recent declines in homicides have been attributed to Mayor Landrieu's new crime fighting program, called: *NOLA for Life: A Comprehensive Murder Reduction Strategy* (see table 6, below). Many of the key initiatives such as focusing on training and jobs and urban renewal in neighborhoods are no doubt long term in their implementation and subsequent effects on violence and murder reduction. Strengthening and rebuilding the New Orleans Police Department in terms of organization, improving community trust, and revamping the Homicide Unit (e.g., proactive hot spot policing and new data-driven law enforcement operations focusing on more efficient and effective deployment of resources such as Data-Driven Approaches to Crime and Traffic Safety [DDACTS]) likewise will take time to impact murder rates in the city. Currently, the NOPD is under a federal consent decree to make numerous changes based on past problems in the department, although many of the deficiencies have been addressed in a comprehensive sixty-five-point plan to completely remake the department by former Chief Ronal Serpas (See chapter 8).

More immediate initiatives to prevent and stop shootings and murders particularly among young males have been implemented shortly after the launching of *NOLA for Life* in October 2012. The Group Violence Reduction Strategy (GVRS) designed by criminologist David Kennedy, involves concentrated law enforcement in high crime areas focused on groups of "known" violent individuals based on the belief that future "crimes can be prevented when the costs of committing a crime are perceived by the offender to outweigh the benefits." Young males at risk of becoming victims of violence as well as violent adult and juvenile offenders who are known chronic offenders have been targeted by the police.

NOLA for Life
Comprehensive Murder Reduction Strategy
September 2013

NOLA FOR LIFE PILLARS	FOCUS	KEY INITIATIVES
Stop the Shootings	Special focus on highest risk population of young men who are killing and being killed. Our message to them: Stop Shooting.	• Project Safe Neighborhoods • Ceasefire New Orleans • Group Violence Reduction Strategy • Multi-agency Gang Unit • Violent Crime Impact Teams
Invest in Prevention	The city cannot arrest its way out of this problem. NOLA for Life puts heavy emphasis on helping our young people and families succeed.	• Mayor's Strategic Command to Reduce Murder • NOLA for Life Midnight Basketball • Trauma Response in Schools • Connect High Need Students with Coordinated System of Care • Family Violence Prevention Strategy • National Forum on Youth Violence Prevention • Real-time Resources Mobile Applications • NOLA for Life Fund • NOLA for Life Community of Practice • NOLA for Life Mentoring • Coordinate and Strengthen the Behavioral Health System • Protect Mental Health Services

Promote Jobs and Opportunity	People need a chance to change their lives. Training and better access to good jobs provides a new path away from violence towards opportunity.	• NOLA Youth Works Summer Jobs Program • Comprehensive Workforce Reentry Strategy • Pathways to Prosperity • Lot Maintenance Pilot Program
Get Involved and Rebuild Neighborhoods	To make New Orleans safe we all need to do our part, get involved and rebuild our neighborhoods. We need everyone to be committed to inclusiveness and making a difference.	• Fight the Blight • NOLA for Life Days • Lighting the City • Quality of Life STAT • NOPD Community Policing • Public Awareness Campaign
Strengthen the NOPD	Continue with the comprehensive 65-point plan to completely remake the police department. We must move full speed ahead to see results.	• NOPD Leadership Training • Proactive Hot Spot Policing • Improve Community Trust with the use of Procedural Justice • Equip NOPD Crime lab • Enhance NOPD Homicide Unit • Project Blood Work • Release Public Calls for Service Data

It has been projected that the impact of the GVRS will be a 35-80 percent reduction in community-wide homicides (City of New Orleans, 2012: p. 19). This is a bold assertion and only time will tell whether this projection is met. Another initiative, "Ceasefire," was announced in April 2012 in a 6th District Central City neighborhood in New Orleans (section bounded by South Claiborne Avenue,

Washington Avenue, Oretha Castle Haley Boulevard, and Thalia Street) in which staff were given the task of "short-circuiting" street violence by sending in "interrupters" (trained community members) to meet personally with individuals involved in conflicts that either have resulted or could result in bloodshed. Interrupters typically meet with victims of violence, their friends, and relatives in the streets, in their homes, and even in hospitals and seek to prevent future revenge violence from occurring.

Early results indicate that while some retaliatory violence has been prevented through the efforts of Ceasefire outreach workers, shooting and murders have not been reduced in the targeted geographical area; in fact they actually increased in the comparable geographical area and times from 2012 to 2013 (e.g., see Vargas, May 23). The selection of a neighborhood in the 6th district to test Ceasefire no doubt was influenced from a report done by the New Orleans Metropolitan Crime Commission (MCC), "Crime and Safety in Central City" (2007), which found that results of a 2006 community survey with residents in the 6th district suggested that citizens had high levels of fear of crime as a consequence of the high number of murders in their residential area and skepticism with the ability of the New Orleans Police Department to prevent crime from occurring. Principal recommendations from the MCC study include: (1) The NOPD should try to build greater community awareness of their presence and activities; (2) The NOPD should work to earn the trust and confidence of the community with residents, which is deemed to be paramount in the criminal justice system's ability to prevent and control criminal activity; and (3) City officials and community groups should engage in activities to clean up Central City, involve children in constructive activities, work to improve police/community interactions, and develop a neighborhood watch program (MCC, 2007b: Executive Summary).

Focusing on perceived problems with the components of the criminal justice system in the city have been voiced in several other studies since Hurricane Katrina, including the Vera Institute of Justice in its 2007 study, *Proposals for New Orleans' Criminal Justice System: Best Practices to Advance Public Safety and Justice*. Unlike other critiques of the criminal justice system, rather than focusing on law enforcement, Vera researchers suggest that New Orleans can improve public safety by pursuing several new policies or programs.

These include:

(1) Early triage of cases and routine communication between police and prosecutors;
(2) A wider range of pretrial release options;
(3) Community-services sentencing and greater use of alternatives to prison; and
(4) More appropriate and cost-effective sanctions for municipal
offenses.

Some of these recommendations appear to have been implemented in the Orleans Parish criminal justice system. For example, while results from the October 14, 2008, Metropolitan Crime
Commission Orleans Parish Criminal Justice Accountability Report
documents relatively large numbers of arrests for minor offenses,
later reports beginning in 2009-11 indicate that arrest trends suggest that the NOPD has been reducing the number of municipal
arrests in favor of municipal citations and significant reductions
have been found in misdemeanor, traffic, and municipal violations
(MCC, May 14, 2012). However, while decreasing trends in minor,
municipal arrests have continued in 2012, there have been increases
in felony arrests and "felony conviction rates compared to previous
years as a result of improved coordination between the police and
prosecutors" (MCC, May 12, 2013).

Ronal Serpas's concluding chapter in this book, "The Future
of Lethal Violence in New Orleans," addresses several of the past
studies that have focused on the New Orleans Police Department
and its role in reducing lethal violence in the city as well as current
strategies and programs. One of these studies, requested by Mayor
Mitch Landrieu and Serpas in the summer of 2010, was conducted
by the Bureau of Criminal Justice Statistics (BCJ), *An Assessment of
the New Orleans Police Department Homicide Section: Recommendations
for Best Practices*, 2010. The BCJ research assessment team (including recognized and experienced homicide investigators, forensic
experts, and researchers) has made recommendations for improvement in fourteen key areas of homicide investigation ranging from
management and human resources, policies and procedures, case
management, relationship with the district attorney, forensic issues, and community and victim relationships and outreach. In all,
eighty-two specific recommendations have been made, all directed

to assist the NOPD in increasing the homicide clearance and conviction rate in the city and preventing future homicides from occurring. Incorporating the BCJ recommendations and others, including a 2010 Civil Rights Investigation by the Department of Justice, Serpas developed a sixty-five-point plan designed to reform the NOPD launched in August 2010, *Rebuilding the New Orleans Police Department – First Steps*, which is reviewed and discussed in chapter 9. Ten principles are employed to guide the reform of the department and implement the plan, which has been in effect since June of 2012. Underpinning the plan are the goals of changing the culture of the department; embracing a community policing philosophy, community outreach, and transparency; improveing hiring, training, and crime fighting, especially to bring down the murder rate. In addition to re-engineering the Homicide Unit of the NOPD (e.g., doubling the number of detectives, better training, proactive community engagement), new advanced software referred to as "Data-Driven Policing" including *Omega* (used to enhance Compstat to direct police activities with pin-point accuracy on crime hotspots), *Data-Driven Violent Crime Trend Strategy* (DDVCTS) (used to chart, link, and analyze offenses such as homicides, shootings, drug, and gun arrests leading to the development of proactive policing and optimization of police resources), and *Data-Driven Approaches to Crime and Traffic Safety* (DDACTS) (used to integrate location-based crime (Part 1 and II UCR offenses), and traffic crash data to deploy law enforcement (See appendix A, chapter 9). Also, the use of social network analysis (SNA) employed by social scientists (e.g., Papachristos and Wildeman, 2013), is being used by the NOPD to analyze known individuals who are at high risk because of their participation in shooting incidents, either as suspected shooters or victims. Such information is being used to identify individuals at highest risk to becoming involved in homicides as perpetrators or victims.

Future Projections and Recommendations

Our attempt at explaining murder at the neighborhood level of analysis finds variations along theoretically relevant dimensions. Some neighborhoods seem to be completely immune to lethal violence while others are saturated almost to the point of ceasing to exist or function in any meaningful way as a neighborhood. That is to say, short of retaliatory murder, informal means of social control do not seem to exist. Street norms and values such as those suggested by Anderson (1999) and Pattillo (1999; 2013) seem to dictate non-cooperation with the criminal justice system undermining the effectiveness of formal social control. This has produced what is known on the streets as the sixty-day homicide rule.[10]

By contrast, the overwhelming majority of neighborhoods in the city are murder free for exactly the opposite reasons others are plagued with lethal violence. These include some neighborhoods that are very poor, but mostly neighborhoods with relatively low levels or no poverty and relatively smaller rates of drug trafficking or felony gun arrests. Based on our path analysis there is a clear connection linking concentrated poverty to the presence of a violent subculture, which in turn seem to drive up the murder rate at the neighborhood level of analysis. However, our study demonstrates that structural features of neighborhoods are a great deal more complex than first imagined, especially when considered from different angles (i.e., longitudinal analysis, cross-sectional analysis, and case study). Neighborhoods, which may represent certain features that persist over time, are not static. Constructing adequate measures of structural and cultural predictors of violence remains a significant research challenge.

It is important to note that if we are to understand the phenomenon of murder at the neighborhood level, we must have more than a simple assessment of its demographic or economic indicators. To more fully explain murder requires a holistic examination of the social context — its structural, cultural, and historical characteristic and intersections.

As has been noted, the public health (PH) perspective is currently being tried in New Orleans chiefly in addressing the problem of youth violence and murder. Despite the lack of long- and short-term data at the present time for many of the initiatives and strategies set forth in the *NOLA for Life*, the emphasis is on reducing the violence risk factors, of which there are three types: (1) institutional/structural and cultural (e.g., familial or neighborhood factors or governmental/policy factors), (2) criminogenic commodities (e.g., guns), and (3) situational (e.g., drug use) (See, Thornton, Voigt, and Harper (2013, p. 23) and Prothrow-Stith, 1991). Key elements of the

---

10. Louisiana law requires that a prisoner be released from custody if in sixty days they have not been indicted for the crime.

PH-based *NOLA for Life* include:

(1) Focus on prevention: preventing violence before it occurs
(2) Data-driven: targeting risk and protective factors
(3) Collaborative: building multi-disciplinary partnerships
(4) Population-base: situating the individual within the larger societal framework (City of New Orleans, December 10, 2012)

There is a real effort to engage youth, parents, and other community stakeholders in the planning process and to coordinate
interagency information sharing and existing resources. Unlike
many past initiatives to reduce violence, *NOLA for Life* does not
exclusively focus on a law enforcement initiative to solve the
crime problem. In fact, the one thing that most people agree on in
trying to prevent or reduce murder in the city is that we cannot
"arrest" our way out of the problem. The PH approach challenges
the moral value about who should be blamed for the problem of
violence, resulting in a more favorable disposition regarding offenders and the victims of violence and particularly a restorative
justice approach.

While there is evidence that New Orleans may be on a path
toward declining murder rates, the city is still experiencing a much
higher rate of homicide (with over 42 per 100,000 registered in
2013) than comparable cities in the United States. There are reasons, however, to believe that further declines in the years ahead
may be realized. For instance, the key quality of life indicators in
New Orleans have been steadily improving in the post-Katrina period (e.g., median household incomes have been rising as has the
rate of home ownership and education has been improving) (2010
Census). Equally important is evidence that educational attainment
levels have been rising. Currently there is a larger percentage of
youth who have the potential to continue on to higher education
and possess the basic credentials to be successful.[11] Evidence also
suggests that there has been a decrease in the at-risk population.
For example, the most criminogenic age group (15-24 year olds)
is projected to further decline in real numbers and as a proportion of the total population. In 2000, 15-24 year olds numbered
77,244. That number declined to 53,429 in 2012 and is projected to

11.   Retrieved from: http://www.louisianabelieves.com/docs/data-management/cohort-
graduation-rates-(2006-2012).pdf?sfvrsn=2)

be around 47,678 in 2015 and 46,610 in 2020 (U.S. Census Bureau; table 2: Projections of the Population by Selected Age Groups and Sex for the United States: 2015-2060). There has also been a decline observed in the volume and rate of violent crimes reported to the police, which are indicators that are used to project lower incarceration rates in New Orleans in the future (Austin, Ware, and Ocker, 2011: p. 12).

Serious challenges, however, still remain in New Orleans despite the demographic trends and the best efforts of all involved. These include:

(1) The deeply ingrained culture of violence in New Orleans, which goes back over a hundred years (see chapter 1).
(2) Extremely high rates of trauma and associated mental health disorders and lack of resources to deal with these problems due to recent cuts in health services.
(3) A need to work with schools on a "bottom up" approach.
(4) Historic distrust of public process.
(5) Little data on youth violence and related risk factors to help inform proactive prevention.

At the time of this writing, December 2014, the volume of murders in New Orleans has continued to decline, but at a slower pace than the substantial drop in 2013. The count appears to be maintaining a decreasing trend for a third consecutive year and there are hopes that at year's end in 2015, the declining trend will continue. However, many criminologists, city officials, police, and the public wonder if the positive effects of programs such as *NOLA for Life* will be negated by retaliatory murders and multiple-victim shootings such as those recently committed on Bourbon Street and in the Lower 9th Ward, which were carried out by a cohort of young men who have often spent more time in prison than in school, and who have very few options for legitimate employment (Daley, 2014: A-6). At this point we cannot predict whether our efforts to come together as a community to address our problems will be successful. However, we can say with certainty that if we fail to try to do something or go back to "business as usual," nothing will change, and our opportunity to make a difference will be squandered.

References

Albanese, J. (1985). *Organized Crime in America*. Cincinnati, OH: Anderson Publishing.

Alexander, Michelle. (2012). *The New Jim Crow: Mass Incarceration in the Age of Colorblindness*. New York: New Press.

American Community Survey 5-Year Estimates. Demographic and Housing Estimates. (2007-2011). Retrieved from: http://www.dof.ca.gov/research/demographic/state_census_data_center/american_community_survey/.

Anderson, Elijah. (1978). A *Place on the Corner*. Chicago, IL: University of Chicago Press.

———. (1990). *Streetwise: Race, Class and Change in an Urban Community*. Chicago: University of Chicago Press.

———. (1999). *Code of the Streets: Decency, Violence and the Moral Life of the Inner City*. New York: W. W. Norton and Company.

Anselin, Luc. (1992). *SpaceStat, A Software Package for Analysis of Spatial Data*. Santa Barbara, CA: National Center for Geographic Information and Analysis, University of California.

Anselin, Luc, Jacqueline Cohen, David Cook, Wilpen Gorr, and George Tita. (2000). "Spatial Analyses of Crime." In David Duffee (Ed.), *Criminal Justice*, Vol. 4, *Measurement and Analysis of Crime and Justice*. (pp. 213-62). Washington, D.C.: National Institute of Justice.

Austin, James, Wendy Ware, and Roger Ocker. (2011). *Orleans Parish Prison Ten-Year Inmate Population Projection*. Washington, D.C.: U.S. Department of Justice.

Baiamonte, John. (1986). *Spirit of Vengeance: Nativism and Louisiana Justice, 1921-1924*. Baton Rouge: Louisiana State University Press.

Baller, Robert, Luc Anselin, Steven Messner, Glenn Deane, and Darnell Hawkins. (2001). "Structural covariates of U.S. county homicide rates: Incorporating spatial effects." *Criminology* 39 (3): 561-91.

Bell, Wendell. (1954). "A Probability Model for the Measurement of Ecological Segregation." *Social Forces* 32: 357-64.

Black, Donald. (1983). "Crime as social control." *American Sociological Review* 48: 34-45.

Blau, J., and P. Blau. (1982). "The cost of inequality: metropolitan structure and violent crime." *American Sociological Review* 47 (1): 114-29.

Blumstein, Alfred. (1995). "Youth violence, guns, and the illicit drug industry." *Journal of Criminal Law and Criminology* 86 (1): 10-37.

Brantingham, Patricia L., and Paul J. Brantingham. (1981). "Notes on the geometry of crime." In Paul J. Brantingham and Patricia L. Brantingham (Eds.), *Environmental Criminology.* (pp. 27-54). Beverly Hills, CA: Sage.

————. (1984). *Patterns in Crime.* New York: Macmillan.

————. (1993). "Environment, routine, and situation: Toward a pattern theory of crime." In Ronald V. Clarke and Marcus Felson (Eds.), *Routine Activity and Rational Choice: Advances in Criminological Theory.* (5: 259-94). New Brunswick, NJ: Transaction Publishers.

Brantingham, Patricia, and Paul Brantingham. (1995). "Criminality of place." *European Journal of Criminal Policy and Research* 3 (3): 5-26.

Brearley, H. C. (1932). *Homicide in the United States.* Chapel Hill: University of North Carolina Press.

Bureau of Justice Assistance (BJA). (2010). *An Assessment of the New Orleans Police Department Homicide Section: Recommendations for Best Practices.* Washington, D.C.: U.S. Department of Justice, Bureau of Justice Assistance.

Bursik, Robert J. and Harold G. Grasmick. (1993). *Neighborhoods and Crime: The Dimensions of Effective Community Control.* Boston, MA: Lexington Books.

Carson, E. Ann., and William J. Sabol. (2012). *Prisoners in 2011.* Washington. D.C.: U. S. Department of Justice, Bureau of Justice Statistics.

Chilton, Roland. (2003). "Regional variations in lethal and non-lethal assaults." In M. Smith, P. Blackman, and J. Jarvis (Eds.), *New Directions in Homicide Research: Proceedings of the 2001 Annual Meeting of the Homicide Research Working Group.* Washington D.C.: Federal Bureau of Investigation.

City of New Orleans. (2012, December 10). National Forum on Youth Violence Prevention.

City of New Orleans. (2012, May). *NOLA for Life: A Comprehensive Murder Reduction Strategy.*

Cloward, Richard, and Lloyd Ohlin. (1960). *Delinquency and Opportunity: A Theory of Delinquent Gangs.* Glencoe, IL: The Free Press.

Cohen, Albert K. (1955). *Delinquent Boys.* Glencoe, IL: Free Press.

Cohen, L.E., and M. Felson. (1979). "Social change and crime rate trends." *American Sociological Review* 44: 488-608.

Comparet-Cassani, J. (2002). "Balancing the anonymity of threatened witnesses versus a defendant's right of confrontation: The Waive Doctrine after Alvarado." *San Diego Law Review* 39: 1165-1240.

Cork, D. (1999). "Examining space–time interaction in city-level homicide data: Crack markets and the diffusion of guns among youth." *Journal of Quantitative Criminology* 15 (4): 379-406.

Corzine, Jay, and Lin Huff-Corzine. (1989). "On cultural explanations of Southern homicide: Comment on Dixon and Lizotte." *American Journal of Sociology* 95: 178-82.

Curriden, M. (1994). "Witness threats: A problem." *American Bar Association Journal* 80 (November): 1019-36.

Daley, K. (2014, August 22). "Murder Rate Falls more in 2014." *Times-Picayune*. A-1, A-6.

Dixon, Jo, and Alan J. Lizotte. (1987). "Gun ownership and the Southern subculture of violence." *American Journal of Sociology* 93: 389-405.

———. (1989). "The burden of proof: Southern subculture of violence explanations of gun ownership and homicide." *American Journal of Sociology* 95: 182-87.

Douglas, J., A.W. Burgess, A.G. Burgess, R. Ressler. (2006). *Crime Classification Manual: A Standard System for Investigating and Classifying Violent Crimes* (2nd Ed.) San Francisco, CA: John Wiley & Sons, Inc.

Durkheim, Emile. (1893/1947). *The Division of Labor in Society*. Glencoe, IL: Free Press.

———. (1897/1951). *Suicide*. New York: Free Press.

Ellison, C.G., and P.L. McCall. (1989). "Region and attitudes reconsidered: Comment on Dixon and Lizotte." *American Journal of Sociology* 95: 174-78.

Finn, Peter, and Kerry Murphy Healey. (1996). *Preventing Gang and Drug-Related Witness Intimidation*. Washington, D.C.: National Institute of Justice.

Frailing, Kelly, and Dee Wood Harper. (2010). "School kids and oil rigs: Two more pieces of the post-Katrina puzzle in New Orleans." *American Journal of Economics and Sociology* 69 (2): 1-19.

Gastil, Raymond D. (1971). "Homicide and a regional culture of violence." *American Sociological Review* 36: 412-27.

Gibbs, J. P., and M. Erickson. (1976). "Crime rates of American cities in an ecological context." *American Journal of Sociology* 82 (November): 605-20.

Guerry, A. M. (1833). *Essai Sur La Statistique Morale de la France*. Paris: Crochard.

Hackney, Sheldon. (1969). "Southern violence." *American Historical Review* 39: 906-25.

Harer, Miles D., and Darrell Steffensmeier. (1992). The differing effects of economic inequality on black and white rates of violence. *Social Forces* 70 (4): 1035-54.

Harper, Dee Wood. (2007). A temporal and spatial analysis assessing risks of murder at the neighborhood level using location quotients. Paper presented at the European Society of Criminology, Bologna, Italy.

Harper, Dee Wood, and Lydia Voigt. (2007). "Homicide followed by suicide: An integrated theoretical perspective." *Homicide Studies* 11 (4): 295-318.

Harper, Dee Wood., Lydia Voigt, and William E. Thornton. (2004). Neighborhood covariates of murder. Paper presented at the Academy of Criminal Justice Sciences, Las Vegas, Nevada.

Hawley, Amos H. (1950). *Human Ecology: A Theory of Community Structure.* New York: Ronald Press.

Hawkins, Darnell. (1990). "Explaining the black homicide rate." *Journal of Interpersonal Violence* 5: 151-63.

Hawkins, D. (1997). Building peace in the inner cities. In J. Grisolia (Ed.), *Violence: From Biology to Society.* (pp. 161–70). Amsterdam: Elsevier Press.

Hipp, John R. (2007). "Income inequality, race, and place: Does the distribution of race and class in neighborhoods affect crime rates?" *Criminology* 45 (3): 665-97.

Horowitz, R. (1983). *Honor and the American Dream: Culture and Identity in a Chicano Community.* New Brunswick, NJ: Rutgers University Press.

Huff-Corzine, Jay Corzine, and David C. Moore. (1986). "Southern exposure: Deciphering the South's influence on homicide rates." *Social Forces* 64 (4): 906-24.

Huff-Corzine, L.G. Weaver, J. Corzine, J. Wittekind, and T. Petee. (2003). "The importance of disaggregation in specifying the southern subculture of violence." In M. Smith, P. Blackman, and J. Jarvis (Eds.), *New Directions in Homicide Research: Proceedings of the 2001 Annual Meeting of the Homicide Research Working Group.* Washington D.C.: Federal Bureau of Investigation.

International Centre for Prison Studies, A partner of the University of Essex. (date unknown). Retrieved from: http://www.prisonstudies.org/highest-lowest.

Jones-Webb, Rhonda, and Melanie Wall. (2008). "Neighborhood Racial/ Ethnic Concentration, Social Disadvantage, and Homicide Risk: An Ecological Analysis of 10 U.S. Cities." *Journal of Urban Health* 85 (5): 662–76.

Keen, James, H. (2004). *Murder Statistical Report 2002 & 2003*. Interoffice Correspondence. New Orleans, LA: New Orleans Department of Police.

Konigsmark, A. (2006). Crime takes hold of new New Orleans. *USA Today*, December 8. Retrieved from: Crime takes hold of new New Orleans – USATODAY.com.htm.

Kovandzic, Tomislav, Lynn Vieraitis, and Mark Yeisley. (1998). "The structural covariates of urban homicide: Reassessing the impact of income inequality and poverty in the post-Reagan era." *Criminology* 36 (3): 569–99.

Kowalski, Gregory S., and Thomas A. Petee. (1991). "Sunbelt effects on homicide rates." *Sociology and Social Research* 75: 73-79.

Kposowa, Augustine J., Kevin D. Breault, and Beatrice M. Harrison. (1995). "Reassessing the structural covariates of violent and property crimes in the USA: A county level analysis." *The British Journal of Sociology* 46: 79-105.

Krivo, Lauren J., and Ruth D. Peterson. (1996). "Extremely disadvantaged neighborhoods and urban crime." *Social Forces* 75 (2): 619-50.

———. (2000). "The structural context of homicide: Accounting for racial differences in process." *American Sociological Review* 65 (4): 547-60.

Kubrin, Charis E. (2003). "Structural covariates of homicide rates: Does type of homicide matter?" *Journal of Research in Crime and Delinquency* 40 (2): 139-70.

Kubrin, Charis E., and Jerald R. Herting. (2003). "Neighborhood correlates of homicide trends: An analysis using growth-curve modeling." *The Sociological Quarterly* 44 (3): 329–55.

Kubrin, Charis E., and Tim Wadsworth. (2003). "Identifying the structural correlates of African-American killings: What can we learn from data disaggregation?" *Homicide Studies* 7: 3-35.

Kubrin, Charis E., and Ronald Weitzer. (2003). "Retaliatory homicide: Concentrated disadvantage and neighborhood culture." *Social Problems* 50 (2): 157-80.

LaFree, Gary, Kriss A. Drass, and Patrick O'Day. (1992). "Race and crime in postwar America: Determinants of African-American and white rates, 1957-1988." *Criminology* 30: 157-85

Land, Kenneth C., Patricia L. McCall, and Lawrence Cohen. (1990). "Structural covariates of homicide rates: Are there any invariances across time and social space?" *American Journal of Sociology* 95 (4): 922-63.

Lee, Matthew. (2000). "Concentrated poverty, race, and homicide." *The Sociological Quarterly* 41 (2): 189-206.

Lee, Mathew R., and John P. Bartkowski. (2004). "Civic participation, regional subcultures, and violence." *Homicide Studies* 8 (1): 5-39.

Levitov, Jana, and Dee Harper. (2012). "You can't do crack on credit: Drugs and Retaliatory Murder." In D.W. Harper, W. E. Thornton, and L. Voigt (Eds.), *Violence: Do We Know It When We See It? A Reader.* (pp. 129-46) Durham, NC: Carolina Academic Press.

Loftin, Colin, and Robert H. Hill. (1974). Regional subculture and homicide: An examination of the Gastil-Hackney thesis. *American Sociological Review* 39: 714-24.

Louisiana Department of Corrections (2014). Retrieved from: http://www.doc.la.gov/wp-content/uploads/statmap/Southeast7-2011.pdf.

Louisiana Department of Education. Retrieved from: http://www.louisianabelieves.com/docs/data-management/cohort-graduation-rates-(2006-2012).pdf?sfvrsn=2.

Louisiana Statistical Analysis Center. (2013). *Crime in Louisiana in 2011.* Baton Rouge, LA: Louisiana Commission on Law Enforcement Uniform Crime Reporting Section.

Massey, Douglas, and Shawn Kanaiaupuni. (1993). "Public Housing and the concentration of poverty." *Social Sciences Quarterly* 74 (1): 109-22.

McCall, Patricia L., Kenneth C. Land, and K. Parker. (2010). "An empirical assessment of what we know about structural covariates of homicide rates: A return to a classic 20 years later." *Homicide Studies* 14, 3: 219-43.

McCall, Patricia L., and Paul Nieuwbeerta. (2007). "Structural covariates of homicide rates: A European city cross-national comparative analysis." *Homicide Studies* 11 (3): 167-88.

Mears, Daniel., and Avinash Bhati. (2006). "No community is an island: The effects of resource deprivation on urban violence in spatially and socially proximate communities." *Criminology* 44 (3): 509-48.

Medaris, M., and C. Sigworth. (2010). An Assessment of the New Orleans Police Department Homicide Section: Recommendations for Best Practices. Washington, D.C.: Bureau of Justice Assistance, U.S. Department of Justice.

Merton, Robert K. (1938). "Social Structure and Anomie." *American Socio-logical Review* 3: 672–82.

Messner, Steven F. (1983). "Regional and Racial Effects on the Urban Homicide Rate: The Subculture of Violence Revisited." *The American Journal of Sociology* 88 (5): 997-1007.

Messner, Steven F., Luc Anselin, Robert D. Baller, Darnell F. Hawkins, Glenn Deane, and Stewart E. Tolnay. (1999). "Spatial patterning of county homicide rates: An application of exploratory spatial data analysis." *Journal of Quantitative Criminology* 15: 423-50.

Messner, Steven F., and Robert Sampson. (1991). "The sex ratio, family disruption, and rates of violent crime: The paradox of demographic structure." *Social Forces* 69 (3): 693-713.

Metropolitan Crime Commission (MCC). (2005). *Performance of the New Orleans Criminal Justice System 2003-2004.* New Orleans, LA: MCC.

———. (2007a). *Orleans Parish Criminal Justice System Accountability Report (Third and Fourth Quarter 2007).* New Orleans, LA: MCC.

———. (2007b). *Crime & Safety in Central City: A Community's Perspective.* New Orleans, LA: MCC. Retrieved from: http://metrocrime.org/wp-content/uploads/2-13/05/CC-Safety-Assessment-Jan-2007-Full report.pdf.

———. (Oct. 14, 2008). *Orleans Parish Criminal Justice System Accountability Report.* New Orleans, LA: MCC.

———. (May 5, 2009). *Orleans Parish Criminal Justice System Accountability Report.* New Orleans, LA: MCC.

———. (May 14, 2012). *Orleans Parish Criminal Justice System Accountability Report.* New Orleans, LA: MCC.

———. (May 12, 2013). *Orleans Parish Criminal Justice System Accountability Report.* New Orleans, LA: MCC.

———. (2013a). *Orleans Parish Criminal Justice Accountability Report, May 2013.* New Orleans, LA: MCC.

———. (2013b). *Orleans Parish Prison Inmate Population Snapshot, July 24, 2013.* New Orleans, LA: MCC.

Michalowski, Raymond. (2013). "The myth that punishment reduces crime." In Robert M. Bohm and Jeffery T. Walker (Eds.), *Demystifying Crime & Criminal Justice.* (pp. 179-91) New York: Oxford University Press.

Miles-Doan, R. (1998). "Violence between spouses and intimates: Does neighborhood context matter?" *Social Forces* 77 (2): 623-45.

Miller, Walter B. (1958). "Lower class culture as a generating milieu of gang delinquency." *Journal of Social Issues* 14: 5-19.

Morenoff, Jeffrey, Robert Sampson, and Stephen Raudenbush. (2001). "Neighborhood Inequality, collective efficacy, and the spatial dynamics of urban violence." *Criminology* 39 (3) 517-58.

Nelson, Candice, Jay Corzine, and Lin Huff-Corzine. (1994). "The violent West re-examined: A research note on regional homicide rates." *Criminology* 32: 149-61.

Newman, Oscar. (1973). *Defensible Space*. New York: Macmillan.

City of New Orleans. (2012, May). *NOLA For Life: A Comprehensive Murder Reduction Strategy*.

O'Carroll, Patrick W., and James A. Mercy. (1989). "Regional variations in homicide rates: Why is the *West* so Violent?" *Violence and Victims* 4: 17-25.

Parenti, Christian. (2000). "Crime as social control." *Social Justice* 27: 43-49.

Park, Robert E. (1925). "The Urban Communty as a Spatial Pattern and a Moral Order." *Publications of the American Sociological Society* 20: 1-14.

Parker, Robert Nash. (1989). "Poverty, subculture of violence, and type of homicide." *Social Forces* 67 (4): 983-1007.

Parker, Karen F., and Patricia L. McCall. (1997). "Adding another piece to the inequality-homicide puzzle." *Homicide Studies* 1 (1): 35-60.

Parker, Karen. F., and Matthew V. Pruitt. (2000). "How the West was one: Explaining the similarities in race-specific homicide rates in the West and South." *Social Forces* 78 (4): 1483-1508.

Pattillo-McCoy, Mary E. (1999). *Black Picket Fences: Privilege and Peril among the Black Middle Class*. Chicago, IL: University of Chicago Press.

———. (2013). *Black Picket Fences: Privilege and Peril among the Black Middle Class 2nd edition*. Chicago, IL: University of Chicago Press.

Peterson, Ruth D., and Lauren J. Krivo. (1993). "Racial segregation and black urban homicide." *Social Forces* 71 (4): 1001-1026.

———. (2005). "Macrostructural analyses of race, ethnicity, and violent crime: Recent lessons and new directions for research." *Annual Review of Sociology* 31: 331-56.

Peterson, Ruth D., Lauren J. Krivo, and Mark A. Harris. (2000). "Disadvantage and neighborhood violent crime: Do local institutions matter?" *Journal of Research in Crime and Delinquency* 37 (1): 31-63.

Quetelet, Adolphe. (1835). *Sur l'homme et le developpement de ses facultes*. Brussels: Muquartd.

Reed, John Shelton. (1972). *The Enduring South: Subcultural Persistence in Mass Society*. Lexington, MA.: D.C. Heath and Company

Redfield, Horace V. (1880). *Homicide, North and South*. Philadelphia, PA: J.P. Lippincott.

———. (2000). *Homicide, North and South: Being a Comparative View of Crime Against the Person in Several Parts of the United States*. Columbus, OH: Ohio State University Press.

Rey, Sergio J., Luc Anselin, David C. Folch, Daniel Arribas-Bel, Myrna Sastre Gutierrez, and Lindsey Interlante. (2011). *Economic Development Quarterly* 25 (54): 54–64.

Roncek, Dennis W. (1981). "Dangerous places: Crime and residential environment." *Social Forces* 60 (1): 74-96.

Rousey, Dennis C. (1996). *Policing the Southern City: New Orleans, 1805-1889*. Baton Rouge: Louisiana State University Press.

Russell, William Howard. (1863). My *Diary North and South*. Boston, MA: T.O.H.P. Burnham. 244-45.

Sabol, W., Heather Coulture, and Paige Harrison. (2007). *Prisoners in 2006*. Washington, D.C.: USDO, BSJ, (NCJ219516).

Sampson, Robert J. (1987). "Urban black violence: The effect of male joblessness and family disruption." *The American Journal of Sociology* 93 (2): 348-82.

———. (1991). "Linking the micro- and macro level dimensions of community social organization." *Social Forces* 70 (1): 43-64.

Sampson, Robert J. (1993). Linking time and place: Dynamic contextualism and the future of criminological inquiry. *Journal of Research in Crime and Delinquency* 30: 426-44.

———. (2012). *Great American City: Chicago and the Enduring Neighborhood Effect*. Chicago, IL: University of Chicago Press.

Sampson, Robert J., and W. Byron Groves. (1989). "Community structure and crime: Testing social disorganization theory." *The American Journal of Sociology* 94 (4): 774-802.

Sampson, Robert J., Stephen W. Raudenbush, and Earls Felton. (1997). "Neighborhoods and violent crime: A multi-level study of collective efficacy." *Science* 227: 1-7.

Sampson, Robert J., and William Julius Wilson. (1995). "Toward a theory of race, crime and urban inequality." In John Hagan and Ruth D. Peterson (Eds.), *Crime and Inequality* (pp. 37-54). Stanford, CA: Stanford University Press.

Shaw, Clifford, and Henry McKay. (1942/1969). *Juvenile Delinquency and Urban Areas.* Chicago, IL: University of Chicago Press.

Sheley, Joseph, and James Wright. (1995). *In the Line of Fire: Youth, Guns and Violence in Urban America.* New York: Aldine and De Gruyter.

Shihadeh, E. S., and Graham C. Ousey. (1996). "Metropolitan expansion and black social dislocation: The link between suburbanization and center-city crime." *Social Forces* 75 (2): 649-66.

Simmel, Georg. (1950). "Metropolis and mental life." In Kurt H. Wolff (ed.) *The Sociology of Georg Simmel* (pp. 409-24). New York: The Free Press.

Skogan, Wesley. (1977). "Public policy and the fear of crime in large American cities." In J. Gardner (Ed.), *Public Law and Public Policy* (pp. 1-18). New York, NY: Praeger.

Skogan, W. (1989). "Communities, crime, and neighborhood organization." *Crime and Delinquency* 35 (3): 437-57.

Skogan, W. (1990). *Disorder and Decline: Crime and the Spiral of Decay in American Neighborhoods.* New York: The Free Press.

Sun, Ivan, Ruth Triplett, and Randy Gainey. (2004). "Neighborhood characteristics and crime: A test of Sampson and Groves' model of social disorganization." *Western Criminology Review* 5 (1): 1-16.

Suttles, Gerald D. (1968). *Social Order of the Slum.* Chicago, IL: University of Chicago Press.

Suttles, Gerald D. (1984). "The cumulative texture of local urban culture." *The American Journal of Sociology* 90 (2): 283-304.

Taylor, Ralph. (1997). "Social order and disorder of street blocks and neighborhoods: Ecology, micro-ecology, and the systemic model of social disorganization." *Journal of Research in Crime and Delinquency* 34 (1): 113-55.

Thornton, William E., and Lydia Voigt. (2007). "Disaster rape: Vulnerability of women to sexual assaults during Hurricane Katrina." *Journal of Public Management & Social Policy* 13 (2): 22-51.

Thornton, W., L. Voigt, and D.W. Harper (2013). *Why Violence? Leading Questions Regarding the Conceptualization of Violence in Society.* Durham, NC: Carolina Academic Press.

Titterington, Victoria B., Scott A. Vollum, and Pamela M. Diamond. (2003). "Neighborhoods & Homicide: Sex- and Type-Specific Variation across Three Cities." *Homicide Studies* 7 (3): 263-88.

Topalli, Volkan. (2005). "When being good is bad: An expansion of neutralization theory." *Criminology* 43 (3): 797-836.

Topalli, Volkan. (2006). "The seductive nature of autotelic crime: How neutralization theory serves as a boundary condition for understanding hardcore street offending." *Sociological Inquiry* 76 (4): 475-501.

U.S. Bureau of the Census, American Community Survey 2007-2011.

U.S. Census of Population (2000-2010) Table 1. Louisiana. Retrieved from: http://www.census.gov/popest/data/intercensal/state/state2010.html.

U.S. Census Bureau; Table 2. Projections of the Population by Selected Age Groups and Sex for the United States: 2015-2060). Retrieved from: http://www.census.gov/population/projections/data/national/2012/summarytables.html.

VanLandingham, M. J. (2007). "Murder rates in New Orleans, La. 2004-2006."*American Journal of Public Health* 97: 1,614-16.

Vargas, Ramon. A. (May 23). Ceasefire hasn't yet reduced Central City violence, but officials remain confident program will work. NOLA.com. Retrieved from: http://www.nola.com/crime/index.ssf/2013/05/ceasefire_hasnt_yet_reduced_ce.html.

Vera Institute of Justice. (2007). *Proposals for New Orleans' Criminal Justice System: Best Practices to Advance Public Safety and Justice.* Washington D.C.: Vera Institute of Justice.

Veysey, Bonita, and Steven Messner. (1999). "Further testing of social disorganization theory: An elaboration of Sampson and Groves' 'Community Structure and Crime.'" *Journal of Research in Crime and Delinquency* 36 (2): 156-74.

Warner, B. (2003). "The role of attenuated culture in social disorganization theory." *Criminology* 41 (1): 73-97.

Wellford, Charles, Brenda J. Bond, and Sean Goodison. (2011). *Crime in New Orleans: Analyzing Crime Trends and New Orleans' Responses to Crime.* Washington, D.C.: U.S. Department of Justice, Bureau of Justice Assistance, Office of Justice programs.

Whyte, William F. (1955). *Street Corner Society* (2nd Ed.). Chicago, IL: University of Chicago Press.

Wilson, William J. (1987). *The Truly Disadvantaged: The Inner City, the Underclass, and Public Policy.* Chicago, IL: University of Chicago Press.

Wilson, William J. (1993). "The underclass: Issues, perspectives, and public policy." In William Julius Wilson (Ed.), *The Ghetto Underclass* (pp. 1-24). Beverly Hills, CA: Sage.

————. (1996). *When Work Disappears: The World of the New Urban Poor.* New York: Alfred A. Knoptf.

Wilson, William Julius, and Kathryn M. Neckerman. (1986). "Poverty and family structure: The widening gap between evidence and public policy issues." In Sheldon H. Danziger and Daniel H. Weinberg (Eds.), *Fighting Poverty* (pp. 232-59). Cambridge, MA: Harvard University Press.

Wirth, Lewis. (1931). "Culture conflict and misconduct." *Social Forces* 9: 484-92.

————. (1938). *Urbanism as a Way of Life.* Chicago, IL: University of Chicago Press.

Wooldredge, John. (2002). "Examining the (ir) relevance of aggregation bias for multilevel studies of neighborhoods and crime with an example comparing census tracts to official neighborhoods in Cincinnati." *Criminology* 40 (3): 681-709.

Wolfgang, Marvin, and Franco Ferracuti. (1967). *The Subculture of Violence.* London: Tavistock.

————. (1982). *The Subculture of Violence: Towards an Integrated Theory of Criminology.* Beverly Hills, CA: Sage.

————. (2001). *The Subculture of Violence.* New York: Routledge.

Wright, James., and James Devine. (1994). *Drugs as a Social Problem.* New York: Harper Collins.

Zimring, Franklin E. (2012). *The City that Became Safe: New York's Lessons for Urban Crime and Its Control.* New York: Oxford University Press.

3 | The Chain of Violence and the Lessons for New Orleans

Peter Iadicola

Criminologists uncover patterns of criminal offending and victimization and theorize about what explains these patterns. No theory provides a comprehensive explanation. There are a multiplicity of factors, some proximate in time sequence and others that are part of the life course of the offenders and victims, that are important elements of the explanation of the cause of the violent event that is the focus of explanation. It is important to think of the unfolding of these events as they are part of a chain of causality. When considering acts of interpersonal violence that are the principle focus of policing and crime control it is important to think of a chain of violence that often begins at the earliest points in one's life. A chain that can begin at the start of one's life as a result of the positions that we are born into and then a result of our participation in the various institutions that make up our society (Iadicola and Shupe, 2013). In responding to the problem of interpersonal violence it is important to address proximate causes for short term impact. However, for long term impact it is necessary to intervene at the beginning of the chain. This paper will discuss the chain of violence and its ramifications for development of strategies to address violence in New Orleans.

Defining Violence

It is important to start with a definition of violence that not only includes the violence that we criminalize and is the focus of policing, but also includes the violence that is part of the nature of our society that plays a central role in the overall pattern of violence in a community. It is crucial to be aware of all the forms of violence in a community and not just the ones that are criminalized because they in the majority of cases are linked to each other. Rarely are the

77

acts of violence that we read about in our newspapers, that are part of police reports, are isolated events. They are part of many forms of violence that are part of the fabric of the community. In our attempt to control criminal violence we often miss the forest for the trees. We first must understand the nature of the forest that the tree has grown within if we are able to develop long-term, root-cause remedies to the problem of violence.

Let's begin with a more encompassing definition to begin our analysis of violence in New Orleans. We have defined violence as any action, inaction, or structural arrangement that results in physical or nonphysical harm to one or more persons (Iadicola and Shupe, 2003). The most recent edition of that work introduces the dimension of other species being victims. This is an important aspect of understanding the totality of the phenomenon, but for our purposes in this discussion about violence in New Orleans we will use a definition that delimits the phenomenon to only human victims.

We readily understand violence as a form of action, and it is uncontroversial to think of violence as inaction. The violence of inaction can be as powerful as the violence of action. Child neglect is one example among many where the failure to act constitutes violence, a violence that can cause lasting harm beyond the immediate trauma. The definition is also uncontroversial in its recognition that the harm that is the result of violence is not just physical, but also is harm to the psyche and to the social relationships that are necessary for human wellbeing. The violence that occurs in the home between a husband and wife causes physical, psychological, and social harm that need to be healed in ones' recovery from their victimization.

What may be perceived as controversial is to think of violence as a result of one's position in a hierarchical arrangement (systems of stratification) within the society or world. In the case of child neglect, it is because of the dependent and relatively powerless position of the child that they are victimized. Violence that stems from one's position in a society is referred to as structural violence. There are other forms of structural violence that are also obvious. No one can deny the violent consequences of slavery, which is often described as the most extreme form of harm, that results from the structural positioning of people. Defining other people as property to be used as one sees fit, with no rights and little concern for their development beyond the need for them to serve the purpose for which they are owned has harmful consequences that we do not deny. However, it is not just the violence of slavery that is structural. There is the violence that is a result of a legacy of violence from slavery that extends beyond the period of slavery in the United States and includes the violence that results from the denial of services and opportunities for human development. It is the violence that stems from ethnic minority status in a society that has organized resource distribution based on cultural/"racial" designation. In the United States, it is important to remember that we are just three generations past the legal system of discrimination (America's apartheid) that existed throughout the country and especially in the southern part of the United States, including the state of Louisiana.

There are also the structures of social class and gender that are important contexts for violence. For example, the denial of services to maintain health as a result of one's inability to pay for the services as a result of class position has direct harmful consequences. Although those who act to deny the services are required to do so because of the rules that reinforce and perpetuate the structure of the society as defined by social class and income levels. Those who are unable to pay for preventive and acute healthcare services are more likely to have a shorter life span with more illness and disease. In general, social class is a crucial factor that establishes a pattern of distribution of resources for human development. It is a common fact in our society that those who are of lower class status receive less opportunities for education, experience less stable families, and live in less safe neighborhoods to grow and develop. Lastly, it is important to recognize the significance of gender position as it relates to violence. Much of the violence that occurs in the society, especially where women are victims, is a result of the enforcement of hierarchical relationships that are rooted in a system of patriarchy. Male power and privilege is part of the structure and the functioning of all social institutions within our society.

Levels of Violence

Furthermore, when we discuss violence that occurs within a community there is a need to focus on the different levels or con-

texts that violence occurs within. Interpersonal violence is the violence that occurs between strangers, friends, and acquaintances.
More precisely it is the violence that occurs between people acting outside of the roles prescribed within social institutions. It is
the violence between rival gang members, the violence that occurs
in public or private places between strangers, acquaintances, and
friends who offend or take advantage of each other, or who respond
to this event in a violent manner. Much of the violence that police
respond to in New Orleans is of this nature.

It is important to distinguish the interpersonal level of violence
from the violence that occurs within an institutional context. Here
the violence follows from one's position and role performance within an organizational context that are functioning within one of the
five basic institutions of a society: family, education, religion, the
state or government, and the economy. The violence within families
occurs because of the nature of the positions and roles within the
home. The violence would not have occurred outside of this context. For example, in the case of violence between a husband and a
wife, we would not expect that the husband or wife who is violent
is likely to be violent in their social interaction with friends, neighbors, or acquaintances. Friends, acquaintances, and co-workers
may be surprised to learn of violence within the home. The parents
who are violent toward their children are not necessarily violent to
other children who are not members of their family. The violence
occurs because of their role of parent, how they define it and how
they act in accordance with the position to maintain order in their
home. This is the case with other forms of institutional violence. The
violence of a police officer or soldier is not likely to occur outside of
the institutional context. This is not to say that violence that occurs
within these institutional contexts cannot extend and be linked to
other areas and levels of violence. Nevertheless, we can identify a
sphere of violence that is distinct from the interpersonal realm that
occurs in the context of social institutions within a society.

Lastly, as mentioned previously in our discussion of the definition of violence, violence occurs within a structural context. This is
the violence that stems from positions that are arranged hierarchi-
cally which result in harmful consequences to the occupants of the
dominated positions. When we look at the morbidity and mortality
patterns within any society, or the world for that matter, those who

are in the most dominated positions as defined in terms of class, gender, or ethnic minority status are more likely to live a shorter life and suffer most from illness, disease, and natural disasters (Wilkinson and Pickett, 2010).

Although we can identify violence that occurs within a context or sphere of action (interpersonal, institutional, and structural), these contexts or spheres may overlap. Important areas of overlap are the ones that occur between the structural level and both the institutional and interpersonal levels. Much of the institutional and interpersonal forms of the violence occurs as a result of the different positions of the actors, and often serve to reinforce the hierarchical position between the actors. Thus in the case of violence within families, economic organizations, religious organizations, educational organizations (schools), or government, those who are more likely to be victims are those who are in dominated positions within the larger society. Thus, not only do we recognize interpersonal, institutional, and structural violence, but there is also violence which occurs at the intersection of these interactional spheres (Iadicola and Shupe, 2013). In discussing forms and patterns of institutional and interpersonal violence, it is important to think of how these acts of violence often reinforce the violence that occurs as a result of the nature of the hierarchical structures of the society.

When we look at the violence that is occurring within a society, we can see how it occurs within these three different contexts. As we examine the scope and consequences of the violence that occurs within any society, and as we go from the interpersonal, to the institutional, and to the structural levels of violence, the level of victimization increases as we move to the higher levels of violence. The level of violence at the interpersonal level is the smallest level of violence when compared to the violence at the institutional level. Whereas the violence at the institutional level is dwarfed in comparison to what Sheper-Hughes and Bourgois (2004) referred to as the "everyday violence" that occurs at the structural level.

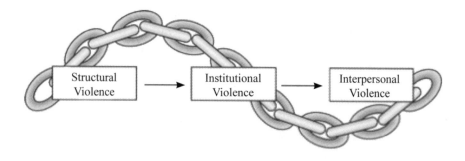

The Chain of Violence

Although we can think of violence within these three interactional contexts, it is important to note how these contexts of violence often occur within a sequence of violence over a lifetime of the offender, and in many cases the victim as well. Most violence that occurs in a society is linked to the other contexts of violence. Violence for many in our society begins at the structural level in the positions that they are born into. It emanates from the structure of the society and is experienced as a result of these structures. In the most fundamental sense, what allows us to victimize others is our ability to think less of and separate ourselves from the others we victimize. This is the case whether it is a rival gang member, an enemy soldier, a wife or a child, a student, a worker or consumer, or a member of one's religious flock or an infidel or heathen. The victim of violence is one who we do not empathize with but rather define as different and less than ourselves.

Those who are victimized at the structural level, often beginning at birth, are more likely to be victimized at the institutional level in families, in schools, in the economy, and in the political system. For example, in the case of family violence, whether we are discussing spousal abuse or child abuse or neglect, they all can occur at any class and income level, however we also recognize that those who are poor are more likely to experience higher levels of victimization. The same pattern exists within each of the areas of institutional violence (Iadicola and Shupe, 2013). In general, those who are victimized at the structural level have higher levels of victimization at the various institutional levels. Lastly, the violence manifests itself at the interpersonal level, where those who experience the higher levels of institutional violence are also likely to experience the higher levels of interpersonal violence. In some cases the interpersonal violence is directed at those who are perceived as victimizers at the higher levels, in most cases it is directed at those who also experience similar victimization at the structural and institutional levels.

Central Role of Inequality

Inequality plays a central role in most forms of violence (Iadicola and Shupe, 2013). Even when we focus on interpersonal violence we find that it is often a result of an insult or affront to one's position or status. As Wilkinson and Pickett note, "One of the most common causes of violence, and one which plays a large part in explaining why violence is more common in more unequal societies, is that it is often triggered by loss of face and humiliation when people feel looked down on and disrespected" (Wilkinson and Pickett, 2010: p. 40). Gilligan (1996) argues that acts of violence are attempts to ward off feelings of shame or humiliation. This is especially the case for those who have little status or position to begin with. This is most likely to be the case with those with an exaggerated self-esteem ("threatened egotism," "insecure high self-esteem," or "narcissism") according to Wilkinson and Pickett (2010).

This is also a manifestation of the chain of violence. As a result of the experience of being a victim of institutional violence in the home, school, the economy, and in relations with the state or government at all levels, often ends in the violence at the interpersonal levels that is triggered by an insult to one's status or position in relation at the interpersonal level. In more unequal societies children experience more bullying, fights, and conflicts. And there is no better predictor of later violence than childhood violence. The authors note that shame and humiliation become more sensitive issues in more hierarchical societies: status becomes more important, status competition increases, and more people are deprived of access to markers of status and social success (Wilkinson and Pickett, 2010). We also know that levels of inequality are related to drug and alcohol abuse, which are catalysts to violence at the interpersonal level and in the case of family violence at the institutional level as well.

In general, Wilkinson and Pickett note that "there is a large body of evidence that shows a clear relationship between greater inequality and higher homicide rates" (Wilkinson and Pickett, 2010: p. 135). The State of Louisiana and the city of New Orleans, in particular, have some of the highest levels of income inequality and the highest rates of homicide in the nation. This is a manifestation of the chain of violence that begins at the structural level and leads to the institutional levels and eventually to the interpersonal levels in New Orleans. Now let's focus on the patterns of violence in New Orleans at all three levels, beginning where we often focus as criminologists, on the police and criminal justice system, and where consequentially there is most information.

Patterns of Violence in New Orleans

Interpersonal Violence–Homicide

New Orleans has a higher rate of overall crime, property crime, and violent crime than the nation. However, the rate of crime in New Orleans is lower than for comparable cities. The one exception is the homicide rate in New Orleans, which is substantially higher than the rate in the nation and for comparable-sized cities. In 2009, the rate of homicide in New Orleans, 49 per 100,000, was more than ten times the national average and more than four times the rate for cities of a similar size (Welford, Bond, and Goodson, 2011). Homicide rates fluctuate in more recent years but remain high through reporting year 2013 (42 per 100,000) as discussed in chapter 2.

The majority of victims were young, with more than 50 percent being twenty-seven years old or younger at death. Most victims were African American males and a plurality of victims were noted as having no gainful employment (46 percent). Surprisingly, few victims had a gang affiliation according to police files. The vast majority of victims had at least one previous formal contact with police before being killed (73 percent), and these one half had at least one violent or property crime offense, two thirds had a drug offense, and two fifths had a firearm possession offense (Welford, Bond, and Goodson, 2011).

The majority of known offenders were younger than the victims, with more than 50 percent being twenty-three years old or younger at the time of the incident. The vast majority of offenders were African American and again they appeared to have no gang

affiliation. Like the majority of victims, the majority of known offenders had no gainful employment (nearly 56 percent), whereas
only approximately 17 percent had a job/occupation listed in the
police record. Like the victim pattern, the vast majority of offenders had a prior offense, the largest category for a violent crime. The
same proportion of offenders as victims had a prior firearms arrest (more than 41 percent of known offenders) (Welford, Bond, and
Goodson, 2011).

Welford, Bond, and Goodson (2011), also found that the most
common official motive listed in police reports was the drug-related label, with approximately 29 percent of the total. In addition to
the drug related motive, revenge killings were almost 24 percent
of homicides, and argument/conflict represented about another 19
percent of incidents. According to Welford, Bond, and Goodson,
gangs and organized drug markets in general appear to play less of
a role in homicides in New Orleans than they do in other cities. Furthermore, most of the homicide incidents took place in some form
or residence or in a residential area. Similar to national patterns, the
most common weapon was the handgun and the homicides were
highly concentrated in the poorest areas of the city. Similar findings
for more recent years, 2012, reveal similar findings; however, the
percentages are smaller (See chapter 2)

Institutional Violence–Family

Let's now turn, to some of the types of institutional violence
where data is available for the city of New Orleans. It is very difficult to get accurate statistics on the number of cases of domestic violence that occur in New Orleans. Up until three years ago, the vast
majority of cases were never prosecuted and those that were prosecuted were prosecuted as misdemeanors. In the spring of 2009, a
new district attorney, requested that the police submit cases to his
office for review (Filosa, 2010). An average of 93 percent of domestic violence cases that were reported to the DA's office, including
many involving serious injury, were booked as municipal violations. As Filosa reports, "nearly all of the roughly 3,000 domestic-
violence arrests made by New Orleans police annually in years past
were sent to Municipal Court, and when they got there, more than
half the cases were dismissed. In those that weren't, the city attorney's office often sent offenders to a twenty-six-week anger man-

agement program in lieu of trial. Though data is spotty, there were few if any trials" (Filosa, 2010). According to retired judge Calvin Johnson, who spent seventeen years on the bench at Tulane and Broad, "The DA before Leon [Cannizzaro] ignored these cases, because we just didn't take domestic violence seriously enough, and that's just true. The fact that men were brutalizing women, on some level, our male-dominated justice system thought it was OK. It was part of our sexism (Filosa, 2010)."

In 2009, more than five times the number of cases was referred to the DA than in the previous year and more than 80 percent were prosecuted successfully. For 2006-2007, Orleans Parish had 3,611 and Jefferson Parish had 3,467 domestic abuse protective orders issued by civil, criminal, and juvenile courts received by the Louisiana Protective Order Registry (LPOR) (Jenkins and Phillips, 2008). The U.S. Department of Justice, Civil Rights division investigation of the New Orleans police department concluded that the department's culture "tolerates and encourages under-enforcement and under-investigation of violence against women (United States Department of Justice, Civil Rights Division, 2011: p. V)." In particular the report noted that the police department systematically under-investigated and under-reported sexual assaults and domestic violence. (This problem is discussed in more detail by Rae Taylor in chapter 6, "Intimate Partner Homicide in New Orleans").

Another important area of domestic violence that is part of the chain of violence which we see in our communities around the nation is the violence directed at children within families. Over 9,600 Louisiana children were victims of abuse or neglect in 2009, over 185 per week, and 40 Louisiana children died from that abuse or neglect (Schaefer, Christeson, and Messner-Zidell, 2012). Based on Widom's estimate determined by the results of a longitudinal study based on court records of the effect of abuse and neglect on future violent criminal behavior, these numbers would result in approximately 384 additional individuals who will be arrested for at least one violent crime beyond the number of those who would have been arrested had the abuse or neglect never occurred (Widom, 2000). Recently the Louisiana Department of Children and Family Services reported that the statewide child abuse and neglect hotline has received 114,000 calls in its first year of operation, and more than 50,000 of those calls reported suspected abuse or neglect (Associated Press, 2012).

The violence within families is very important in the chain of violence. This is one area of violence within New Orleans in which there must be better records to monitor the occurrence and determining the need for intervention. The difficulty in finding public records for the city of New Orleans on this type of violence is a significant problem. This information not only needs to be regularly collected but also publicized to make citizens aware of the occurrence of this form of violence in the community. Without the recognition of and communication about family violence, it will be impossible to break the chain that results in the interpersonal violence that the police focus on and of which the community is well aware.

Institutional Violence–Schools

Another important area of institutional violence is the violence that occurs within the educational system. The violence within schools can take many forms. There is the violence that occurs between students and teachers, students and administrators, and students themselves. There is also the violence that occurs from outsiders to the school who direct their violence at those within the schools. The phenomenon that is referred to as "running amok," committing acts of violence as a result of an uncontrollable rage have targeted schools. However, there is little evidence that this is systematic, the target can be a workplace or other public setting. Nevertheless, the violence can take many forms; from the physical violence of assault or homicide, to the psychological violence of bullying and the symbolic violence of the denigration and exclusion of one's culture from the curriculum in schools, to the social violence of denial of educational resources that allow students to grow and develop their talents and abilities (Iadicola and Shupe, 2013). Very little information is collected and made public on all the incidences of violence that occurs within the school. Only when it is defined as criminal is there much of a record of occurrence. However, most of the violence that occurs within the schools rarely reaches the stage of criminal violence. Nevertheless, it is these other forms of violence that may lead to violence that is criminal in nature at the end of the chain.

Overall, the New Orleans public school system has been failing large numbers of minority and poor children in the city for quite

some time. The public schools in New Orleans have performed below average in the state of Louisiana, a state that has some of the
lowest levels of public school success in comparison to other states
in the nation. For 2009, the State of Louisiana had the lowest percentage of students who passed the fourth grade basic proficiency
reading test on the National Assessment of Educational Progress in
comparison to all other states in the nation (United States Department of Education, 2009). This is an important part of the chain
of violence in general and the criminal violence that we experience in New Orleans, in particular. Those who are most involved
in homicide either as offender or victim were victimized earlier in
their years of schooling. Most had withdrawn from schools initially
psychologically and socially, but eventually physically, dropping
out or being forced out prior to their graduation. As Quigley and
Finger note in their "Katrina Pain Index," less than 60 percent of
Louisiana's public school students graduate from high school with
their class. Among public school children with disabilities in New
Orleans, the high school graduation rate is 6.8 percent (Quigley and
Finger, 2011).

When the levees broke in August 2005, all but 16 of the city's
126 school buildings were damaged. Three months later, the state
legislature transferred authority over 112 city schools to a state-run
"Recovery School District." This was accompanied by the rapid
privatization of control over the public system. New Orleans has
the highest concentration of "charter schools" in the nation. Almost
70 percent of the public schools in New Orleans are now charter
schools. Although the charter schools' transformation are heralded
as a success in improving student performance, it is impossible to
compare school performance before and after Katrina as a result
of the selective depopulation of New Orleans in the wake of the
storm. According to the U.S. Census Bureau, New Orleans's population stood at 343,829 people in 2010. Ten years earlier, the city's
population was 483,663, reflecting a 29.1 decline in the population
from 2000 to 2010 (Chinni, 2011; Robertson, 2011). Those areas of
the city hardest hit by the storm and who did not recover and return to New Orleans were poorer and African American. In general, natural disasters reveal the structural violence in a community
by systematically having the greatest impact on those who are in
the most dominated structural position as defined in terms of class,

race, and gender. Those who are in the most dominated positions within a society are most vulnerable because of where they live and the structures that they live in, often lacking resources both familial and financial to recover, and often experiencing less government assistance because of their lack of political power. This is the pattern that we see in the aftermath of Katrina in New Orleans.

What we do know about the effect of charter schools is they often re-segregate children in schools based on the parents' differential ability to choose schools for their children. This ability to choose may be based on differential knowledge and appreciation for differences in the quality of education, and differences based on the ability to provide transport to schools that may be outside of their immediate area. According to the Cowen Institute's public school parent's public opinion poll, transportation in particular was noted as an important factor for 64 percent of parents overall, and 91 percent of parents reporting an annual income below $15,000 (The Scott S. Cowen Institute for Public Education Initiatives, 2012). One underappreciated aspect of housing segregation is that it is by far mostly class based in which we have low, medium, and high income neighborhoods in our communities. Thus neighborhood schools are also generally class and often racially segregated. This differential benefit to choose may also be based on the family resources to pay for additional resources (school materials, uniforms, class trips) that are necessary for those schools that have the highest levels of performance. In general, families with the least resources and stability are less likely to be able to exercise the freedom of choice that the charter school models promise.

Lastly, it is also important to recognize that the schools that are the highest performing have admissions and retention requirements that prevent open choice. For example, of the four charter schools that provided elementary school education and received the highest letter grade from the State of Louisiana (A or A+), three of them had admissions requirements (New Orleans Parent Organizing Network, 2012; The Scott S. Cowen Institute for Public Education Initiatives, 2012). Quigley and Finger state that "the reorganization of the public schools has created a separate but unequal tiered system of schools that steers a minority of students, including virtually all of the city's white students, into a set of selective, higher-performing schools and most of the city's students of color

into a set of lower-performing schools (Quigley and Finger, 2011)."
In the state of Louisiana for the most recent official data (2009-
2010), 67 percent of students graduated high school in four years,
for the New Orleans Recovery School District, it was 49.7 percent —
less than half of the students graduated in four years (Louisiana
Department of Education, 2011).

Another important area of school violence is the exclusion from
education that can result from suspension and expulsion from
school. The Southern Poverty Law Center in its report *Access Denied*
found that Recovery School District students, of whom 98 percent
are African American and 79 percent are low income, are suspend-
ed at a rate that is more than three times the rate of suspensions in
neighboring, mostly white, affluent school districts (Belway, 2010).
Almost 29 percent of the students at the RSD schools received an
out of school suspension during the 2007-2008 school year. The rate
of suspension in RSD schools was also more than twice the state
average and more than ten times the national rate. The report also
notes that the schools do not track the number of students who are
subject to abusive security practices including handcuffing, shack-
ling, and physical assaults by security personnel. However, Belway
argues that anecdotal evidence suggests this is also a problem.

Institutional Violence–Government
In April 2012, five former New Orleans police officers were
sentenced to prison for their involvement in the shooting of civilians in the aftermath of Hurricane Katrina, one of those shot died.
Three of the police officers were directly involved in the assault
and two were responsible for covering up the killings. According
to the court testimony, "Sgt. Kenneth Bowen and Sgt. Robert Gise-
vius and Officers Anthony Villavaso and Robert Faulcon jumped
in a Budget rental truck with several other officers and raced to the
Danziger Bridge in eastern New Orleans, responding to a distress
call (Robertson, 2012)." Witnesses at the trial stated that soon after
the officers arrived on the scene they began firing on members of
a family who were trying to find a grocery store in the area. A sev-
enteen-year-old named James Brisette, a friend who was with the
family, was killed and four others were gravely wounded. Police
chased two of the family members, one a forty-year-old man who
was mentally disabled, was shot in the back and then "stomped

on by another officer as he lay wounded." A cover-up of the shootings began soon afterward that included made-up witnesses and a planted gun at the scene.

This case of police misuse of authority and outright violence directed at citizens is unfortunately not an isolated instance. Earlier in 2011, the U.S. Department of Justice issued a report on their investigation of the New Orleans police force. In their investigation they found that "officers in NOPD routinely use unnecessary and unreasonable force in violation of the Constitution and NOPD policy" (United States Department of Justice, Civil Rights Division, 2011: p. vi). The report noted that minority populations and those who were mentally disabled were particular targets of unnecessary and unreasonable force. Furthermore, the Justice Department concluded that even in cases of the most serious uses of force, such as officer-involved shootings and in-custody deaths, there was no investigation or the investigation was so mishandled that it appeared intentional. The report noted the following practice to prevent investigation of their offices; "For a time, NOPD had a practice of temporarily assigning officers who had been involved in officer-involved shootings to the Homicide Division, and then automatically deeming the statements officers provided to homicide investigators to be 'compelled,' effectively immunizing the use of these statements in any subsequent criminal investigation or prosecution. It is difficult to interpret this practice as anything other than a deliberate attempt to make it more difficult to criminally prosecute any officer in these cases" (United States Department of Justice, Civil Rights Division, 2011: p. VII).

The report also noted that detentions without reasonable suspicion are routine by the NOPD, and they often lead to unwarranted searches and arrests without probable cause. In general, they concluded that policing in New Orleans was done in a discriminatory manner such that African Americans and those of the LGBT community were particularly targeted for harassment. Furthermore, juveniles who were African American were disproportionately arrested.

> Arrest data provided by NOPD indicates that in 2009, the Department arrested 500 African American males and eight white males under the age of 17 for serious offenses, which range from homicide to larceny over fifty dollars. During this same period the

Department arrested 65 African American females and one white female in this same age group. Adjusting for the population, these figures mean that the ratio of arrest rates for both African American males to white males, and African American females to white females, was nearly 16 to 1 (United States Department of Justice, Civil Rights Division, 2011: pp. IX-X).

National ratios of minority to majority juvenile arrests are approximately three to one.

Lastly, the report noted that the New Orleans police often failed to provide police services to those who did not speak English. Their investigation found that "NOPD has virtually no capacity to provide meaningful access to police services to LEP community members, who in New Orleans are predominantly Latino or of Vietnamese descent" (United States Department of Justice, Civil Rights Division, 2011: p. XII). In July, 2012, the United States government entered into a comprehensive, cooperative consent decree with the city of New Orleans to resolve allegations of unlawful police misconduct by the New Orleans Police Department (NOPD) (Department of Justice Office of Public Affairs, 2012).

The pattern of abuse and discriminatory treatment of its citizens is not a recent occurrence in the history of the city of New Orleans. As Adler in chapter one points out, going back to the early part of the twentieth century it was a core mission of the police to maintain a racial hierarchy against the social disorder the minority twentieth century, the police focused their patrols to responding to the needs of white citizens, often ignoring crime that occurred between members of the black population. Furthermore the abuse of police authority specifically directed at black residents is also part of this history. Adler notes that street justice was often used by police when blacks were suspected of committing crime against the white residents. As he states, "If early twenty-first-century police brutality is the horrifying exception, in early twentieth-century New Orleans such treatment was routine and publicly defended, further undermining African American confidence in local law enforcers." Thus, given this history and the most recent investigation by the Department of Justice, it is quite understandable as to why the minority community has little trust and use for the police in resolving their own problems, problems that oftentimes lead to violence, their own version of "street justice," as they attempt to resolve them. Adler also notes that the justice system provided little protection or justice for black New Orleanians. He notes that the courts responded quite differently if the victim was black or white. If the victim was white and the offender black, punishment was quite harsh; if the victim was black and the offender white the response was quite lenient. In particular, he notes that convictions of whites for killing blacks was rare.

In short, institutional violence and discriminatory treatment by the police and local government has a long history in New Orleans. These acts of police violence in particular are an important part of the chain of violence that must be considered as part of the story of violence in New Orleans. Those who are the victims or offenders of the acts of interpersonal violence that is defined as the problem of violence in New Orleans were also often the victims of institutional violence that included the violence committed by the police directed at young minority members of the New Orleans community.

Structural Violence

The greatest violence as a result of a single event that has occurred in New Orleans, certainly during the last fifty years, if not the entire twentieth and twenty-first centuries, is the violence that occurred in the wake of Hurricane Katrina. On August 29, 2005, Katrina's storm surge caused more than fifty different levee breaches in greater New Orleans that resulted in approximately eighty percent of the city submerged. More than nine hundred people died in the aftermath. The victims were for the most part poor, elderly, ill, or disabled. (Brunkard, Namulanda, and Ratard, 2008). The largest portion of victims (40 percent) died by drowning, as some areas of the city were covered with up to fifteen feet of water from broken levees. Another 25 percent died of trauma and injury, and another 11 percent died from heart conditions.

They were disproportionately African American. According to Dyson, 80 percent of New Orleans's minority households lived in the flooded area, while only 54 percent of the city's white population did. He also notes that "the average household income of those in the flooded area trailed those who lived on New Orleans's higher ground by $17,000" (Dyson, 2005: pp. 31-32). It was the concentrated poverty that rendered poor African Americans much more vulnerable to the hurricane's effects. Naomi Klein opens the chapter entitled "Disaster Apartheid" in her book *Shock Doctrine* with a quote from Hein Marais, a South African writer. "Shelve the abiding fiction that disasters do not discriminate—that they flatten everything in their path with 'democratic' disregard. Plagues zero in on the dispossessed, on those forced to build their lives in the path of danger" (Klein, 2007: p. 513).

This is the story of structural violence. It is "the everyday violence of infant mortality, slow starvation, disease, despair, and humiliation that destroys socially marginalized humans with even greater frequency" (Scheper-Hughes and Bourgois, 2004: p. 2). However, the everyday violence that manifests itself in terms of disparities in mortality or morbidity rates becomes accelerated with natural disasters. It is also the story of the Titanic, one's class position was defined in terms of where one's cabin was located on the ship, which was the major factor in determining who would live and who would die as a result of the ship's collision with the iceberg. In cases of natural disaster, because of our position as defined in terms of class, gender, or ethnicity, we have a greater or lesser chance of escaping the calamity. As Klein describes the victims,

> The 120,000 people in New Orleans without cars, who depended on the state to organize their evacuation, waited for help that did not arrive, making desperate SOS signs or rafts out of their refrigerator doors. Those images shocked the world because, even if most of us had resigned ourselves to the daily inequalities of who has access to health care and whose schools have decent equipment, there was still a widespread assumption that disasters were supposed to be different. It was taken for granted that the state— at least in a rich country—would come to the aid of the people during a cataclysmic event (Klein, 2007: p. 516).

These positions and what they mean in terms of chances to live is the form of violence that becomes more accelerated and transparent during the occurrence of natural disasters or accidents. It is not the hurricane that was violent, it was the fact that some were valued as less and thus there was less of an effort to protect them from the storm. There were reports years in advance of Katrina that predicted what would happen when a severe storm would strike New Orleans (Dyson, 2005). Dyson cites a 2001 FEMA report that concluded that a catastrophic hurricane in New Orleans was "among the three likeliest . . . disasters facing this country" (Dyson, 2005: p. 78). He notes that articles in such general periodicals as *Popular Mechanics* and *Scientific American*, along with the PBS science program, *Nova*, provided dire warnings of the impending calamity once a severe hurricane struck New Orleans, a city which is approximately 49 percent below sea level and is protected by a series of levees that were in need of being strengthened.

The United States Army Corp of Engineers was responsible for maintaining the Southeast Louisiana Urban Flood Control Project (SELA). More than one quarter of a billion dollars in projects that were to strengthen the levees that were weakened or eroded by previous storm activity was cut from the budget by the George W. Bush Administration in order to continue funding two wars and the development of the homeland security system (Dyson, 2005). A bipartisan congressional committee to investigate the preparation for and response to Hurricane Katrina defined the cause of the disaster as "a failure of initiative" (Select Bipartisan Committee to Investigate the Preparation for and Response to Hurricane Katrina, 2006). Others may define it as inaction to prevent the deaths of almost one thousand people in New Orleans because of their lack of power and influence in a system in which the government, as well as all other institutions, is more responsive to those who have the influence to make it responsive to them and not responsive to those who do not have the power or influence. The failure to protect through the maintenance of the levee system and the failure of an adequate evacuation system for those without transportation is not only the story of the calamity of the storm, but a case of institutional, structural violence.

Another example of this violence related to the hurricane is the uneven nature of the government-supported efforts to rebuild after the storm. In general, those people who were most harmed have been provided the least support to return and rebuild their lives. Those who did not own the dwelling they resided in, did not have insurance to cover the loss, or did not have the necessary funds to rebuild experienced the least amount of support. Instead the rebuilding has become an opportunity for those who had more resources to recover, to receive more support from local, state, and federal government. Since the hurricane, there is less available housing for the lower income residents, the neighborhood schools where they sent their children have been transformed into charter schools, to which they must apply to attend, and the principle hospital (Charity Hospital) that was in the city and whose mission was to care for the poor and minority population (85 percent of patients had income below $20,000 and 75 percent were African American) in the city was closed and has never reopened. A recent report documents how lower income and minority residents were disadvantaged by the reconstruction activities including the lack of employment opportunities in the rebuilding effort and a loss of schools and access to affordable housing (Jenkins, Thukral, Hsu, Kunakemakorn, and Haberle, 2012). As noted earlier, the city has also shrank in population by approximately 30 percent, the majority of those who have not returned have been African American (118,000 less blacks and 24,000 less whites since the 2000 census) (Chinni, 2011), most of them were poor, and most of them had previously resided in the area that experienced the greatest destruction. Despite these changes in the population the levels of inequality have increased in the city (Eichler, 2012).

Katrina highlighted and exacerbated the structural violence that was occurring on a daily basis in the city of New Orleans. The beginning of the chain of violence lies in the structures of inequality that is part of the everyday life of citizens in New Orleans. This violence comes to light most dramatically during times of natural disasters. Those areas with the highest concentration of the poor are the most vulnerable to the non-responsiveness of government to protect them. The state of Louisiana is second only to the state of Mississippi in having the greatest concentration of poverty in the nation. The poverty rate in New Orleans is approximately twice the national average (Quigley and Finger, 2011). The rate of poverty among children is also significantly higher than the rate for the United States as a whole, 34 percent versus 20 percent (Annie E. Casey Foundation, 2011). The State of Louisiana ranks forty-seventh in the nation in overall child welfare. The city of New Orleans also has the second highest levels of income inequality compared to other places in the nation with a population of 100,000 or more. This is the beginning of the chain of violence where because of one's position in terms of class, ethnicity, and/or gender you are defined as less to be invested in, whether the investment is in education, health, or protection by the government.

Mapping the Intervention Strategies

The local government, in partnership with the federal government's response to the violence in New Orleans, has focused on all levels of violence that have been discussed. This in part is a credit to the public health approach that plays an important part in recognizing that violence goes beyond the homicides to which police respond. However, it is also important to point out that the Justice Department's response to the violence of police and its unresponsiveness to the poor and minority community in New Orleans has had an even greater impact on promoting changes to reduce the problems of the institutional violence of the police and make them more accountable to all segments of the community.

Nevertheless, in reviewing the efforts in the community to reduce violence the focus has been on proximate causes of the interpersonal violence, with less attention on the larger institutional and structural forms of violence. *NOLA for Life: A Comprehensive Murder Reduction Strategy* is the outline of the strategy used to combat violence in New Orleans. Strategies like Project Safe Neighborhoods, Violent Crime Impact Teams, Ceasefire New Orleans, and the Kennedy's Group Violent Reduction Strategy, as well as necessary improvements in the crime lab, evidence collection, and increasing the size of police homicide unit along with the improvement in the training for police are all important measures that focus on improving the police response to the immediate problem of interpersonal violence (See chapters 2 and 9 for more details about these strategies).

The strategies that focus on trying to improve relations between the police and the local community, especially in those areas where the police have been seen as more of a threat than an aid to combatting violence, are also very important. Included in these efforts are the releasing to the public of police records on calls for service and the improvement in police-community relations through the use of a procedural justice model that provides a greater degree of transparency in law enforcement activities. There are additional steps within the *NOLA for Life* strategy that focus on strengthening the community. Programs such as improvement of lighting in the inner city, the expansion of recreational opportunities for inner city youth, efforts to fight blight through the Lot Maintenance Program, the *NOLA for Life* neighborhood Volunteer Days Program, efforts to connect residents to mental health services in the community, and the development of a quality of life indicator program are all important efforts to strengthen neighborhoods in the city.

Lastly, the efforts to assist in the reentry of those who have been convicted and incarcerated are extremely important in assisting in providing a place for the large number of people who everyday are being released back into the community with the stigma of the label of felon and little resources to start a new life. New Orleans incarcerates a larger percentage of its population than any other U.S. city its size. Equal efforts to those spent prosecuting and incarcerating these individuals must be spent in assisting their reentry into the community. Punishment will be insufficient to protect the community if these individuals are not helped in finding a place where they can be contributors and not threats to the community. The Comprehensive Reentry Strategy outlined in the *NOLA for Life* plan is scheduled for implementation next year and includes greater assistance to former inmates to acquire employment, housing, and mental health counseling, which will be a very important component of the plan, to reduce the level of violence in the community.

The *NOLA for Life* plan also focuses needed attention on the forms of institutional violence that occur in the home and the school. The Family Violence Prevention Strategy, which is part of the Healthy Start Program, is an important effort in identifying problems of family violence that go unreported. The Family Justice Centers and the efforts of the police and prosecuting attorney's office to respond more effectively to cases of family violence and intimate partner violence are very important steps. Youth mentoring programs such as the "Saving Our Sons Mentoring Program" that targets one hundred young males in New Orleans who are at risk of exposure to or involvement in violence can also be important in aiding families in the socialization of their children. Nevertheless these are all relatively small steps given the long history of neglect of these areas of violence and much more will be needed in providing the necessary support to families in response to the violence in their homes.

Similarly in the area of school violence, the promotion of conflict resolution strategies to prevent violence and the development of the School Community Response Program are important steps.

However, the greater problem may be the problem of school exclusion (suspensions, expulsions, and drop outs) that reflect the failure of the school in meeting the educational needs of the majority of youth who are likely to commit violent acts in the community. As noted earlier, given that the city population has declined by 29 percent since the last census as a result of more than 100,000 poor or low income and minority residents (there are 56,193 fewer children, a drop of nearly 44 percent from 2000 to 2010 [Robertson, 2011]) not returning to the city, in most cases a result of the lack of rebuilding of low income housing in the areas where they principally resided and in the areas of New Orleans that experienced the greatest destruction as a result of Katrina, measures which show an improvement in dropout rates for the newly converted charter schools are highly suspect. It is more likely a result of the change in the population served than any efforts of the schools to prevent exclusion. As mentioned previously, charter schools may be using more restrictive admission strategies that prevent those who pose the greatest educational challenges from attending.

Lastly, the efforts to address the problem of structural violence in the community are the weakest. Given that New Orleans has one of the highest poverty rates in the nation and a recent census report indicates that the levels of inequality have only increased in the community since 2005, a much greater effort needs to be made in providing employment in the community at livable wages. Economic development strategies that focus on tourism, which provide generally lower wage employment, needs to be coupled with a strategy that promotes the increase in wages in the community. Solely relying on traditional economic development strategies that provide tax abatements without the requirement of paying a livable wage are likely to have minimal impact on the levels of inequality in the community. Furthermore, despite the national and regional climate to suppress unionization efforts like "right to work laws," unionization has been the principal means by which lower skilled workers have been able to elevate their standard of living and provide necessary resources for their families. The city government needs to be more aggressive in establishing a livable wage and right to organize requirements as part of its economic development strategy. Furthermore, the exploration of alternative economic models that do not rely solely on the investment of individuals, but provides programs of community investment that subsidize and encourage the development of profit and non-profit cooperatives where the resources (both monetary and labor) of middle and lower income residents are pooled to form neighborhood businesses in the areas that have the greatest needs for services and highest levels of unemployment should be considered (Zeuli and Radel, 2005).

In addition to the use of economic development strategies that focus on increasing wages and creating alternatives to the private ownership model, the providing of needed housing and medical services to the lower income population is essential in reducing the levels of structural violence in the community. A community re-development strategy that is more responsive to those who have capital to invest and are looking for the highest returns on their investment is likely to exclude consideration of the needs of the poorer segments of the community. There must be a concerted ef-fort to ameliorate the conditions of poverty as a result of lack of ad-equate housing and the need for medical services in their commu-nity, and the development of economic strategies that build upon the resources that are available in the community and not just rely on those who are outside the community to uplift it, if the levels of violence are to be reduced.

Conclusion

It is first important to commend the community and its politi-cal leadership for the development of a plan that is more compre-hensive than most efforts in addressing violence in cities around the nation. The city government is also to be commended for in-corporating measures to monitor the effectiveness of these efforts. However, I fear that the overall impact will be much less than if the efforts were redirected to incorporate more emphasis on the larger forms of violence in the community.

As noted earlier, violence occurs in a sequential chain that be-gins with structural violence that often begins at birth, which is then linked to forms of institutional violence, and finally to the in-terpersonal violence that is the focus of much of the police and lo-cal government's attention and resources in combatting violence. In general, when one reviews the efforts of the government to re-duce the levels of violence in New Orleans, the focus is princi-

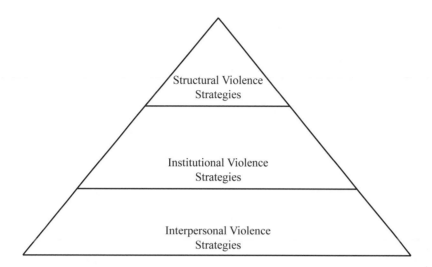

pally a response to the interpersonal violence and its proximate causes. The graphic below illustrates the focus of the efforts in New Orleans.

The violence within New Orleans is foremost a violence of poverty that begins at the earliest point in a person's life and then is reinforced by violence in the homes, the schools, an inadequate economic system and an unresponsive system of government, or worse a brutalizing response from the police, all of which leads to the interpersonal violence that is one of the highest in the nation. High rates of homicide are at the end of the chain and are the area (despite being comparably high) that is one of the smallest areas of violence that is occurring in New Orleans. There are much greater levels of violence at the structural and institutional levels occurring within New Orleans that need to be measured and defined as violence and not just seen as potential causes. There needs to be a shift in focus, resources, and intervention to match the chain of violence that is occurring in New Orleans. As illustrated below more focus must be on the highest levels and greatest amount of violence that are occurring at the structural and institutional levels.

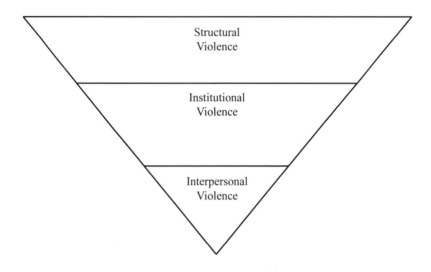

This will not be easy. There is much resistance to making changes in the structure of the community and the functioning of institutions that are more responsive to those with the most influence and power. However if there are not more efforts to address these forms of violence, we will continue to respond at the end of the chain after all the other levels of violence have occurred. To reduce the levels of interpersonal violence that plague the community we must break the chain by addressing the violence at the structural and institutional levels.

References

Annie E. Casey Foundation. (2011). *Kids Count 2011.* New Orleans: Annie E. Casey Foundation.

Associated Press. (2012, July 12). "Louisiana child abuse hotline logged 114,000 calls its 1st year." *Times-Picayune.*

Belway, S. (2010). *Access Denied: New Orleans Students and Parents Identify Barriers to Public Education.* New Orleans: Southern Poverty Law Center.

Brunkard, J., G. Namulanda, and R. Ratard. (2008). "Hurricane Katrina Deaths, Louisiana, 2005." *Disaster Medicine and Public Health Preparedness* 2: 215-23.

Chinni, D. (2011, February 10). *Census Data Start to Show Katrina's Long-*

Term Impact on New Orleans . Retrieved December 18, 2012, from PBS Newshour-Patchwork Nation. http://www.pbs.org/newshour/ rundown/2011/02/census-data-start-to-show-katrinas-long-term-impact-on-new-orleans.html.

Department of Justice Office of Public Affairs. (2012, July 24). *Justice Department Announces Consent Decree with City of New Orleans to Resolve Allegations of Unlawful Misconduct by New Orleans Police Department.* Retrieved December 11, 2012, from The United States Department of Justice. http://www.justice.gov/opa/pr/2012/July/12-ag-917.html.

Dyson, M.E. (2005). *Come Hell or High Water: Hurricane Katrina and the Color of Disaster.* New York: Basic Books.

Eichler, A. (2012, April 26). *New Orleans Grew More Unequal After Hurricane Katrina: Report.* Retrieved December 28, 2012, from Huffington Post. http://www.huffingtonpost.com/2012/04/26/new-orleans-unequal_n_1456445.html.

Filosa, G. (2010, May 16). "Recent domestic violence tragedies in New Orleans couldn't be prevented by moving cases to state court." *Times-Picayune.*

Gilligan, J. (1996). *Violence: Our deadly epidemic and its causes.* New York: G.P. Putnam.

Iadicola, P., and A. Shupe. (2003, 2013). *Violence, Inequality, and Human Freedom.* Lanham: Rowman and Littlefield.

Jenkins, A., J. Thukral, K. Hsu, N. Kunakemakorn, and M. Haberle. (2012). *Promoting Opportunity through Impact Statements: A Tool for Policymakers to Assess Equity.* Washington, D.C.: American Constitution Society.

Jenkins, P., and B. Phillips. (2008). "Domestic Violence and Disaster." In *Katrina and the Women of New Orleans.* G. a. Group (pp. 65-70). New Orleans, Louisiana: Tulane University, Newcomb College Center for Research on Women.

Klein, N. (2007). *The Shock Doctrine.* New York: Picador.

Louisiana Department of Education. (2011). *Cohort Graduation Rate.* Retrieved December 7, 2012, from LDOE Lousiana Department of Education. http://www.louisianaschools.net/topics/cohort_rates.html.

New Orleans Parent Organizing Network. (2012). *New Orleans Parent's Guide to Public Schools.* New Orleans: New Orleans Parent Organizing Network.

Quigley, B., and D. Finger. (2011, August 22). Katrina Pain Index 2011. *Counterpunch.* Petrolia, California, U.S.A. Retrieved November 30, 2012. http://www.counterpunch.org/2011/08/22/katrina-pain-index-2011/.

Robertson, C. (2011, February 4). "Smaller New Orleans After Katrina, Census Shows." *The New York Times*, p. A11.

———. (2012, April 4). "5 Ex-Officers Sentenced in Post-Katrina Shootings." *The New York Times*, p. A10.

Schaefer, S., W. Christeson, and S. Messner-Zidell. (2012). *Breaking the Cycle: How Home Visiting Can Reduce Child Abuse and Neglect and Prevent Crime in Louisiana*. Washington, D.C.: Fight Crime: Invest in Kids.

Scheper-Hughes, N., and P. Bourgois. (2004). *Violence in War and Peace: An Anthology*. Malden: Blackwell Publishing.

Select Bipartisan Committee to Investigate the Preparation for and Response to Hurricane Katrina. (2006). *A FAILURE OF INITIATIVE: Final Report of the Select Bipartisan Committee to Investigate the Preparation for and Response to Hurricane Katrina*. Washington, D.C.: United States Government Printing Office.

The Scott S. Cowen Institute for Public Education Initiatives. (2012). *The State of Public Education in New Orleans*. Tulane University. New Orleans: Cowen Institute for Public Education Initiatives.

United States Department of Education. (2009). United States Education Dashboard: Percent of public school 4th graders Proficient on the NAEP in Reading. Washington, D. C. Retrieved November 29, 2012. http://dashboard.ed.gov/statecomparison.aspx?i=c4&id=2&wt=0.

United States Department of Justice, Civil Rights Division. (2011). *Investigation of the New Orleans Police Department*. Washington, D.C.: The United States Department of Justice.

Welford, C., B.J. Bond, and S. Goodson. (2011). *Crime in New Orleans: Analyzing Trends and New Orleans Responses to Crime*. Washington, D.C.: Bureau of Justice Statistics.

Widom, C.S. (2000, January). "Childhood Victimization: Early Adversity, Later Psychopathogy." *National Institute of Justice Journal* : 3-9

Wilkinson, R., and K. Pickett. (2010). *The Spirit Level: Why Greater Equality Makes Societies Stronger*. New York: Bloomsbury Press.

Zeuli, K., and J. Radel. (2005). "Cooperatives as a Community Development Strategy: Linking Theory and Practice." *Journal of Regional Analysis and Policy* 35 (1): 43-54.

4 | The Public Health Approach to Violence Prevention

David Hemenway

Components of the Approach

Public health was a late entry into the field of violence prevention. In the twentieth century, after successfully helping to reduce the scourge of infectious disease, public health gradually turned its attention to the other sources of death and disability — chronic disease, injury, and violence. Public health made its initial foray into the violence field in 1979 when the U.S. Surgeon General's Report, *Healthy People*, identified stress and violent behavior as one of fifteen priority areas for action. The following year, the Department of Health and Human Services promulgated the first measurable ten-year objectives for violence (i.e., child abuse, homicide, suicide, handguns, and reliable data). In 1983 the Centers for Disease Control and Prevention (CDC) established a Violence Epidemiology Branch. Today, thirty years later, violence is generally recognized in the United States as a public health issue. For example, in 2008 the U.S. Conference of Mayors declared violence to be a "public health crisis" (Dahlberg and Mercy, 2009).

As a late entry to the violence field, public health has tried to distinguish itself from criminology and criminal justice, which historically have been the principal form of study and of response to violent acts. This essay explains the main aspects of "the public health approach." It then contrasts public health with criminology and with criminal justice, focusing on what public health adds to the mix. Finally, the essay provides multiple examples of the approach in action, with particular emphasis on illustrations from Boston and from the Harvard Youth Violence Prevention Center. These examples are not presented as illustrations of public health at its best — they are simply the examples I know best.

Both the Centers for Disease Control and the World Health Organization describe the public health approach as a four-step model: Define the problem, identify risk and protective factors, develop and test prevention strategies, and ensure widespread adoption of effective programs. Yet these steps are little more than the scientific approach to any problem. I believe instead that the public health approach has these five key overlapping components (Hemenway and Miller, 2013).

First, the approach is population-based and rarely involves identifiable individuals. For example, the interest is not why Peter killed his wife, but why so many intimate partner homicides occur, why they occur more often in Louisiana than in Massachusetts, and how to reduce them everywhere.

Second, the approach focuses on prevention — usually as far upstream as possible. It is often more effective to affect the instrument of violence (e.g., the gun) and the environment (e.g., improved lighting for schools, streets, parks) in which the problem occurs than it is to focus on changing the individual with the last clear chance to prevent the problem (e.g., victim or perpetrator). The public health approach is thus quite attuned to the idea of crime prevention through environmental design (CPTED) (Clarke, 1997). Crime in the Washington, D.C. metro appears to be much lower than in Boston, Chicago, or New York subways in large part because of the design of the metro rather than the inherent criminal tendencies of the community or the subway riders (Hemenway, 2009).

Third, public health uses a systems approach — borrowing from human-factors engineering, it tries to create a system where (a) it is difficult to behave inappropriately and, since some people will still behave badly, (b) the inappropriate behavior does not lead to serious injury. For presidential assassination, for example, the goal would be to make it difficult for a potential perpetrator to gain access to the president (ID checks) and less likely for a serious injury if a shooting occurred (e.g., bullet-proof glass, body armor).

Fourth, the approach is broad and inclusive. It examines all possible interventions, including changing social norms, passing new laws, and improving the enforcement of old laws. It also tries to engage and mobilize as many people and institutions as possible in a multifaceted way. The scores of groups to be mobilized include foundations, undertakers, hairdressers, reporters, physicians, Hollywood writers, and the faith community. At the city level, the big tent approach includes such government agencies as social services, public works, economic development, zoning, and recreation and parks. Law enforcement and suppression activities are crucial, but alone are not typically sufficient for effective prevention.

Fifth, the approach emphasizes shared responsibility over blame. Prevention works best when everyone is trying to help and institutions as well as people take responsibility. By contrast, assessing blame can sometimes be counterproductive to the goal of public health, which is to prevent the problem from occurring (Hemenway, 2013).

Public health does sometimes emphasize blame and punishment, particularly in areas where the social norm has winked at truly dangerous behavior such as intimate partner violence or drunk driving. But, in general, public health does not usually actively push for the blame and punishment of offenders. While punishment is often an appropriate response to violent crime, far too many people seem to view it as the only necessary response. Allocating blame appears to permit too many people to wash their hands of the problem rather than also considering and taking effective upstream actions to prevent future violence. Since criminologists and criminal justice already focus on punishment — and the potential benefits of deterrence, incapacitation, and rehabilitation — public health, I believe correctly, sees that its main contribution is to emphasize other aspects of prevention.

The success story of motor vehicle injuries helps to illustrate the public health approach. In the 1950s, almost all crashes were classified as due to driver error, and most deaths were "caused" by deliberate driver misbehavior (e.g., speeding, drunk driving, running red lights). The obvious solution was to do something about the "nut behind the wheel" — drivers training to reduce errors and traffic enforcement to reduce misbehavior. But in the 1950s, public health physicians began asking a different question, not "who caused the collision?" but "what caused the injury?" It became clear that drivers were being killed by spear-like steering columns that would rupture vital organs; faces and major arteries were ripped apart by windshields; occupants were being thrown from the cars and their skulls would hit the hood or the pavement. Motorist were dying when their vehicle left the road and hit unyielding lights, signs, and trees that lined the road ways. The physicians asked, why can't cars have energy-absorbing steering columns, padded interiors, safety glass, seat belts, and airbags? Why can't the roadways be made safer? After all, society was not placing unyielding impediments along the sides of airport runways (Eastman, 1981).

Over the past six decades, cars and roads have been made safer, and the emergency medical system has improved. Traffic safety experts do not think that drivers today are any better than they were sixty years ago (alcohol use is down, but distracted driving is up), yet fatalities per mile driven have fallen by more than 80 percent! Modern traffic safety does not neglect the driver, but it also emphasizes the importance of upstream prevention.

The motor vehicle success was due to a multifaceted approach. For example, the key to the reduction in drunk driving was a combination of stronger laws and enforcement, changes in social norms about the acceptability of drinking and driving, creative new solutions such as the "designated driver," more crashworthy cars, better roads, and an improved emergency medical system.

Public Health contrasted to Criminology

Public health is different than criminology, and these differences help public health add to our knowledge about crime and violence. While the core discipline of criminology is sociology, the core discipline of public health is epidemiology. This makes a difference in terms of the theories presented and the factors that tend to be highlighted. Thus, criminologists are more apt to discuss issues such as social disorganization, social strain, and deviance, while public health researchers may emphasize the similarities of violence with contagious disease. My personal experience has been that public health experts are more likely than criminologists to incorporate positive and negative feedback loops (e.g., contagion) into their models as main factors explaining crime trends.

The different approaches of sociology and epidemiology make a difference in terms of the research methods used: criminologists are taught how to use factor analysis, while public health professionals are more likely to employ case-control studies. Thus public health experts were the first to examine whether a gun in the home was a "risk factor" for homicide, and naturally used a case-control approach (e.g., Kellermann et al., 1993).

The social institutions criminologists are likely to turn to for data and for policy action are law enforcement agencies (e.g., police, corrections). By contrast, the social institutions most aligned with public health are medical organizations (e.g., physicians, hospitals). The differences extend to the sources of data and the statistical approaches preferred. Criminologists tend to use police data, while public health researchers are more likely to use emergency department, hospital, or death certificate data. Even this simple difference can be profound. Physicians see different arrays of violence than do police (e.g., physicians are more likely to see the results of bullying and certain forms of family violence—child abuse and elder abuse—compared to police). Not surprisingly, relative to criminologists, public health researchers have tended to focus more on these issues.

Finally, and perhaps most important, public health is more than the study of an issue. It is not "public health-ology." Public health researchers are expected not just to increase understanding of the problems, but to do something about them to improve society's health and well-being. Thus it is common that public health researchers are involved in advocacy and action, not only presenting information but often helping to rally social and political support for solutions.

Public Health contrasted to Criminal Justice

Two decades ago, Mark Moore, professor of Criminal Justice at Harvard, wrote thoughtful and insightful essays about the differences between the criminal justice approach and the public health approach (Moore, 1993, 1995). While criminal justice sees violence as a threat to community order, public health is more likely to see it as a threat to community health. Public health thus is more likely to emphasize the importance of responding to the needs of victims (and to point out that perpetrators frequently have been or will be victims). Victims often appear to receive short shrift from criminal justice—which seems most interested in them in their role as potential witnesses. Public health not only wants to help victims—whose victimization has increased their risk for violence perpetration—but also wants to organize them to act socially and politically to reduce violence levels.

While the criminal justice approach tends to be case-oriented and reactive to crimes, public health emphasizes upstream prevention, with a concern to preventing not only subsequent offenses, but first offenses. Criminal justice tends to focus on apprehending and punishing the perpetrators of violence; public health has more interest in changing the environment that promotes violence (e.g., reducing the number of alcohol outlets in crime areas). Many public health successes — sewer and water systems to eliminate typhoid epidemics; immunizations to solve polio and smallpox problems; and road and car design to ameliorate the problems of automobile crashes — involved environmental changes having little directly to do with changing individual behavior. While some claim that lessons learned in traffic safety (where crashes are unintentional) cannot be applied to homicide (where actions are intentional and illegal), in fact the underlying cause in most motor vehicle *deaths* is intentional and illegal behavior (e.g., speeding, drunk driving).

Criminal justice is often seen as a morality play — bringing bad guys to justice. Public health recognizes the need to get dangerous offenders off the street (and out of the home), but also remembers that, historically, people with leprosy, plague, cholera, and tuberculosis were often considered as morally bad and suffered not only stigma but sometimes were burnt at the stake or thrown down wells (Slutkin, 2013). Public health strongly believes that focusing almost exclusively on punishing bad behavior is not the most effective way to reduce violence.

An activity of law enforcement consistent with the public health approach is community (or problem-oriented) policing, which holds that the local community is a crucially important partner, perhaps even the first line of defense, in responding to violence and disorder. Public health emphasizes that violence is also a threat to community health and tries to empower communities to solve their own problems — with and without police help (Roth and Moore, 1995).

Community policing emphasizes that arrest is only one of the tools available to police responding to incidents. Police can also offer informal mediation, refer people to services, and mobilize other agencies (Roth and Moore, 1995). This notion of police as part social worker resonates well with public health. Public health believes that police in schools (school resource officers) and elsewhere can often accomplish more if their role model is Mayberry's Sheriff

Andy Taylor (from *The Andy Griffith Show*) rather than Rambo.

For criminal justice, if one thousand people walk along a street, but only one engages in criminal violence, the focus should be on getting that dangerous offender off the street. That violent behavior is an anomaly that needs correcting. This view resonates, but somewhat less strongly, for public health professionals; they have seen it before. For example, one thousand cars typically get safely through intersection A before one motorist has a serious crash. If we care about prevention, should our main focus be on that one motorist — and others like him? Perhaps not — if we know there is a similar intersection B three blocks away, where ten thousand cars typically get through safely before a motorist has a serious crash. Public health believes it may be most effective to modify intersection A to have the same characteristics as intersection B. We may be able to reduce serious crashes by 90 percent, without punishment or directly changing human behavior.

The first tool taught to public health students studying violence prevention is the Haddon Matrix (Haddon, 1970, 1980), which combines the epidemiology triangle (host, agent, environment — with environment often divided into physical and social) with the three levels of prevention (pre-event, event, post-event). The Haddon Matrix is useful in brainstorming about the many countermeasures that can help reduce various types of violence (e.g., gun violence, school violence, intimate partner violence). Table 1 illustrates the Haddon Matrix as applied to workplace violence, with a few examples in each cell (Runyan, undated). The Haddon Matrix emphasizes that there may be many more cost-effective interventions to reduce violence than primarily focusing on changing the morality of the perpetrator.

The Public Health Approach in Action

A public health involvement in violence prevention has had many beneficial consequences. It has added new data sources (e.g., Youth Risk Behavior Surveillance System, National Violent Death Reporting System), new analytic tools (e.g., case control analyses), and new research professionals from the medical and public health communities. It has added many important organizations that now include violence prevention as part of their mission (e.g., Centers for Disease Control, National Institutes of Health, U.S. Public Health Service). Public health has the added benefit of being able to attract and mobilize the efforts of disparate groups, such as physicians, women's and youth organizations, civil rights groups, consumer organizations, and the faith community. Public health brings with it a pragmatic, positive attitude drawn from its many successes in reducing other harms (e.g., polio, measles, smoking, motor vehicle crashes).

Among the many diverse examples of a public health approach to reduce violence are: the Nurse Family Partnership that trains public health nurses to make regular home visits to low-income, first-time mothers, which can lead to reduced aggression and violence among children, and reduced violence when these children become adults (Karolyn, 1998); enlisting salon hairdressers to help reduce intimate partner violence, with the catchy slogan—"cut it out" (Salons against Domestic Abuse, 2013); the training of students in conflict resolution; helping impede the flow of guns to criminals by ensuring that local communities require firearms dealers to obtain business licenses, operate out of store fronts, and abide by local zoning ordinances; and promoting violence prevention strategies in the workplace (Weiss, 1996).

One of the better known public health approaches to youth violence prevention is the Ceasefire/Safe Streets program. Pioneered by physician Gary Slutkin in Chicago, it treats violence like a contagious disease (Slutkin, 2013). A major component of the program is street outreach workers, many of whom are former gang members, who go out in urban areas and develop relationships with at-risk youth. These individuals serve as positive role models for the youth and steer them to resources such as jobs and training. Special outreach workers act as "violence interrupters" who work around the clock to identify and intervene at the site to resolve potentially dangerous conflicts before they escalate into shootings. The program also attempts to change social norms, sending a message that using guns to resolve disputes is unacceptable (Webster et al., 2013).

Boston exemplifies the use of the public health approach to prevent violence. Street workers and clergy played key roles in the so-called Boston Miracle, which saw a reduction of 80 percent in city homicides in the decade of the 1990s. The Miracle relied heavily on innovative policing strategies, described in detail elsewhere (Kennedy, 2012). Among the public health aspects of the approach was having community stakeholders brought into deliberations from the beginning. Part of the strategy was that gang youth were offered positive alternatives to a life of violence on the streets. The alternatives included jobs, job training, mentoring, and after-school programs. One of the programs was helping these young men to become good fathers. Among the many stakeholders important for the success of the project were the Boston clergy who worked on the streets, the Roman Catholic cardinal who publicly supported the efforts of the black Protestant clergy in a city with a predominantly Irish Catholic police department, and the many grassroots community organizations that worked with troubled youth and taught dispute resolution skills to help change adolescent norms concerning violence (Pruitt, 2001; Hemenway, 2009).

The activities of the Harvard Youth Violence Prevention Center (HYVPC) in Boston further illustrate the public health approach (Azrael and Hemenway, 2011). Physician Deborah Prothrow-Stith was the first female and the youngest Commissioner of the Massachusetts Department of Public Health and probably more than any other person brought the public health message of violence prevention to local communities, and to the nation, through her presentations and a series of popular books (e.g., Prothrow-Stith, 1993; 2003). Two of her many accomplishments were creating one of the initial grade-school curricula on violence prevention and organizing a community of violence survivors. Survivor communities can bring knowledge to and support for other survivors, and can play a social and political role in changing social norms and promoting beneficial public policies.

The first step in the public health approach to violence prevention is to create data systems that provide rich, detailed consistent and comparative data across sites and over time. HYVPC core faculty was instrumental in helping create the National Violent Death Reporting System that provides data on all violent deaths (Hemenway et al., 2009). Now under the auspices of the Centers for Disease Control and Prevention (CDC), the system assembles data from four sources: death certificates, medical examiner/coroner reports, police reports, and crime labs. Currently available for eighteen states, the system can provide information on such topics as home invasions, self-defense gun use, and homicide-followed-by-suicide (Barber et al., 2013). Many school shootings and other mass murders, as well as intimate partner homicides, are murder/ suicides (Logan et al., 2008).

HYVPC built a data system for youth violence in Boston (Azrael et al., 2009). The data system was composed of biennial surveys of high school students and of adults, in addition to violence-related data from administrative sources (e.g., police, schools, hospitals). The youth (high school) survey asked many questions about fear, witnessing, victimization, and perpetration of violence, broken down into peer, sibling, and dating violence. A few of the many interesting findings from that survey were: (1) the place more students were afraid was not home, nor school, nor the streets, but the Boston subway system (Boston police changed its policies in response to that information); (2) hours of sleep was related to the likelihood of aggressive behavior, and the school starting time largely determined the average number of hours slept; (3) soda consumption was strongly related to aggressive behavior, even after controlling for many family variables (Solnick and Hemenway, 2012); and (4) community social capital and social efficacy reduced the likelihood of individual aggressive behavior, even after controlling for neighborhood poverty.

HYVPC was able to use the Boston data system to support the work of city agencies — including school, police, public health, and the mayor's office — and to respond to their needs and requests. For example, after a cluster of homicides within the city's Cape Verdean community, the data were used to show that Cape Verdean youth were not more violent than other Boston adolescents. Similarly, when "No Snitching" t-shirts became popular among some city youth, HYVPC added questions about snitching to the youth survey — which showed clear risk and resilience factors for such behavior (Azrael and Hemenway, 2011).

HYVPC helped support the innovative work of physician Bob Sege with the Massachusetts Medical Society and the American Academy of Pediatrics to help doctors teach patients how to reduce and respond to violence. Pediatricians and other primary care providers (PCPs) have a role and a duty to help keep their patients healthy. In the modern era, this means being immunized against disease, wearing seat belts, not smoking or taking illicit drugs, washing hands, eating and sleeping well — and reducing violence.

Violence includes corporal punishment (spanking), bullying, dating violence, and peer youth violence. Sege helped create and disseminate a variety of tools for PCPs, such as simple tip cards to be given to parents (e.g., how to use a "time-out" rather than a strap), videos for the waiting room, and easily digestible information for physicians. These have been distributed and used by thousands of physicians in Massachusetts and throughout the United States (American Academy of Pediatrics 2013).

HVYPC helped many non-profit organizations involved in reducing violent harm. Girls are often victims of violence. Girls LEAP provides self-defense skills to girls, but more important empowers them with a strong sense of self-worth (Girls LEAP 2011). In most school shootings, there were students who knew beforehand that a shooting might occur. The Center to Prevent Youth Violence teaches youth to "speak up" if they hear about something bad that is going to happen (tell a trusted adult or call 1-866-SPEAKUP) (CPYV, 2013). The Louis D. Brown Peace Institute helps survivors of violence. HYVPC worked with the Peace Institute to create a toolkit for first responders on the scene of a homicide [e.g., ten things that emergency medical technicians (EMTs) should say, and ten things they should never say] (LDB Peace Institute, 2013).

HYVPC worked with a non-profit organization to create a computer model of gang involvement in Boston. A key was to involve both gang members and community members in the process. Input from both groups emphasized the importance of trauma as a "positive" feedback loop in the model — trauma led to more violence and more trauma (Bridgewater et al., 2011).

Trauma (e.g., PTSD) is a risk factor for aggressive behavior. Witnessing, victimization, and even the perpetration of violence increase the likelihood of being traumatized, and thereby the likelihood of further aggression and violence. Working with the Boston Public Health Commission (BPHC), HYVPC applied for funds to create trauma-sensitive schools. While shootings and other tragedies in suburban schools bring hosts of social workers and other responders, the same has not been true for Boston tragedies. Creating trauma-sensitive schools can help reduce the likelihood that those exposed to trauma will respond with further violence.

The work of the Boston Public Health Commission (BPHC) helps illustrate the public health approach. BPHC has engaged in many community activities designed to reduce violence, including providing services to victims of violence to reduce trauma-related aggression; intervening with assault victims in emergency departments to reduce retaliation; and teaching 11-14 year olds about individual and group strategies for dating violence prevention. BPHC often employs neighborhood residents to organize, lead, and implement community-based solutions to reduce violence (BPHC, 2013).

One of the most important community mobilization activities of HYVPC was the creation of a coalition of ten grassroots Boston community organizations who met monthly. These partners included community health centers, faith-based organizations, ethnic groups (Massachusetts Alliance of Portuguese Speakers), and nonprofits focused on youth violence prevention (e.g., Teens Against Gang Violence). All the groups had been working with youth to reduce violence, but most had little knowledge of each other. HYVPC brought these groups together, not only to learn from and support each other, but to create an effective group that could provide a unified voice from the various Boston neighborhoods.

The academics and the community partners learned much from each other. For example, the partners provided real-world input for survey instruments, developed questions of relevance to them (e.g., about youth who had lost someone to a homicide), and provided access to a broad spectrum of community youth (some of whom joined the HYVPC youth advisory board). Academics provided training, technical assistance, and scientific feedback to the partners. HYVPC's academic stature facilitated partners' access to policy makers, while Partners' local reputation facilitated academic's credibility with schools, the police, and the mayor.

Of particular note, the public health approach to violence prevention was a galvanizing framework for these practitioners, who saw in it the intellectual validation for their hands-on work in the community. HYVPC training to the partners, which emphasized community assets as well as liabilities, helped promote partners' growth into an active public health-oriented coalition.

Guns

In the United States, most intentional violent deaths (i.e., homicides, suicides) are gun deaths. Note that public health is concerned about all gun injuries, not just from assaults. After all, to a surgeon, it doesn't matter whether a bullet wound to the head was intentionally self-inflicted or other-inflicted, or due to an accidental shooting.

HYVPC core faculty have written close to one hundred journal articles on firearms—investigating such issues as training, storage, carrying, intimidation, self-defense, road rage, as well as guns at college, public attitudes about guns, and gun use in homicides, suicides, and unintentional shootings (Harvard Injury Control Research Center, 2013)

Many HYVPC studies have demonstrated that across all U.S. states, for both genders and all age groups, higher levels of household gun ownership and weaker gun laws are associated with higher rates of homicide (because of more gun homicides), higher rates of suicide (because of more gun suicides), and higher rates of unintentional gun deaths. These studies have controlled for such variables as rates of urbanization, poverty, alcohol consumption, divorce, unemployment, education, depression, suicide attempts, and even violent crime (Miller et al., 2007; Miller et al., 2012; Fleegher et al., 2013).

One HYVPC study used data from the Boston youth survey. We found that students wildly overestimated the ease with which other students could obtain firearms, and the percentage of their classmates illegally carrying guns. The degree of overestimation was strongly correlated with the likelihood that that particular adolescent would carry a gun (Hemenway et al., 2011). Correcting the perceptions to reflect reality might reduce gun carrying.

Most of the gun carriers claimed they were carrying because they were afraid; they were carrying for self-defense because they believed other students were carrying guns. The Boston high school students were also asked what kind of world they would like to live in—where it was easy, difficult, or impossible for teens like themselves to obtain guns. Similar to previous studies (Hemenway et al., 1996), the large majority of students wanted to live in a world where it was impossible for teens like themselves to obtain firearms. Even the majority of students who had already illegally carried guns wanted it to be impossible for themselves and their classmates to obtain guns (Hemenway et al., 2011). The HYVPC endeavored to fulfill their wish by helping with various attempts to reduce gun trafficking into the city.

Massachusetts has strong gun laws and low levels of gun ownership. Not surprisingly, most guns used in crime in Boston come from outside the state—brought into the city by adults for profit. HYVPC works with Boston's non-profit Citizens for Safety which encourages reporters and the general public to ask, whenever there is a street shooting: "Where Did the Gun Come From?" The campaign is designed to expand awareness beyond the shooter and the victim to the system of gun trafficking where additional programs and policies can make a difference. While most straw purchasers are male, a woman purchasing a firearm has a much higher likelihood of being a straw purchaser than does a man. A Citizens for Safety initiative is designed to reduce the willingness of women to engage in straw purchasing, using peer-to-peer education in hair salons, churches, battered women's shelters, and other places where women gather. The goal is to create a network of educated, active, engaged, and vocal female leaders who are key partners with law enforcement to keep illegally trafficked guns out of our communities.

Applying a Public Health Approach to New Orleans

A public health approach to gun violence prevention in New Orleans would be wide and encompassing. An initial first step would be to examine the data in detail, trying to understand the specific aspects of the problem and whether and why New Orleans is different than other cities (See chapter 5, "Criminal Homicide and Firearms in New Orleans"). The CDC provides data on states (Centers for Disease Control, 2013). Table 2 below provides a simple comparison of Louisiana with my state, Massachusetts, in terms of homicide, suicide, and unintentional gun deaths, without any controls. The data are suggestive—indicating that gun prevalence and gun policies may play an important role in explaining the differences in rates of violent death. Louisiana has many more guns (e.g., a 46 percent household gun ownership rate in 2002, compared to 13 percent for Massachusetts) and weaker state gun laws (the Brady Campaign website, accessed August 2013 gives Louisiana a "2" or 4th weakest and Massachusetts a "65" or 3rd strongest). Perhaps not surprisingly, compared to Massachusetts, Louisiana has more than four times the rate of gun homicide, gun suicide, and accidental gun death. Table 3 provides similar data from the CDC broken down by race (white/black).

A public health approach to *firearm* violence would involve ensuring that firearm manufacturers help reduce the problem. For example, all guns produced should have unique serial numbers that are difficult to obliterate; pistols should allow ballistic fingerprinting to make it easier to convict criminals and link incidents involving the same gun; guns should be personalized so they are not profitable to steal; and manufacturers should exert strong oversight over their distributors to reduce the likelihood of guns getting into the wrong hands. The firearm distribution system should be improved. For example, there should be universal background checks on virtually all gun transfers, and dealers should be expected to follow best practices that limit the likelihood of straw purchasing (Hemenway and Miller, 2013). Many social norms should also be changed, particularly the ones that promote gun use as a symbol of power and masculinity. Too often when an inner-city youth feels disrespected, the norm requires that he respond violently, sometimes with a gun. A better norm would be that only "wusses" have to use guns, that hand-to-hand combat, or better still a nonviolent resolution, is a more manly response. The current inner-city norm is reminiscent of the old dueling norm among high status whites — that disrespect required a formal response with a gun. Fortunately the norm of dueling was gradually eliminated (Hemenway, 2013).

Conclusion

Public health is idealistic — it believes that health can be improved. But public health also is resourceful. It focuses on the pragmatic. There is none of the defeatist rhetoric about first having to eliminate the "root causes" of violence (e.g., poverty, racism, inequality) or wait until people become more kind, moral, and saint-like before violent injury can be substantially reduced. Instead, public health innovatively looks for low-hanging fruit — from brief alcohol interventions in the emergency department to changing high school starting times to increase sleep and reduce aggression.

Moore (1995) discusses the "determinedly empirical and experimental" nature of the public health approach. He provides two illuminating examples. (1) After an Infant Death Review Board found that several deaths occurred shortly after the mothers were sent to jail, a program was created that ensured greater continuity of care for convicted women with young children and reduced this type of death. (2) After examining assaultive injuries, a public health practitioner recommended that plastic "glasses" be substituted for traditional glassware in bars to reduce the damage occurring from drunken fights. "The ad hoc, opportunistic, preventive aspect of these efforts becomes apparent only when one looks, as many public health epidemiologists do, at the details of violence as well as at broader structural forces."

The public health approach focuses on prevention. It gathers the data, then steps back and asks, what can be done? It recognizes that many policies and programs can reduce violence—and don't involve apprehending and punishing perpetrators and that don't need to involve police or corrections. Public health asks: what can doctors do to help? What can social workers, teachers, undertakers, and hairdressers do? Indeed, how can all aspects of society—including police and corrections—work together to reduce violence? Then public health tries to ensure that these various groups are effectively mobilized, have the right tools, and are able to respond pragmatically and effectively. The can-do attitude of public health, combined with its past successes (Hemenway, 2009), brings hope and inspiration to all who seek to make the world a safer place.

Table 1

Phases	Host (victim)	Agent/Vector (assailant & weapon)	Physical Environment (structures & facilities)	Social Environment (norms, policies, & procedures)
Pre-Event (pre-assault)	Train workers to identify potentially violent customers Train managers in conflict resolution and proper dismissal strategies	Provide oversight of volatile employees Make weapons less easily concealable	Modify structure to decrease access by unauthorized persons Install metal detectors Install bullet proof shields	Reduce easy access to weapons Prohibit solo workers in high risk establishments Practice plan for responding to threats
Event (assault)	Train workers in methods of signaling for help during robberies Train employees in self-protection when confronted with violent customers	Reduce lethality of weapons (e.g., fewer firing rounds)	Install/maintain easy to operate alarms Reduce isolation of work spaces Ensure easy escape routes	Ensure security backup for threatened workers
Post-Event (post-assault)	Train workers in first aid Provide workers with counseling after the assault	Improve ability to trace firearms and apprehend suspects	Ensure access to the worksite by emergency vehicles Install cameras to help identify & apprehend assailants	Provide adequate insurance for acute and long term physical and mental health care

Source: Carol Runyan, available on-line

David Hemenway

**Table 2: Violent Deaths in Louisiana (pop 4.5 million)
and Massachusetts (pop 6.5 million) for 2010 by gun and non-gun**

	Louisiana		Massachusetts		
Death type	#	Age-adjusted rate	#	Age – adjusted rate	Mortality rate ratio: LA/MA
Firearm homicide	432	9.6	126	1.9	5.0
Non-firearm homicide	109	2.4	78	1.2	2.0
Total homicide	541	12.0	204	3.1	3.9
Firearm suicide	385	8.5	138	2.0	4.2
Non-firearm suicide	172	3.8	460	460	0.6
Total suicide	557	12.3	598	8.7	1.4
Unintentional firearm death	43	0.9	6	0.1	9.0
Total firearm death	864	19.1	270	4.0	4.5

Source: CDC WISQARS data, Accessed August 2013

**Table 3: Violent Deaths in Louisiana (pop 4.5 million; 65% white)
and Massachusetts (pop 6.5 million; 85% white) for 2010 by race**

	Louisiana		Massachusetts		
Death type	#	Age-adjusted rate	#	Age-adjusted rate	Mortality rate ratio: LA/MA
Total homicide					
White	138	4.8	117	2.2	2.2
Black	397	25.7	83	13.3	1.9
Total suicide					
White	486	16.1	556	9.4	1.7
Black	63	4.4	26	4.4	1.0
Total firearm death					
White	464	15.8	193	3.3	4.8
Black	396	26.7	75	11.9	2.2

Source: CDC WISQARS data, Accessed August 2013

References

American Academy of Pediatrics. Connected kids: safe, strong, secure. http://www2.aap.org/connectedkids/. Accessed August 2013.

Azrael, D., and D. Hemenway. (2011). "Greater than the sum of their parts: the benefits of Youth Violence Prevention Centers." *American Journal of Community Psychology* 48: 21-30.

Azrael, D., R.M. Johnson, B.E. Molnar, M. Vriniotis, E.C. Dunn, D.T. Duncan, and D. Hemenway. (2009). "Creating a youth violence data system for Boston, MA." *The Australian and New Zealand Journal of Criminology* 42: 406-21.

Barber C., D. Azrael, and D. Hemenway. (2013). "A truly national National Violent Death Reporting System." *Injury Prevention* 19: 225-26.

Boston Public Health Commission (BPHC). http://www.bphc.org/programs/cafh/violenceprevention/Pages/Home.aspx. Accessed August 2013.

Bridgewater, K., S. Peterson, J. McDevill, D. Hemenway, J. Bass, P. Bothwell, and R. Everdell. (2011). "A Community-Based Systems Learning Approach to Understanding Youth Violence in Boston." *Progress in Community Health Partnerships: Research, Education and Action* 5: 67-75.

Center to Prevent Youth Violence (CPYV) http://www.cpyv.org/programs/what-is-speak-up-2/kids-and-teens/materials/. Accessed August 2013.

CDC (Centers for Disease Control and Prevention) WISQARS. http://www.cdc.gov/injury/wisqars/fatal_injury_reports.html. Accessed August 2013.

Citizens for Safety. http://citizensforsafety.org/. Accessed August 2013.

Clarke R.V., ed. (1997). *Situational Crime Prevention: Successful Case Studies.* 2nd ed. Guilderland, NY: Harrow & Heston.

Dahlberg, L.L., and J.A. Mercy. (February 2009) "History of violence as a public health issue." *AMA Virtual Mentor* 11 (2): 167-72.

Eastman, J.W. (1981). "Doctor's orders: the American medical profession and the origins of automobile design for crash protection, 1930-1955." *Bulletin of the History of Medicine* 55: 407-24.

Fleegher, E.W., L.K. Lee, M.C. Monuteaux, D. Hemenway, R. Mannix. (2013). "Firearm legislation and firearm-related fatalities in the United States." *JAMA-Internal Medicine* 173: 732-40.

Girls LEAP. http://girlsleap.org/wordpress/wp-content/uploads/2010/11/Girls-LEAP-Overview.pdf. Accessed August 2013.

Haddon, W. (1970). "On the escape of tigers: an ecological note." *American Journal of Public Health* 60: 2229-34.

———. (1980). Options for the prevention of motor vehicle crash injury. *Israeli Medical Journal* 16: 45-65.

Harvard Injury Control Research Center, http://www.hsph.harvard.edu/hicrc/firearms-research/. Accessed August 2013.

Hemenway, D. (2013). "Three common beliefs which are impediments to injury prevention. *Injury Prevention* 19: 290-93.

———. *While We Were Sleeping: Success Stories in Injury and Violence Prevention.* Berkley, CA: University of California Press, 2009.

Hemenway, D., C.W. Barber, S.S. Gallagher, and D.R. Azrael. (2009). "Creating a National Violent Death Reporting System: a successful beginning." *American Journal of Preventive Medicine* 37: 68-71.

Hemenway, D., and M. Miller. (2013). "Public health approach to the prevention of gun violence." *New England Journal of Medicine* 368: 2033-35.

Hemenway, D., D. Prothrow-Stith, J.M. Bergstein, R. Ander, and B.P. Kennedy. (1996). "Gun carrying among adolescents." *Law and Contemporary Problems* 59: 39-54.

Hemenway, D., M. Vriniotis, R.M. Johnson, M. Miller, D. Azrael. (2011). "Gun carrying by high school students in Boston MA: does overestimation of peer gun carrying matter?" *Journal of Adolescence* 34: 997-1003.

Karolyn, I.A. (1998). "Investing in our children; what we know and don't know about the costs and benefits of early childhood interventions." Rand Corporation.

Kellermann, A.L, F.P. Rivara, N.B. Rushforth et al. (1993). "Gun ownership as a risk factor for homicide in the home." *New England Journal of Medicine.* 329: 1084-91.

Kennedy, D. (2012). *Don't Shoot.* New York: Bloomsbury USA.

Logan, J., H.A. Hill, M.L. Black, A.E. Crosby, D.L. Karch, J.D. Barnes, and K.M. Lubell. (2008). "Characteristics of perpetrators in homicide-followed-by-suicide incidents: National Violent Death Reporting System 2003-2005." *American Journal of Epidemiology* 168: 1056-64.

Louis D. Brown Peace Institute. http://www.ldbpeaceinstitute.org/. Accessed August 2013.

Miller, M., D. Azrael, C. Barber. (2012). "Suicide mortality in the United States: The importance of attending to method in understanding population-level disparities in the burden of suicide." *Annual Review of Public Health* 33: 393-408.

Miller, M., D. Azrael, and D. Hemenway. (2012). "State-level homicide victimization rates in the U.S. in relation to survey measures of household firearm ownership, 2001-2003." *Social Science and Medicine* 64: 656-64.

Moore, M.H. (1995). "Public health and criminal justice approaches to prevention." *Crime and Justice* 19: 237-62.

———. (1993). "Violence prevention: criminal justice or public health?" *Health Affairs* 12: 34-45.

Prothrow-Stith, D.(1993). *Deadly Consequences.* New York: Harper.

Prothrow-Stith, D., and H.R. Spivak. (2003). *Murder is No Accident.* Jossey-Bass.

Pruitt, B.H. The Boston strategy: a story of unlikely alliances. The Robert Wood Johnson Foundation. Boston Strategy website. http://sasnet.com/bostonstrategy/downloads/BS_StoryPruitt.pdf. 2001. Accessed August 2013.

Roth, J.A., and M.H. Moore. (1995, October). "Reducing violent crimes and intentional injuries." NIJ Research in Action.

Runyan, C. Introduction to injury prevention. http://www.npaihb.org/images/epicenter_docs/injuryprevention/CompletedHaddonMatrixWorkplaceViolence.pdf. Accessed August 2013.

Salons against domestic abuse. http://www.cutitout.org/. Accessed August 2013.

Solnick, S.J., and D. Hemenway. (2012). "The twinkie defense: the relationship between carbonated non-diet soft drinks and violence perpetration among Boston high school students." *Injury Prevention* 18: 259-63.

Slutkin, G. (2013). "Violence is a contagious disease." Institute of Medicine. Contagion of Violence, workshop summary. Washington D.C.: National Academies Press.

Webster, D.W., J.M. Whitehill, J.S. Vernick, and F.C. Curriero. (2013). "Effect of Baltimore's Safe Streets program on gun violence: a replication of Chicago's CeaseFire Program." *Journal of Urban Health* 90: 27-40.

Weiss, B.P. (1997). "A public health approach to violence prevention: The Los Angeles Coalition." In R.L. Hampton, P. Jenkins, T.P. Gullotta. *Preventing Violence in America*. Thousand Oaks, CA: Sage.

5 | Criminal Homicide and Firearms in New Orleans

Sean Goodison

In a 2010 survey conducted by the Kaiser Foundation, residents of New Orleans reported that crime was the most serious problem facing their city. Crime ranked higher than the economy, housing, education, or health care. The media have focused on New Orleans and its police department in recent years regarding how crime is addressed in the city. Such attention, however, can over generalize. It may be implied that if New Orleans has a "crime problem," then all crime is high. "Dangerous" is a powerful label and potential master status for a city. Violent crime, property crime, Part I offenses, Part II offenses, aggregated, disaggregated crime must all be equally as bad. Everyone is at equal risk of being victimized for anything. It is a slippery slope because people become afraid. But as Frank Herbert once wrote, "fear is the mind-killer." Sometimes fear blinds our vision. As result, we may be unable to prioritize when faced with a potential tangle of pathologies.

For this reason, it is best to start with a general examination of New Orleans's crime in context using the FBI's Uniform Crime Reports. These data allow for a general comparison of New Orleans with the nation, similar-sized cities, and cities with similar characteristics. Of course, there are known pitfalls and limitations of comparative analysis using UCR data, as noted in the warnings and caveats at the beginning of the FBI's *Crime in the United States*. However, the purpose here is illustrative rather than explanatory. Orlando was picked as a city of similar size, in the South, and with a heavy base in tourism. Beyond the FBI caveats, certainly no city is a fully apt comparison to New Orleans, especially post-Katrina. Therefore, with any conclusions here sufficiently nuanced, we can examine the general state of crime in New Orleans.

Crime in New Orleans

For Total Crime rate, New Orleans is within an expected range, as seen in chart 1. Urban areas will typically have higher crime than seen nationally, and New Orleans finds itself consistent with similar-sized cities while Orlando is slightly higher in this regard. The same pattern holds for property crime and for violent crime. Based on this, one may conclude that New Orleans is unremarkable regarding crime. However, the FBI does warn us to not draw substantive conclusions based on these data, and one reason is that aggregate figures may mask smaller trends within different areas.

Still, one can expect that this ranking pattern would hold while looking at specific crime types. In fact, it does for almost all Part I Property and Violent crimes (see charts 2 and 3). Homicide stands apart though, and here we see what may be classified as the primary crime problem in New Orleans. Chart 4 shows how in 2009, the homicide rate far outpaced any of these comparisons. Over time, this is not necessarily an outlier year for New Orleans, as seen in charts 5 and 6. Obviously in the post-Katrina period there is substantial difficulty in determining a proper denominator for rate calculations. Yet, going back to 1985, the lowest estimated homicide rate in New Orleans was just under 30 per 100,000. Looking briefly at the counts, we see the same general trend as seen in the rate calculation, though with more stability in recent years. The lowest homicide count in the past few decades was the year of Katrina, and that was the only year it dipped below 150.

The people of New Orleans are certainly right to identify crime as a serious problem, but the primary problem seems to be that which clearly sets New Orleans apart—homicide.

Homicide in New Orleans, 2009-2010

This is the context in which Charles Wellford, Brenda Bond, and I analyzed homicide data and responses to crime during the second half of 2010 (Wellford, Bond, and Goodison, 2011). Before describing this research, I want to thank the New Orleans Police Department and their Homicide unit. They welcomed us warmly, were incredibly helpful, and went the extra mile a number of times in order to assist our project.

The purpose of our analysis was to get a snapshot of homicide at the time in New Orleans. The benefit of a snapshot is that you can see the overall picture but then also focus on the details in the background. I have already reviewed some of that overall picture. Homicide is a clear problem in New Orleans, as it sets the city far apart from a variety of comparisons. But some obvious "details in the background" questions remain. Foremost, is the nature of homicide in New Orleans also drastically different than what has been seen elsewhere?

To examine this question and others, our work addressed a number of topics. We collected qualitative and quantitative data on both crime trends and police responses, specifically in regards to homicide. However, this work will focus on the portion of research that examined the patterns of criminal homicide in New Orleans from 2009 through 2010. We collected detailed information from two hundred consecutive cases reported from April 2009 through May 2010. The data were examined in September and October of 2010, allowing sufficient time for any cases in our sample to have been actively investigated. We felt that studying two hundred consecutive cases would present a comprehensive sample of the nature of homicide in New Orleans at the time. While we started with a basic listing of the cases including general victim, offender, and incident data, we expanded the collection by individually reviewing each case jacket. These jackets had numerous reports such as evidence catalogues, interviews, and detailed narratives, along with criminal history information for both victims and known offenders. Often, relevant information was found in both paper copies and through the electronic records management system, so we were given access to both for the project. In addition to the static records, some of the data collection relied on discussion with the homicide detectives. These interactions were invaluable to the process and helped fill out our data collection.

Some of what we discovered is not surprising to those who study homicide. There was a considerable overlap between victim and known offender traits. We examined all two hundred victims and the 102 known first offenders. There are three important points regarding our offender counts. First, we only used closed cases. We did not include information based on potential suspects, partially because of the uncertainty and partially because critical information was often missing in cases with a general suspect. Second, we tended only to look at the first offender in cases where there were multiple offenders. Over 80 percent of cases had a single offender, and detailed data often was not available for secondary offenders. Third, we kept the incident as the unit of analysis with offenders and therefore did not remove duplicates among the thirteen individuals responsible for multiple homicides. We were interested in offender characteristics within the context of the incident — for example, if a seventy-eight-year-old was responsible for a triple homicide, then we felt it was most accurate from an incident-based perspective to present three murders by that individual rather than to treat all offenders uniformly (i.e., a triple murderer is given the same weight in the analysis as an offender who killed only one person).

As seen in table 1, the vast majority of those involved in homicide in our sample are male and black. Both victims and offenders tend to be in their twenties with known offenders on average slightly younger. This is unsurprising given the well-documented male, intraracial nature of homicide and research suggesting that more serious violent crime involves a shifted age-crime curve with a peak in the early twenties rather than mid to late teens.

We captured data on known employment based on the documented police investigation. We had three categories: employed, unemployed, and unknown. To be classified as either employed or unemployed, there had to be declarative statements in the investigation towards that end. Employment was often demonstrated by interviews of those described as co-workers. If there was no reference to employment status, the individual was flagged as unknown. As a result, these unemployment figures represent a conservative estimate as an undetermined percentage of unknowns are actually unemployed.

Vast majorities had a prior criminal record, according to our data.[1] Of those with a criminal record, majorities had a violent crime in their history. Violence was defined as Part I violent offenses and other assaults. Interestingly, about 40 percent of each sample had a prior gun-related charge on their record. This could range from crimes involving a gun, for example a robbery with a gun, to illegal possession. I will discuss this finding more when discussing gun

---

1. For criminal record, we captured police "contacts" rather than "arrests." For more detail on this differentiation, please refer to Wellford, Bond, and Goodison (2011).

homicide in New Orleans in greater detail. One final note about the criminal history data: the violent and firearms categories are not mutually exclusive and were coded as independent binary variables. For example, a victim with an armed robbery would be classified as having both a violent and a firearm prior. An additional caveat is that since we only collected homicide data, we do not currently have data of other crime victims or offenders as a comparison.

Most commonly, these homicides involved an escalating argument of some sort. We collected multiple factors regarding motive in order to grasp some of the complexities. From this, the most common clear themes were altercations, or an argument escalating in the moment, and retaliation, or an argument escalating over time. Drug-related motives were the next most common, but we only found this clearly established in about 27 percent of cases; in most of those cases, the drug motive did not seem to be the primary motivation but rather a secondary issue. Through our reading of case jackets, though, we found less definitive documentation of drug-related motives. Additionally, we were less likely to assign a single, clear motive in cases that were not yet closed. We recognize that this methodology will produce more conservative estimates, but we felt this process was best for our goal of a precise analysis of the trends.

Table 2 shows further descriptive characteristics of these homicides. The modal victim-offender relationship (among the closed cases) was acquaintance with over 40 percent of cases. For our purposes, acquaintances are those who recognize each other but who do not seem to travel in similar small groups. One may see an acquaintance at a large party or in the neighborhood, but an acquaintance would never be individually invited to a small gathering. In contrast, less than 10 percent of the known relationships were classified as a type of friend and nearly 14 percent percent were strangers.

The setting for the typical homicide was outdoors and in a residential area. Over 74 percent of cases took place outside, with about 59 percent in or around a residential building, most commonly a single-family home. While these findings may not be particularly shocking, they have a distinct significance. Homicides in this setting most likely have witnesses. These killings are not taking place in isolated areas, even taking into account that many residential areas were plagued by blight as a result of Katrina. The potential for witnesses exists, though of course the cooperation of said witnesses with law enforcement is a more open question. Many studies have examined community attitudes towards helping police and how factors such as a lack of trust, lack of incentive, or even a neighborhood code discouraging cooperation play a role in limiting witnesses. In a separate analysis of this data examining factors impacting clearance outcomes, cooperating witnesses at the onset of a case was the strongest positive and significant predictor of closure while controlling for numerous extralegal and case characteristics.

We also saw evidence that New Orleans had a decentralized gang and drug structure. We saw this both through our direct experience reviewing case jackets and from interviews with investigators. In other words, we found suggestive evidence that the street-level criminal organizations that would be involved in homicide tend to not be hierarchical in nature. This was manifest within the homicide motives. Gang and drug-related motivations were generally seen as secondary motives, when seen at all. Only 8 percent of the cases we examined had either gangs or drugs as the clear primary motive. More commonly, the dispute was interpersonal in which gang activity or drugs was not a necessary or sufficient condition for the homicide.

During our study, gangs in New Orleans seemed to generally be small, fluid, and highly linked to a small geographic place. Similar small, transitory, unstructured gangs are referenced throughout criminological research, whether it was by Thrasher and Whyte in the distant past or Klein and Decker during more contemporary times (see Decker and Van Winkle, 1996; Klein, 1995; Thrasher, 1963 [1927]; Whyte, 1943). Such structure is seen even today in modern cities, such as Washington, D.C., in which local crews lead to neighborhood conflicts. In our sample, these were not the Bloods and the Crips. There seemed to be no formal leaders or national organization. These are often kids who grew up on the same block who engage in a popular group-level activity called delinquency.

The same considerations apply for issues involving drug territory. Homicides regarding drugs were generally smaller scale and not pitting large organized processes against each other. There did not seem to be constant rivalries to defend drug turf or seemingly endless waves of armed drug dealers and armed robbers pushing up the homicide rate, as was seen in the late 1980s. I'll speak more to the issue of being armed momentarily, but for now the key take-away is the apparent small scale nature of the gangs and drug markets.

Of course, small scale does not mean it is less of a problem for New Orleans. Decentralized organizations provide their own challenges if law enforcement is going to attempt to address violence, and many tactics that were successful against organized groups may be less successful against the lesser-organized (Klein, 1996; McGloin, 2007). As it stands based on our data, though, gang and drug factors are not the driving forces behind homicide during this time. That in and of itself can be either a good or a bad thing for New Orleans, which I discuss later as potential policy recommendations.

Guns and New Orleans

These findings so far do not suggest a significant differentiation in the nature of homicide in New Orleans. However, this changes somewhat when one examines method. Nearly 90 percent of all homicides we reviewed were committed by firearms. To put that in perspective, according to the FBI's Uniform Crime Reports only 67 percent of homicides nationally were by gun in 2009-2010. This increases slightly within urban areas, generally in the low 70s depending on the population. Larger cities with reported gun violence can be higher still, such as Washington, D.C., which had 75 percent of its homicides committed with guns during this time period and Chicago with about 80 percent in 2010. Then, there is New Orleans at 90 percent. The issue goes even deeper than that, though. If you break down the firearm category, you would see that 78 percent of all homicides are by handguns alone. Again, in context, this means that the percentage of murders by *handgun* in New Orleans was larger than the percentage of murders by *all types* of firearms in Washington, D.C., over the same time. Additionally, 8 percent of all homicides were by rifle. Nationally, this figure generally peaks at about 3 percent.

Coupled with these data, approximately 40 percent of both victims and known offenders with a prior arrest have at least one firearms-related prior. Think of it this way: when looking at the whole sample, almost 30 percent of all victims and over one-third of all known offenders come to a homicide incident having enough familiarity with guns that they had been involved in a gun-related police contact. These contacts are a conservative measure here, since people are unlikely to be detected each time they have a weapon. While not a perfect measure, this can serve as a rough proxy as to how common these firearms are among homicide participants.

It is clear that guns are an issue in these homicides. So what types of specific challenges do guns introduce when attempting to address lethal violence? The following listing is by no means exhaustive, however it should highlight some of the major issues facing New Orleans and the gun homicide problem. I will discuss gun-related challenges in general first, and then apply a more New Orleans-specific lens to the problems.

Firearms carry a great deal of history and precedent in this country. Guns and gun rights were central to the formation of the American Republic. Following the armed rebellion against the British Crown, firearms rights were codified through the Second Amendment. These rights have been central to recent debates regarding federal power, as seen in *DC v. Heller* (2008) where the Supreme Court affirmed that the right to bear arms does apply to the individual. Of course, this right is not unlimited and can be regulated. Still, this context of guns and the law provides a significant backstop to the role of government in regulating or confiscating firearms.

Additionally, guns can enter the market in many illegal ways, including thefts or straw purchases, and ultimately serve those who may already have a propensity to not follow the law. It is reasonable to assume that individuals who can legally purchase firearms are less likely to seek out an underground market and accept the level of risk involved when compared to those unable to procure a legal weapon due to prior criminal history.

Next, gun homicides are often tied to gang or drug activity (see Blumstein and Rosenfeld, 1998; Klein, 1996). By this, I specifically mean that a large portion of gang or drug-related violence uses firearms, typically easy to conceal handguns, rather than the large amount of gun violence is itself gang or drug-related. Studies examining the great homicide decline following the collapse of crack markets have shown the potential for variability in gun homicides. Fagan and colleagues (1997) found that the non-gun homicide rate was stable throughout the large spike and decline in homicides through the 1990s. It was the gun-related, and particularly the drug-related killings, that showed great variability. In an examination of the recent sharp decline in homicide within Washington, D.C., since 2006, a similar phenomenon occurred where non-gun homicides were stable over time but firearm fatalities coupled with drug and some gang rates dropped (Goodison, forthcoming). The purpose here is not to determine whether guns or motive is the spurious relationship, but rather to show how conflated the two issues typically are in data. Fighting gun homicide typically will involve fighting drug and gang homicide at the same time.

Finally, there is the lethality component. Firearms themselves are efficient tools for injuring, especially with the widespread use of rifling over the past two centuries. Depending on the range and caliber, considerable damage can be done with a single gunshot. At the same time, given the same variables people may survive multiple gunshots relatively easily. Certainly, the ability and accessibility of techniques to treat wounds and subsequent infection (which from a health perspective can often be worse than the initial wound) have improved dramatically over the long term. This facet is only the most manifest public health element to homicide, though others pose a more general challenge for homicides, such as increased stress, strain, and mental health problems that contribute to violence.

So, what does this all mean for gun homicide in New Orleans? In addition to the national history and precedent, guns are no strangers to New Orleans. Firearms, including cannon, saved the city from foreign invasion during the Battle of New Orleans in 1815. Guns were seen as considerably less helpful over time, and this culminated in New Orleans being the first U.S. municipality to sue gun manufacturers in 1998. This was an attempt to use litigation rather than legislation in handling a public problem, as was done with success against tobacco companies in the years prior. In *Morial v. Smith & Wesson Corp.* (1998), the city argued that it was entitled to compensation for the cost of gun violence since handguns were "unreasonably dangerous." In response the following year, the state legislature in Louisiana passed a bill "abolishing the City's right of action and reserving the authority to bring these suits to the state." The Supreme Court of Louisiana found this action by the legislature to be legal in 2001, thus ending New Orleans's participation in such lawsuits. What this means is that the toolbox of new tactics may be somewhat more limited than other areas and enforcement would then focus on the laws already in place. Multiple legal remedies have been attempted, where now much of the emphasis could be placed in reactive enforcement of the current laws.

As previously noted, gangs and drugs are often related to high firearms usage in homicide. Yet, New Orleans has a particular conundrum in that gun homicides are a very large percentage while clear gang and drug motives may be rather low. Other areas of the nation have seen guns and gangs/drugs drop together. What this means for New Orleans is that the tactics and approaches to specifically fight gangs and drugs may not be as effective here in producing a drop in gun homicides. It is a double-edged sword — while it is positive that the city is not awash in highly-organized gang or drug homicides, the drawback is that many tools used elsewhere may not be as applicable while the overall gun usage remains staggeringly high. In research, the gun homicides were the variability in long-term trends, resulting in many lows in homicide rates and counts in recent years. New Orleans has not seen a continued drop since the fall of crack markets. While there was a post-crack decrease, the homicide rate started to grow again in the late 1990s (see charts 5 and 6). The homicides and guns remain high, without the widespread gang or drug-related explanations. It is possible that cracking down on drugs and gangs would not change the gun-related homicide rate considerably.

Lastly, the lethality challenge presented by gun homicides is acute in New Orleans. While the importance of medical care and treatment remains significant, the fact is that for these homicides 74 percent of the victims are dead at the scene, according to our data. Though we did not have specific response time information, it seemed that most victims were found within five minutes of the incident. The nature of these shootings renders much of the post-shooting treatment and life-saving options moot. Of course, a fuller analysis of this question would likely include various gun assaults as well in order to develop a true gun lethality rate. Still, this challenge highlights the other public health issues beyond mere treatment in dealing with gun homicides. The degree of arguments being settled at the barrel of a gun certainly suggests larger public health pathologies at work, independent of the precise weapon used.

What can be done to address gun violence and homicide? This work focuses on the potential role of law enforcement. Obviously, this is not to diminish or ignore other solutions. Other researchers involved in this symposium discussed social and cultural structural factors, and obviously, these factors play an important role in long-term solutions and prevention. Root causes of crime are critical to address. Yet, crime can be reduced without targeting root causes. In 1933, August Vollmer, a founding figure in policing research and a New Orleans native, noted the potential of police to impact crime without expanding their scope into the roots of crime. He argued that law enforcement cannot fight poverty, but could address crime in a way that could clear the field for other agencies to have an opportunity in addressing the root causes. This philosophy has found considerable support in recent policing research, most importantly in the hot spots perspective where crime is impacted through tailored deterrence strategies within a small geographic area (see Braga, 2005; Braga and Weisburd, 2010; Weisburd and Eck, 2004). Directed, targeted deterrence can contribute to crime prevention without needing to solve larger social problems first. In other words, treating the symptoms directly may yield greater immediate results rather than simply waiting for long-term changes to follow through. Even shallow problem-solving by police, which involves a less coordinated analysis of data and a range of actions by law enforcement, has demonstrated significant reductions in crime (Braga and Weisburd, 2006). But towards the usefulness of addressing the roots, some studies suggest the greatest decreases in crime are in hot spots treated by police that have subsequent follow-up by other non-enforcement agencies (see Braga, Papachristos, and Hureau, 2012, for a general review).

While we justifiably seek to build-up communities and reduce violence as long-term projects, whether it be through collective efficacy, public health, legitimacy, or cultural factors, there are also some law enforcement actions that could be implemented and see results in the short-term. A number of specific tactics have received empirical support from well-planned studies suggesting significant reductions in gun violence. The first tactic is directed police patrol in gun hot spots (see Koper and Mayo-Wilson, 2006 for a review). It is important to focus on guns in the highest risk areas. These hot spots must be small or "micro-places" as they are sometimes called. Research suggests the focus should be in units of blocks. Using larger areas can dilute the police presence and introduce heterogeneity as a tailored solution for one small area may not be the same solution for a nearby region. As Anthony Braga noted (2012), the majority of violence tends to occur on a very small percentage of blocks within a city. A study of gun violence in Boston suggested that as few as 5 percent of intersections or blocks citywide can account for nearly 75 percent of all shootings.

Some research suggested that gun violence can be significantly reduced through traffic enforcement tactics (McGarrell, Chermak, Weiss, and Wilson, 2001; Sherman and Rogan, 1995). Vehicular stops within gun hot spots can have an incapacitation effect, through the recovery of firearms and associated arrests, as well as a deterrent impact on gun violence.

In order to best identify these hot spots and evaluate the tactics, there must be a robust crime analysis unit able to geographically analyze crime patterns using multiple methodologies. These analysts should work as investigative support, bringing specialized knowledge and a focus on larger trends to assist with decision making. It is critical for these hot spots to be evidence-based with objective techniques in order to help justify decisions, efficiently allocate resources, and assess the crime control results.

Pulling levers is a slightly different perspective, in that the tactic focuses on high risk individuals rather than high risk places. This technique is best known through the Boston's Operation Ceasefire (see Braga, 2008; Braga, Kennedy, Waring, and Piehl, 2001). Pulling levers involves specialized, targeted delivery of multiple criminal justice organizations. Like hot spots policing, this is a deterrence-based approach that is actually made possible because of other failures in the criminal justice system. For example, deterrence may be reduced among criminals who have experience avoiding conviction or never had follow-up done on outstanding warrants. Pulling levers aims to correct that among a high-risk pool of prior offenders. Such offenders are made aware that all parts of the criminal justice system will be on alert to maximize punishment for further gun crimes. In addition to the specific deterrent among the individuals warned, there is a general deterrence when said individuals are part of organized structures or central to networks of others.

This policing research suggests that many of the best solutions are tailored and of limited focus, whether it be on high-risk places or people. Large one-rule-fits-all approaches seem to be less successful in reducing gun crime. A common example of a large-scale approach is gun regulation, often in the context that the main path to safety from guns is to have government highly regulate and/or ban firearms. I have noted from a legal perspective that *Heller* establishes a backstop to regulation by making the Second Amendment apply to individuals. The Court ruled that the prospect of gun violence does not trump a Constitutional protection, though the protection is far from absolute. Yet, gun-related research suggests that regulation may not be an effective policy anyway for police, as it is a non-tailored, non-focused approach to crime. Looking at the results of the *Heller* decision in Washington, D.C., may be illustrative of that point. Numerous *amicus* briefs predicted that gun crime and homicide would drastically increase without the 1976 handgun ban in place. While no comprehensive study has yet been conducted in D.C., and knowing well that correlation is not causation, the fact remains that subsequent years saw reductions in gun-related crime. If nothing else, this suggests that a large-scale policy may not be the most important predictor of gun violence. Towards that point, the general themes seen in the literature would certainly tend to agree.

Can these recommendations work in New Orleans? I believe they can, though the solutions have to be tailored to the specific challenges. Nothing I have encountered in this city suggests its people shrink in the face of adversity, no matter how daunting the challenge. The problems with violence and guns are quite significant but solutions are possible. Of course, the most lasting changes will require long-term shifts within the community, whether it be in terms of social control, culture, legitimacy, or health services. My recommendations are more immediate and can help between the present and a better future. The disease of violence in New Orleans can be treated but first we have to stop the bleeding, both literally and figuratively. Undoubtedly, this triage can be done now and I believe law enforcement can have a significant role. In fact, some of the ideas I discussed have been implemented to various degrees. Project Safe Neighborhoods began work in New Orleans in 2010. In January of this year, Mayor Landrieu and the NOPD launched a program called "SOS: Saving Our Sons" that focuses on hot spots, pulling levers, and law enforcement professionalism. Recent plans have started involving David Kennedy, one of the key researchers in the development and evaluation of the pulling levers approach in Operation Ceasefire. Such plans suggest a commitment to evidence-based policing that can have a positive impact in the community. There are a few helpful concepts that may allow these plans to work better and more efficiently in The Crescent City.

Recommendations

First, hot spot determination requires significant resources within crime analysis units. These resources are both physical and personal. Proper GIS software and support are mandatory. Options exist that are either for purchase as well as can be downloaded for free. Computers with sufficient processing power provide the most efficient results, since GIS software is graphics-heavy and can use far more memory than other standard computer applications like word processors or Internet browsers. Another physical requirement often forgotten is data. As the old saying goes, "garbage in, garbage out." A department can have the most sophisticated software, computers, and analysts, but if the data is not clean or has serious validity and/or reliability issues, then any potential benefit of the crime analysis is lost. This does not necessarily mean "more" data though. A limited scope of good, clean, actionable data is always going to beat endless tables of which nothing can be trusted. While no data will ever be perfect, steps are still necessary to ensure a high degree of data quality at all stages from entry to analysis. From the personnel side, analysts must be well-trained to use research and scientific principles to the study of crime and its distribution. The obvious point is that the skills and background knowledge are necessary. Proper identification of a hot spot cannot always be done through a single geographic method just as researchers understand that not every question can be answered with a linear regression model, even if these single method approaches can have a remarkable elasticity. The point remains that analysts need to fully understand their methodologies, how to maximize them, how to correct for problems, and how to go outside of the box for additional techniques when necessary. The less obvious point is that analysts can help police be more effective if these analysts are integrated into the larger investigative picture. I believe this provides analysts with key qualitative information, and such data allows for a clearer vision of purpose and more useful questions to address in their research. Having a number-crunching table-maker without any contextual knowledge of what dynamics are going on within neighborhoods may, not surprisingly, produce a volume of descriptive work with little practical use.

In regards to traffic enforcement and gun violence, there are multiple general protocols available in research that could serve as basic templates. Work has been done in numerous cities such as Indianapolis and Kansas City directly addressing the prevention of gun crime (McGarrell et. al., 2001; Sherman and Rogan, 1995), and there are national efforts such as the DDACTS program (Data-Driven Approaches to Crime and Traffic Safety), which seeks to develop "how to" manuals for law enforcement to impact overall crime through traffic enforcement. There are no inherent reasons why such programs could not be used in New Orleans, and re-search has suggested that shifting resources to such tactics within gun hot spots could be a worthwhile enterprise to reduce gun violence. However, a general caution about these programs is that they have not been subject to a large degree of evaluation. Even those that have been evaluated show there may be difficulties in obtaining the optimal results, and the reasons for this lead to my next point in addressing whether these ideas can work in New Orleans.

Any program needs to have implementation fidelity and monitored dosage of treatment. In order words, clear communication of a program's goals and tactics is necessary but not sufficient. If people involved in planning are not supervised and held accountable, there will be a great deal of variation in how a plan is carried out. In structured programs, unplanned variation can be bad. Even worse, though, is not knowing if you have unplanned variation. Reliable monitoring is critical to ensure a program is being rolled out as intended. It is also essential for the eventual evaluation of the plan by helping account for alternate explanations of either success or failure. This is the only way to have confidence in results and an understanding of what works and what does not.

The criminological body of knowledge shows that solutions with evidence of "working" to reduce crime independent of other factors need to be tailored to the specific problems of a community. The principle crime problem in New Orleans is homicide, as that rate clearly stands apart from other areas of the country. Within this problem, a critical issue is that handguns and rifled-weapons each make up a staggering percentage of homicide methods when compared to other regions. Guns present a number of challenges for both law enforcement and the community, and many of these challenges are enhanced in New Orleans. Still, research shows that programs exist that can work to reduce gun violence, and there is no fundamental reason why New Orleans cannot learn from these. In fact, some of these programs have been implemented to a degree already. However, it is critical that these programs and policies be implemented and properly evaluated.

At the end of the day, the answers as to whether these ideas can work in New Orleans resides within the city itself, both in the leadership and in the community. The problem of gun violence requires a buy-in from all parties involved. Tailoring solutions to the community and working with the city's residents who remain fearful is how any program must start. Government cannot, and should not, do this alone. President Obama was in New Orleans earlier this year (2012) and noted that, "government alone can't fill" the missing elements within those who engage in gun violence. Yet, government, specifically law enforcement, can find ways to address problems in the short-term, determine potential solutions, and evaluate results so future programs can build on experiences constructively and systematically. It may not be easy and it will require considerable determination to ensure the gun violence is handled systematically and with accountability, but ultimately New Orleans has shown this determination in the face of tragedy before and deserves no less determination from those seeking to help this great American city.

Chart 1: Total Crime Rates, 2009

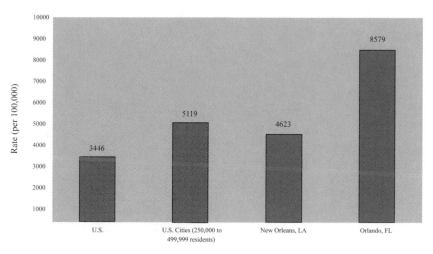

Source: Crime in the United States (Uniform Crime Report), 2009

Chart 2: Violent Crime Rates, 2009

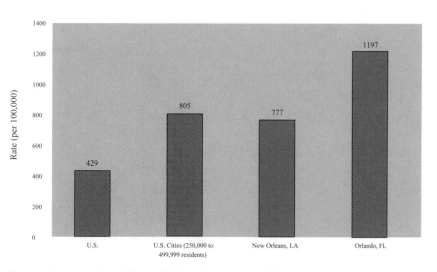

Source: Crime in the United States (Uniform Crime Report), 2009

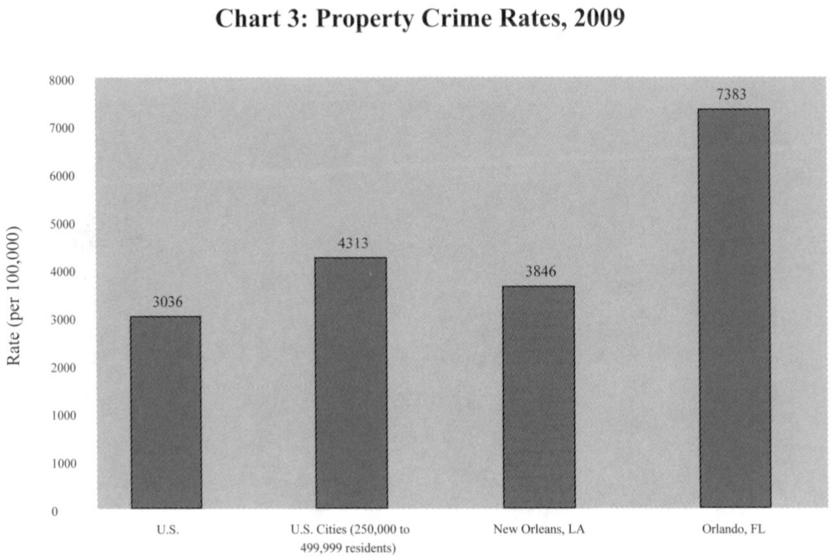

Chart 3: Property Crime Rates, 2009

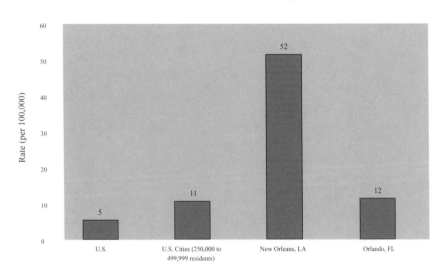

Source: Crime in the United States (Uniform Crime Report), 2009

Chart 2: Violent Crime Rates, 2009

Source: Crime in the United States (Uniform Crime Report), 2009

Chart 5: Homicide Rate, New Orleans 1985-2009

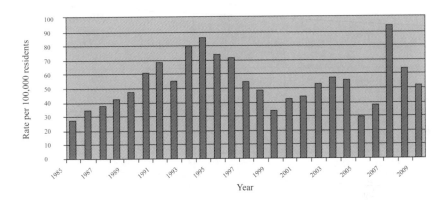

Chart 6: Homicide Counts, New Orleans 1985-2010

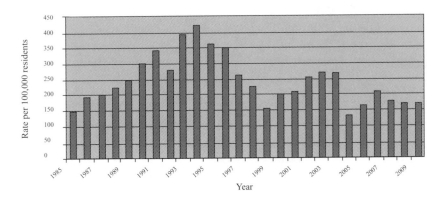

Table 1: Victim and Offender Profiles

Trait	Victims (N=200)	Known Offenders (N=102)
Male	87%	95%
Black	92%	97%
Median Age (Yrs.)	27	23
Unemployed	46%	56%
Criminal History (CH)?	73%	83%
Of those with CH...		
Violent Prior	58%	59%
Firearms Prior	40%	41%

Table 2: Homicide Characteristics

Characteristic	Incidents (N=200)
Victim-Offender Relationship	
Acquaintance	40%
Stranger	14%
Friend (includes Boyfriend/ Girlfriend)	10%
Outdoors	74%
General Residential Area	59%
Primary Motive	
Drug- or Gang-related	8%

References

Blumstein, A. and R. Rosenfeld. (1998). "Explaining recent trends in U.S. homicide rates." *Journal of Criminal Law and Criminology* 88: 1175-1216

Braga, A.A. (2005). "Hot spots policing and crime prevention: A systematic review of randomized controlled trials." *Journal of Experimental Criminology* 1: 317-42.

————. (2008). "Pulling levers focused deterrence strategies and the prevention of gun homicide." *Journal of Criminal Justice* 36: 332-43.

————. (2012, February). Understanding the Nature of Urban Gun Violence Problems. Congressional Briefing on Reducing Gun Violence. U.S. House of Representatives. Washington, D.C.

Braga, A.A., and D. Weisburd. (2006). "Problem-oriented policing: The disconnect between principles and practice." In D. Weisburd and A.A. Braga (Eds.), *Police innovation* (pp. 133-54). New York: Cambridge University Press.

Braga, A.A., and D. Weisburd. (2010). *Policing problem places: Crime hot spots and effective prevention.* New York: Oxford University Press.

Braga, A.A., A.V. Papachristos, and D.M. Hureau. (2012). *Hot spots policing effects on crime.* Campbell Systematic Reviews 2012: 8.

Braga, A.A., D.M. Kennedy, E.J. Waring, and A.M. Piehl. (2001). "Problem-oriented policing, deterrence, and youth violence: An evaluation of Boston's Operation Ceasefire." *Journal of Research in Crime and Delinquency* 38: 195-225.

Decker, S.H., and B. Van Winkle. (1996). *Life in the gang.* New York: Cambridge University Press.

Fagan, J., F.E. Zimring, and J. Kim. (1997). "Declining homicide in New York City: A tale of two trends." *Journal of Criminal Law & Criminology,* 88 (4): 1277-1324.

Goodison, S.E. (forthcoming). Homicide Trends in Washington, D.C.: 2006-2011. Washington, D.C.

Klein, M.W. (1995). *The American street gang.* New York: Oxford University Press.

Koper, C.S., and E. Mayo-Wilson. (2006). "Police crackdowns on illegal gun carrying: a systematic review of their impact on gun crime." *Journal of Experimental Criminology* 2: 227-61.

McGarrell, E.F., S. Chermak, A. Weiss, J. Wilson. (2001). "Reducing firearms violence through directed police patrol." *Criminology and Public Policy* 1: 119-48.

McGloin, J.M. (2007). "The organizational structure of street gangs in Newark, New Jersey: A network analysis methodology." *Journal of Gang Research* 15 (1): 1-34.

Sherman, L. W. and, D.P. Rogan. (1995). "Effects of gun seizures on gun violence: 'Hot spots' patrol in Kansas City." *Justice Quarterly* 12, 673-94.

Thrasher, F.M. (1963 [1927]). *The gang: a study of 1,313 gangs in Chicago.* Chicago: University of Chicago.

Vollmer, A. (1933). "Police progress in the past twenty-five years." *Journal of Criminal Law and Criminology* 24 (1): 161-75.

Wellford, C., B.J. Bond, and S. Goodison. (2011). Crime in New Orleans: Analyzing crime trends and New Orleans' responses to crime. BJA: Washington, D.C.

Weisburd, D., and J.E. Eck. (2004). "What can the police do to reduce crime, disorder, and fear?" *The Annals of the American Academy of Political and Social Science* 593: 42-65.

Whyte, W.F. (1943). *Street corner society.* Chicago, IL: University of Chicago.

6 | Intimate Partner Homicide in New Orleans

Rae Taylor

While New Orleans is widely considered one of the most violent cities in the United States, annually ranking among the highest in lethal and non-lethal violence rates, the city has not been the focus of a great deal of violence research, relative to cities such as Chicago and New York. Intimate partner homicide (IPH) research focusing specifically on New Orleans is virtually non-existent in the scholarly literature. The key objective of this chapter is to provide commentary on the nature of violence in New Orleans generally, structural and organization responses to intimate partner violence, and challenges within the field of domestic violence in the New Orleans area. Using data provided by the New Orleans Police Department (NOPD), descriptive analyses of IP homicides in the city from 2007-2012 provide initial insights into the nature and scope of intimate partner homicide in New Orleans. This is followed by some thoughts regarding the rather low rate of IPH in the context of a fairly high rate of arrests for domestic violence.

National IPH Context

Intimate partner violence perpetrated against women has been deemed an important human rights issue and a major public health and criminal justice issue on a global level (Heise and Garcia-Moreno, 2002; Tjaden and Theonnes, 2000). A recent national-based study in the U.S. revealed that nearly 60 percent of the women in the sample had experienced physical, sexual, or stalking violence in their adulthood (at least eighteen years of age), usually by a current or former intimate partner (Moracco, Runyan, Bowling, and Earp, 2007). Findings from the National Violence Against Women Survey revealed that 64 percent of women compared to 16.2 percent of men had experienced IP-perpe-trated physical, sexual, or stalking violence in adulthood, with lifetime

149

abuse victimization rates of 22.1 percent for women compared to 7.4 percent for men (Tjaden and Thoennes, 2000: p. iii).

The most severe form of intimate partner violence is homicide, the majority of which are *femicides*, defined as "the killing of women by intimate male partners, that is, current or former legal spouses, common-law partners, and boyfriends" (Dawson and Gartner, 1998: p. 383). According to the Bureau of Justice Statistics, there were 1,181 intimate partner murders perpetrated against women in the United States in 2005 (Fox and Zawitz, 2007). This number represents nearly one-third of the total number of female murder victims, as compared to 3 percent of males who were murdered by an intimate. Similarly, CDC data (via the National Violent Death Reporting System) reveal that 65 percent of intimate partner homicides in their 2005 sample involved female victims (Karch et al., 2008). These statistics are likely underestimates, however, since the victim-offender relationship may not always be known and an actual intimate partner homicide may not be classified as such in official reports, mainly due to the lack of an ex-dating partner category in supplemental homicide reports (e.g., Frye, 2008).

The Violence Policy Center issues a report annually titled "When Men Murder Women: Females Murdered by Males in Single Victim/Single Offender Incidents," wherein they rank states' femicide rates. As shown in the chart below, Louisiana is nearly always in the top five for highest femicide rates.

Table 1: Louisiana Femicide Rankings from 2002-2011

Year	National Ranking
2002	#2
2003	#3
2004	#4
2005	#3
2006	#5
2007	#1
2008	#12
2009	#3
2010	#4
2011	#9

While these dismal annual rankings and the consistency with which Louisiana is represented among the worst states for femicide might suggest New Orleans has very high rates of IPH, this trend surprisingly does not hold for the city. Relative to other types of homicides, namely, what David Kennedy (2012) refers to as "street" homicides, IP homicides constitute a very small portion each year.

New Orleans Violence and Homicide Culture

New Orleans is a city known worldwide for its rich and diverse culture. Unfortunately, it is also known for violence and social disorganization in certain concentrated areas. What many outside of the city find surprising is that homicide is often an expected part of these communities, and is even celebrated in certain circumstances. NOPD officers share stories of working crime scenes crowded with people standing around visiting with neighbors while the processing of a homicide occurs in the background. The locals sometimes bring radios to play music and dance and ice chests with drinks to share. It is commonplace for children to run around and play, as well as to interact with investigators. One officer told of a small child asking what kind of gun he had (after asking the officer if it was one of several specific types), and showed enthusiasm for the notion of being able to legally shoot someone. Another officer said he once had a highly emotional woman drive up to a murder scene he was working and was shocked to hear why the woman was so upset. According to the officer, he assumed she was hysterical over the death of a neighbor and walked to her car to try to offer help. Instead, the woman was shouting at him to move the crime scene tape so that she could get through and be home in time for her favorite television show.

In addition to partying at homicide scenes (what one officer literally referred to as "homicide parties"), law enforcement officers and New Orleans residents from these violence infested areas have described a phenomenon where the celebration of "street homicide" victims are memorialized in a particularly unique way in the design and distribution of a memorial t-shirt for the slain. While such memorial t-shirts are not altogether uncommon in urban U.S. cities, the disturbing aspect to this phenomenon in New Orleans is that the victims (usually young black males) have typically de-

signed the t-shirt themselves with the assumption, if not anticipa-
tion, of their own murder. Upon the death of the victim, the family will have the t-shirts printed, and they are worn by family and
friends in honor of the victim, sometimes even to the funeral. After
the body of his son was carried away, one father (as witnessed by
an NOPD officer), ran out of his house with his son's t-shirt proto-
type and shouted "this is the proudest day of my life."

These anecdotal accounts of desensitization to homicide are all
too common among police officers, residents of the areas in which
most homicides occur, and in media stories (or lack thereof) about
these kinds of cases. The desensitization is troubling and has led
to the assumption, if not acceptance, that New Orleans possesses a
culture of homicide. Locally and beyond, this assumption is accepted
by many as part of the history and culture of the city, just as food
and music are, while a growing number of concerned citizens and
officials see the problem of violence as detrimental to the well-being of the city and its residents.

The notion of a subculture of violence can be traced first to the
seminal work of Wolfgang and Ferracuti (1967), where they discussed violence more generally, and then to Gastil (1967), who applied the theory of subculture of violence to homicide in the South
specifically. Gastil argued that the more traditionally southern the
values and traditions of an area are, the more homicide will occur.
Further, he contended that the high rates of homicide in the U.S.
generally are due to the southern states and their historically-based
culture of homicide. The geographic and cultural "southernness"
of Louisiana, as well as the historical persistence of violence may
be explained by a subcultural theory more generally, but this is not
likely to explain IPH, particularly in New Orleans. If the rates of
IPH in New Orleans were more consistent with murder rates in
general in the city, or even with other cities, perhaps this theory
may help shape our understanding of New Orleans IPH, but the
low rates do not indicate this is an appropriate framework.

While the general desensitization to violence in New Orleans,
including the possibility of a "subculture of homicide" persists, intimate partner homicide appears to be a puzzling outlier within
the larger context of homicide in New Orleans. In a recent study
by Jana Levitov and Dee Wood Harper (2012) linking neighborhood racial isolation and poverty to types of murder by motive, the

researchers found that IP homicides occurred in areas marked by moderate racial isolation and moderate concentrated poverty (between 40 percent and 60 percent black and between 40 percent and 60 percent in poverty) while drug and revenge/retaliatory murder was more characteristic of neighborhoods with extreme levels of isolation (>60 percent black) and over 60 percent poor. (p. 143). Their data set was all murders in New Orleans for 2003-2005. In the present study 42 percent of all IP homicides occurred in the 5th and 7th police districts in similar neighborhoods described by Levitov and Harper.

Anecdotal accounts by police and service providers suggest an extraordinary number of non-lethal domestic violence calls each year with few cases of lethal violence. This seems counterintuitive; one would expect high levels of domestic violence calls for service to correlate with higher levels of IP homicide. The reasons for this disjunction perhaps lies with the manner in which police in New Orleans have been handling domestic violence calls for service going back to 2003.

Intimate Partner Violence and Homicide in New Orleans
Policing Domestic Violence

In the spring of 1999 Capitan Louie Dabdoub, commander of the 2nd Police District, was enrolled at Loyola University New Orleans majoring in criminal justice.[1] That spring he took a special seminar on Women and Crime convened by Professor Dee Wood Harper, who had in the previous summer attended a National Institute of Justice week-long institute at the University of Michigan on the same topic. Capitan Dabdoub was perplexed with how difficult it was for the police to make a real difference in handling domestic calls for service. In the next few months Dabdoub and Harper collaborated on developing a domestic violence initiative to be piloted in the 2nd Police District; if results were favorable, the initiative would go city-wide. The initiative was funded by a local foundation and fiscally managed by the New Orleans Police Foundation (later New Orleans Police and Justice Foundation).

---

1. Dabdoub graduated with honors and went on to receive a Master of Criminal Justice from Loyola.

By the end of the first year of a three year grant, the initiative was already departmental wide. On the police side one of the key practices initiated was the training and appointment of a domestic violence detective. Their primary duty was the post-incident interview. Each day the district domestic violence detectives would go visit both the perpetrator and victim of the previous day's incidents. The detectives were provided with scripted information that they delivered verbally and in person to both parties. The purpose was to make both parties very much aware that the police department was engaged and watching the results. Where arrests had been made and an automatic restraining (stay-away) order was in place, the contact with the perpetrator was more on the order of a "knock-and-warn." The script went something like this: "You have a restraining order against you, and we are watching you and will continue to watch you. If you violate the order for any reason you will go to jail."

For the first six months of the process in the second district 273 domestic violence calls for service were received with no call backs from the same location. In effect domestic violence was not allowed to escalate, whereas in the past the average number of calls for DV at a location was as many as seven, escalating with each call and in some instances ending in the worst case with a homicide. IP homicides for New Orleans went from between 23 and 28 from 1990 to 2002 (mean 26.33) to 8 in 2003 and have continued to decline through the period of this study at a remarkable 7.5 average for the six years.

During the grant period in addition to the above initiative the following was accomplished: training was initiated for officers following the Duluth model, training for 911 operators in how to handle DV calls for service, vertical prosecution for DV cases, a victim advocate was assigned to each court case, victimless prosecutions were initiated, dual arrests were virtually eliminated in DV cases, and a domestic violence officer was trained and placed in all eight police districts. While it is not provable in any scientific sense, this initiative seems to have affected a cultural shift regarding lethal intimate partner violence. There are still plenty of calls for service in New Orleans for domestic violence but in only rare instances does it become lethal.

In striking contrast, in March 2011 the U.S. Department of

Justice issued a 158-page report at the conclusion of an extensive investigation of NOPD. The scathing report contained findings of inadequacies in the way NOPD handled domestic violence, from policies, procedures, and training to investigations of cases. The report noted that the department receives a significantly high number of domestic violence calls (6,200 by July of 2010) and that they are severely short-staffed and undertrained to handle these unique cases. Other troubling findings included failure to adequately investigate domestic violence cases, including purposeful delays or non-responses to domestic violence calls, particularly in cases with non-English speaking callers. The report noted a positive effect on policing domestic violence resulting from the New Orleans Family Justice Center (NOFJC), but cautioned that poor policies and training, understaffing, inadequate response to calls, and failure to properly investigate were serious problems in NOPD's responses to domestic violence. The report draws heavily on anecdotal material regarding domestic violence investigations collected through a survey conducted by NOFJC. One thing of note in the report is that although the creation of a centralized Domestic Violence Unit in NOPD may be laudable with three detectives assigned, it certainly represents a step backwards from the earlier model with a DV detective assigned in each police district with the charge to specifically address follow-up of arrests and restraining orders with a "knock and warn," which seemed to be related to the significant drop in IPH that occurred in 2003 and continues to remain low to the present.[22]

Prosecuting Domestic Violence

In 2008 then District Attorney Kelva Landrum-Johnson collaborated with Tania Tetlow, the director of the Tulane Law School's domestic violence clinic, to assist police officers to book more DV cases on state battery charges and have them prosecuted in state court. Up until this point most DV cases ended up as misdemeanors tried in Municipal Court and handled by the city attorney's office. At that time the city attorney's office claimed that prosecution

2. The NIJ report is not a social scientific document. This is clear from the single paragraph concerning domestic violence in the document's executive summary. Assertions like, "We also find systemic deficiencies in NOPD's handling of domestic violence cases...we find significant weaknesses in Department policies and practices in responding to these cases" (p.xi) have no supporting evidence in any social scientific sense.

of DV cases was a priority of their office (Maggi, 2008). The city attorney's office was collaborating with the Family Justice Center that had opened the previous fall to provide a centralized place for domestic violence victims to get help. The city attorney's office had also received federal funds to hire two more assistant city attorneys to handle DV cases.

Beginning in March 2009, newly elected District Attorney Leon Cannizzaro asked NOPD to bring DV arrests to his office to be reviewed in order to charge abusers under state DV statutes and put them in jail. Up until this point 93 percent of DV cases, even those involving serious injury, were booked as municipal violations (Filosa, 2010). During the remainder of 2009 the D. A.'s office reviewed 1,923 domestic violence arrests and agreed to prosecute 80 percent of the cases. Cannizzaro's office reported an 85 percent conviction rate for these cases (Filosa, 2010).

During this period there were some particularly horrendous domestic murders involving former defendants in DV cases that "slipped through the cracks." However, Mary Claire Landry, director of the Family Justice Center, citing tremendous progress in the system, said "While we have focused recently on several high-profile cases where we were unable to prevent violent acts, during this time we were also able to assist hundreds of survivors with support, life-saving strategies and effective prosecution and batterer accountability that never becomes public or is known by anyone other than those of us involved in the case. It's an incredible engine for a wide range of life" (Filosa, 2010).

In 2011, the Louisiana House of Representatives passed a resolution authored by Rep. Nita Hutter, charging the Louisiana Coalition against Domestic Violence (LCADV) to appoint and convene a task force to evaluate existing court-approved batterers intervention programs, to study similar programs in other states, and to report their findings to the state legislature. After completing the study, the LCADV Task Force issued their report in February 2012. Among the key findings was that Louisiana has no central organization to bring batterer's intervention programs together, define best practices, and monitor program quality. Also, unlike most states, Louisiana has no minimum standards for batterer's intervention programs, which are often proprietary in nature in Louisiana. Half of respondents in a survey conducted by the Task Force identifying as prosecutors, court officials, or as working for a corrections agency had no list of court-approved batterer's intervention programs, and only 15 percent identifying as professionals in child protective services had such lists.

Victim Services

The status of victim services in New Orleans can best be described as "in transition." One of the most vital sources of victim services is the New Orleans Family Justice Center (NOFJC), a federally-funded "one-stop shop" where victims of domestic violence have access to police, prosecutors, family law attorneys, and victim advocacy. The NOFJC opened in 2007 and was originally under the management of Catholic Charities, though that has recently changed.

One critical area of victim services severely lacking in New Orleans is emergency shelter for domestic violence victims and their children. Although an exact number of "beds" available city-wide for those fleeing a dangerous home is unknown, estimates range from fifteen to twenty-five. This is a very low number of emergency spaces for a city the size of New Orleans, especially given the high incidence of non-lethal domestic violence annually in the city. This number is also substantially lower than the emergency shelter services before Hurricane Katrina. Reports from professionals in domestic violence services suggest that other emergency shelter services will be available soon, but severe state-level cuts in social services have led to major budget cuts to every domestic violence agency across Louisiana, including eliminating entire programs. Many are now operating on very small budgets with inadequate staff. In addition to the budget constraints, agencies have seen persistent staff turnover in recent years.

IPH in New Orleans from 2007 to 2012

NOPD provided basic homicide data on domestic homicide cases from 2007 through October 2012. In those six years, there were forty-five cases of domestic homicide, thirty-four of which were IPH. Other cases included child abuse-related murders and other non-intimate family members. Given the relatively low number, our statistical analyses are limited to univariate description.

Findings

Frequencies were determined for victim and perpetrator age, race, and sex, weapon used, and NOPD district where the incident occurred. The results of these analyses are shown in the tables below.

Table 2. Victim Age[1]

	2007		2008		2009		2010		2011		2012		Total	
	n	%	n	%	n	%	n	%	n	%	n	%	n	%
Juvenile	0		0		1	10	0		2	18	0		3	6
Young Adult	0		1	20	0		2	20	4	36	0		7	15
Adult	3	75	4	80	6	60	8	80	4	36	5	100	30	67
Senior	1	25	0		3	30	0		1	9	0		5	11
Total	4		5		10		10		11		5		45	

[1]Age Defined: Juvenile 0-17; Young Adult 18-25; Adult 26-64; Senior 65+.

Table 3. Perpetrator Age

	2007		2008		2009		2010		2011		2012		Total	
	n	%	n	%	n	%	n	%	n	%	n	%	n	%
Juvenile	0		0		0		0		0		0		0	
Young Adult	0		0		0		2	20	4	36	0		6	14
Adult	4	100	5	100	9	90	3	30	7	63	4	100	32	71
Senior	0		0		1	10	5	50	0		0		6	14
Total	4		5		10		10		11		4[2]		44	72

[1]Age Defined: Juvenile 0-17; Young Adult 18-25; Adult 26-64; Senior 65+.
[2]2012 lacks one perpetrator age.

Most victims were adults between 26 and 64 years of age (67 percent overall), over three times as many as young adults ages 18 to 25 (15 percent overall), and six times as many as those in the senior category. Nearly the same results can be seen for perpetrator age, shown in Table 3. The majority of perpetrators were adults between 26 and 64 years of age (71 percent overall), with young adults and seniors compromising 14 percent each.

Table 4. Victim Race

	2007 n	%	2008 n	%	2009 n	%	2010 n	%	2011 n	%	2012 n	%	Total n	%
Black	4	100	5	100	7	70	10	100	9	82	4	80	39	86
White	0		0		2	20	0		2	18	0		4	10
Hispanic	0		0		0		0		0		1	20	1	2
Asian	0		0		1	10	0		0		0		1	2
Total	4		5		10		10		11		5		45	

Table 5. Perpetrator Race

	2007 n	%	2008 n	%	2009 n	%	2010 n	%	2011 n	%	2012 n	%	Total n	%
Black	4	100	5	100	6	60	10	100	9	82	4	80	38	84
White	0		0		3	30	0		2	18	0		5	11
Hispanic	0		0		0		0		0		1	20	1	2
Asian	0		0		1	10	0		0		0		1	2
Total	4		5		10		10		11		5		45	

The majority of victims and perpetrators were black in all five years. Black women were victims in 86 percent of cases, as were Black men as perpetrators in 84 percent. Whites made up the next category, with 10 percent of victims and 11 percent of perpetrators. There were two Hispanic and two Asian victims and perpetrators.

Table 6. Sex of Victim

	2007		2008		2009		2010		2011		2012		Total	
	n	%	n	%	n	%	n	%	n	%	n	%	n	%
Male	2	50	3	60	3	30	2	20	5	45	2	40	17	38
Female	2	50	2	40	7	70	8	80	6	55	3	60	28	62
Total	4		5		10		10		11		5		45	

Table 7. Sex of Perpetrator

	2007		2008		2009		2010		2011		2012		Total	
	n	%	n	%	n	%	n	%	n	%	n	%	n	%
Male	2	50	2	40	10	100	10	100	9	82	3	60	36	80
Female	2	50	3	60	0		0		2	18	2	40	9	20
Total	4		5		10		10		11		5		45	

There is much left to investigate regarding victim and perpetrator sex. Tables 6 and 7 reveal that 62 percent of victims were female and 38 percent were male, while 20 percent of perpetrators were female and 80 percent were male. We have to assume some of the perpetrators of murder-suicides were also counted as victims, as was the case of a man who stabbed his wife to death and then hung himself in 2010. Cases of female-perpetrated murders usually indicate self-defense, as with a 2010 case where a man was attacking his girlfriend and her mother and was stabbed in his hand, resulting in him bleeding out and dying. In the cases identified with multiple victims, usually the victims were all female. The sex category of the study warrants much further research before conclusions can be drawn.

Table 8. Weapon Used

	2007		2008		2009		2010		2011		2012		Total	
	n	%	n	%	n	%	n	%	n	%	n	%	n	%
Handgun	1	25	2	40	1	10	3	27	8	72	3	60	18	39
Shotgun	1	25	1	20	2	20	4	36	0		0		8	17
Knife	1	25	2	40	1	10	1	9	1	9	1	20	7	15
Hands[1]	0		0		3	30	0		1	9	0		4	9
Arson	0		0		0		1	9	0		0		1	2
Miscellaneous[2]	1	25	0		3	30	2	18	1	9	1	20	8	17
Total	4		5		10		11		11		5		46	

[1]Hands refers to physical damage incurred during a fight.
[2]Miscellaneous includes a brick, scissors, crossbow, fire extinguisher, and sharp objects.
[3]2011 data represents a single incident in which both a shotgun and a handgun were used.

Guns were used in over half of the incidents (56 percent). Knives and other objects (i.e. a brick, scissors, a concrete block, and other sharp objects) accounted for 32 percent, fist fighting and other forms of physical attacks were the cause of homicide in 9 percent of cases, and arson was the cause in 2 percent. In one particularly gruesome case, a man shot and killed his wife with a crossbow. His first shot travelled through her, severing her spine, and he then shot a second time through her face.

Table 9. NOPD District Where Incident Occurred

	2007		2008		2009		2010		2011		2012		Total	
	n	%	n	%	n	%	n	%	n	%	n	%	n	%
1	0		0		2	20	3	30	2	18	1	20	8	18
2	0		1	20	3	30	0		1	9	0		5	11
3	1	25	0		0		0		1	9	0		2	4
4	0		2	40	0		0		3	27	1	20	6	13
5	0		2	40	0		4	40	1	9	1	20	8	18
6	2	50	0		0		2	20	0		0		4	9
7	1	25	0		4	40	1	10	3	27	2	40	11	24
8	0		0		1	10	0		0		0		1	2
Total	4		5		10		10		11		5		45	

With the exception of districts 3, 6, and 8, domestic homicides in New Orleans were relatively evenly distributed across the NOPD districts. District 7 had the most incidents (24 percent), followed by districts 1 and 5 with 18 percent each. This finding is similar to that of Levitov and Harper (2012), discussed earlier, where more homicides were committed in areas of moderate isolation and moderate poverty in New Orleans. Figure 1 shows the NOPD districts.

Figure 1. NOPD Districts

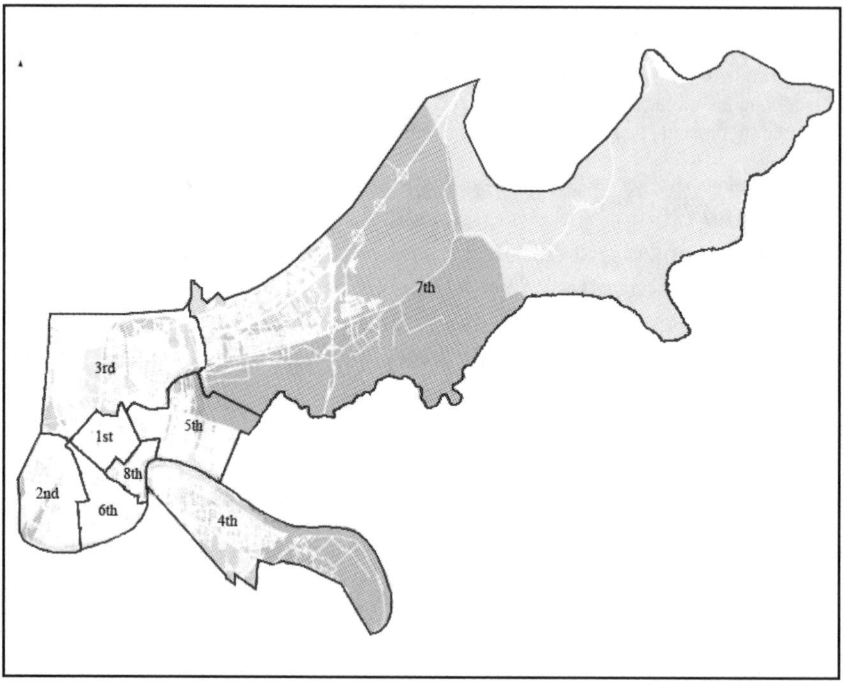

Conclusion

The aim of this chapter is to provide a context of homicide in New Orleans and some insight into IPH, as very little research has addressed these unique areas. While the majority of homicides in New Orleans are drug, retaliation, and revenge-oriented, the general desensitization regarding violence is troubling. This desensitization may also apply to homicides of all sorts, including domestic and intimate partner homicides. "Homicide parties," memorial t-shirts, and a general expectation and acceptance of violence make for a culture conducive for higher rates of violence across all contexts.

Certain issues are particularly concerning with regard to domestic violence. First, the criminal justice system has historically failed victims of domestic violence. A history of ineffective and inadequate policing, as revealed in the Department of Justice's investigation of NOPD includes prolonged or complete lack of police response and sometimes total dismissal of non-English speaking victims. Shifting the criminality of domestic violence from municipal court to criminal court and back to municipal court has caused confusion across the criminal justice system and disconcertment among victims of domestic violence. Finally, the statewide lack of effective and organized batterer's intervention programs severely impedes efforts toward intervention and treatment for offenders after conviction.

Victim services have suffered nationwide with budget cuts and politicization of women's rights, and this is particularly apparent in Louisiana where we see consistently high rates of intimate partner femicide each year. Rapid turnover in victim service agencies, debilitating budget cuts, and generally insufficient resources have led to a crippled victim services network in the state. Given the suggestion from local law enforcement officials and victim service providers that non-lethal domestic violence rates are likely exceptionally high in the city, the lack of a sufficient network of victim services is particularly concerning. Further research is needed to determine the extent of these rates and where additional resources are needed.

The small number of domestic homicides in the data set for this study from 2007 to 2012 precluded the option of statistical analyses, but frequencies of the variables allowed for some insight into the nature of these incidents. The predominant racial category of both victims and perpetrators is black, and both victims and perpetrators were more likely to be adults over the age of twenty-four. These findings are consistent with national trends in sociodemographics for IPH as well (e.g., Campbell et al., 2007; Goodwin et al., 2000). While the sex of victims was predominately female and perpetrators were mostly male, further context of these crimes is needed for better understanding the nature of IPH in New Orleans in particular. For example, one male victim and his girlfriend were stabbed to death by the woman's ex-husband, but both cases were labeled as domestic homicides in the NOPD data. In reality, the murder of the woman would be considered IPH, and the murder of her boyfriend would be considered IPH-related, but not counted as an IPH in the current study. More qualitative data, such as police narratives, will be used to bolster these initial findings in further research.

There is much work to be done in the way of research to better understand IPH in New Orleans. The nature and scope are curious with the little data provided, but further analyses with more extensive quantitative and qualitative data would provide a way for much needed empirical understanding of IPH in New Orleans. In addition to research, victim services and criminal justice policies are in need of evaluation and greater support to provide appropriate prevention and intervention in domestic violence. Finally, research into non-lethal cases in comparison to lethal cases will help explain why New Orleans has lower numbers of IPH in proportion to other cities with high homicide rates, and will help identify areas of potential prevention and intervention.

References

Campbell, J.C., N. Glass, P.W. Sharps, K. Laughon, and T. Bloom. (2007). "Intimate partner homicide: Review and implications of research and policy." *Trauma, Violence, & Abuse* 8 (3): 246-69.

Dahlberg, L.L., J.A. Mercy, A.B. Zwi, R. Lozano (Eds.) *World report on violence and health* (pp. 89-121). World Health Organization: Geneva.

Dawson, M., and R. Gartner. (1998). "Differences in the characteristics of intimate femicides: The role of relationship state and status." *Homicide Studies* 2: 378-99.

Filosa, G. (2010, May 16). "Killings put new focus on domestic violence - Do DA's changes make system tougher on the batterers?" *Times-Picayune* A, 01

Fox, J.A., and M.W. Zawitz. (2007). Homicide trends in the U.S. Washington, D.C.: Bureau of Justice Statistics. Retrieved from www.ojp.usdoj/bjs/.

Frye, V., and S. Wilt. (2001). Femicide and social disorganization. *Violence against Women* 7 (3): 335-51.

Goodwin, M.M., J.A. Gazmararian, C.H. Johnson, B. Colley Gilbert, L.E. Saltzman, and The PRAMS Working Group. (2000). "Pregnancy intendedness and physical abuse around the time of pregnancy: Findings from the pregnancy risk assessment monitoring system, 1996-1997." *Maternal and Child Health Journal* 4 (2): 85-92.

Gastil, R. D. (1971). "Homicide and a regional culture of violence." *American Sociological Review* 36 (3): 412-27.

Heise, L., and C. Garcia-Moreno. (2002). "Violence by intimate partners." In E.G. Krug, L.L. Dahlberg, J.A. Mercy, A.B. Zwi, and R. Lozano (Eds.), World report on violence and health. World Health Organization [WHO], Geneva, Switzerland, 87-121.

Karch, D.L., K.M. Lubell, J. Friday, N. Patel, and D.D. Williams. (2008). Surveillance for violent deaths—National Violent Death Reporting System, 16 states, 2005. Retrieved from http://www.cdc.gov/mmwr/preview/mmwrhtml/ss5703a1.htm.

Kennedy, D. (2012, October). "Stopping the Killing in New Orleans: Focus, Legitimacy, and Common Ground." Presented at "Preventing Lethal Violence in New Orleans" symposium at Loyola University New Orleans, New Orleans, LA.

Levitov, J.L., and D.W. Harper. (2012). "'You can't do crack on credit:' Drug and retaliatory murder." In D.W. Harper, L. Voigt, and W. E. Thornton (Eds.), *Violence: Do we know it when we see it?* (pp. 129-46). Durham: Carolina Academic Press.

Louisiana Coalition against Domestic Violence. (2012). Findings and recommendations Relative to the status of batterer intervention programming in Louisiana. Baton Rouge, LA.

Maggi, L. (2008, May 7). Orleans DA targets domestic violence—Tulane scholars to aid prosecution. *Times-Picayune.* p. B1.

Moracco, K., C. Runyan, J. Bowling, and J. Earp. (2007). "Women's experiences with Violence: A national study." *Women's Health Issues* 17 (1): 3-12.

Tjaden, P., and N. Thoennes. (2000). Full report of the prevalence, incidence, and consequences of violence against women. Washington, D.C.: National Institute of Justice.

Wolfgang, M., and F. Ferracuti. (1967). *The subculture of violence.* London: Tavistock Publications.

United States Department of Justice Civil Rights Division. (2011). Investigation of the New Orleans Police Department. Washington, D.C.: U.S.

Violence Policy Center. (2013). When Men Murder Women: An Analysis of 2011 Homicide Data. Retrieved from http://www.vpc.org/studies/wmmw2011.pdf.

———. (2012). When Men Murder Women: An Analysis of 2011 Homicide Data. Retrieved from http://www.vpc.org/studies/wmmw2010.pdf.

———. (2011). When Men Murder Women: An Analysis of 2011 Homicide Data. Retrieved from http://www.vpc.org/studies/wmmw2009.pdf.

———. (2010). When Men Murder Women: An Analysis of 2011 Homicide Data. Retrieved from http://www.vpc.org/studies/wmmw2008.pdf.

———. (2009). When Men Murder Women: An Analysis of 2011 Homicide Data. Retrieved from http://www.vpc.org/studies/wmmw2007.pdf.

———. (2008). When Men Murder Women: An Analysis of 2011 Homicide Data. Retrieved from http://www.vpc.org/studies/wmmw2006.pdf.

———. (2007). When Men Murder Women: An Analysis of 2011 Homicide Data. Retrieved from http://www.vpc.org/studies/wmmw2005.pdf.

———. (2006). When Men Murder Women: An Analysis of 2011 Homicide Data. Retrieved from http://www.vpc.org/studies/wmmw2004.pdf.

———. (2005). When Men Murder Women: An Analysis of 2011 Homicide Data. Retrieved from http://www.vpc.org/studies/wmmw2003.pdf.

———. (2004). When Men Murder Women: An Analysis of 2011 Homicide Data. Retrieved from http://www.vpc.org/studies/wmmw2002.pdf.

7 Life and Death in the Big Easy: Homicide and Lethality in Twenty-First-Century New Orleans

Jay Corzine, Lin Huff-Corzine, Aaron Poole,
James McCutcheon, and Sarah Ann Sacra

New Orleans is one of the best known and most frequently visited cities in the United States. It is beyond dispute that the unique
cultural, culinary, and musical contributions of the Crescent City
have had a significant and positive impact on the mainstream of the
larger society. On the other hand, the city has a dark side that goes
well beyond the quasi-seedy nightlife of Bourbon Street, its best
known thoroughfare to the millions of tourists who visit it annually. Specifically, New Orleans has a long history of lethal violence
that also distinguishes it from most other large cities in the United
States (see Adler in this volume).

The roots of homicide and other forms of serious violence
run deep in the Big Easy.[1] In 1891, New Orleans was the site of
the bloodiest documented lynching in U.S. history; the killing of
eleven Sicilians by a mixed race lynch mob composed mainly of
Irish and black residents.[2] The lynching was triggered by a local
jury's not guilty verdicts in the trial of six of nineteen Sicilians accused of assassinating David Hennessy, the Police Chief of New
Orleans, during the previous year (Gambino, 1977). As his surname
implies, Hennessey was of Irish descent, and the mass lynching of
Sicilians reflected longstanding ethnic tensions within the city. As
with many nineteenth-century lynchings, a local grand jury failed

---

1. In this chapter, the terms "homicide," "murder," and "killing" are used interchangeably.

2. The term "mob" is often a misnomer when applied to the perpetrators of lynchings,
because it implies a disorderly and disorganized group. The New Orleans citizens responsible for the killing of the eleven Sicilians had recognized leaders and predetermined roles
(Gambino, 1977).

to return any indictments for the murders, although some of the participants took public credit for their deeds.

In the twenty-first century, however, New Orleans is no longer known for intergroup violence but instead for a very high level of homicide occurring among the city's residents. Although the city had consistently tallied one of the higher homicide rates in the United States (often placing in the top five for cities with 250,000+ population), the number of killings per capita spiked after the widespread social dislocations wrought by Hurricane Katrina in 2005. Until being displaced by Detroit in 2012, New Orleans led the nation in urban homicide rates for several years, with an unparalleled rate of over 90 per 100,000 population in 2007 (Wellford, Bond, and Goodison, 2011). Although New Orleans's homicide rate for 2012, 53 per 100,000 residents represents a decrease of almost 50 percent from this high point, it is still approximately ten times the homicide rate for the United States.[3]

The authors were aware of the current homicide problem in New Orleans that has received widespread local and national media coverage. However, the impetus for this chapter occurred in 2011 when the first author received a call from a reporter with the *New Orleans Times-Picayune* who was seeking a comment on New Orleans Police Superintendent Ronal Serpas's public statements that, overall, New Orleans was a safer city than Orlando (Maggi, 2011). This claim was surprising because the authors knew that Orlando typically has a moderate homicide rate for cities of a similar size. On the other hand, Superintendent Serpas, who is well known in law enforcement circles and among criminologists, is not a police executive who would make unsupportable claims (see his contribution in this volume). In fact, his statement is supported by a 2009 study that reported the overall violent crime rate in Orlando as 1,197 per 100,000 compared to 777 per 100,000 in New Orleans (Wellford et al., 2011). Typically, homicide is positively correlated with the other violent felonies; robbery, sexual

---

3. As of this writing, the Federal Bureau of Investigation had not released official crime data for 2013. The number of homicides decreased from 193 in 2012 to 158 in 2013, so using the 2012 population estimate for the city would produce a homicide rate in 2013 of 43.34 per 100,000. A difficulty in calculating homicide rates for the city in 2005 and 2006 is the varying population estimates for these anomalous post-Katrina years, but there is a consensus that the level of killing increased significantly from that in 2004 (VanLandingham, 2007).

assault, and aggravated assault, that comprise the Uniform Crime Report's (UCR) Violent Crime Index, but there are exceptions. New Orleans, in the twenty-first century, stands out as something of an anomaly, a major city with a very high homicide level but an overall low to moderate level of violent crime (Wellford et al., 2011). Perhaps the Crescent City's contemporary homicide problem can better be described as a lethality problem. This suggestion requires some clarification.

While the notion of homicide is a straightforward concept and well understood by the general public, lethality is a term used mostly by violence researchers in public health and the social sciences (Weaver et al., 2004). The concept recognizes that only a small percentage of violent encounters that could result in a death actually have a fatal outcome. The factors that affect the odds of a physical altercation resulting in a fatality are multiple, including the use of a firearm, the quality of emergency medical care, and the speed of ambulance service. It is important to note that several variables that affect lethality, e.g., the presence of a trauma center, do not increase violent crime but instead affect its outcome. Therefore, a high homicide rate may reflect an above average level of violence with a low to moderate rate of lethality or an above average level of lethality coupled with a moderate or even low level of violence. Thus, even though the overall 2009 violence rate was higher in Orlando than in New Orleans, the more meaningful statistic is the lethal violence rate, described below. When comparing the 2009 lethality of serious assaults, Orlando had 1.01 deaths per 100, whereas New Orleans experienced 10.78 lethal outcomes for every 100 aggravated assaults. The importance of the distinction between a city's violence and lethal violence rate for public policy is that different types of interventions may be needed to reduce homicide, depending on whether the rate reflects overall violence, the level of lethality, or both.

The purpose of this chapter is to apply the concept of lethality to contemporary New Orleans to determine if it can provide increased understanding of its homicide problem. Before turning our attention back to the Crescent City, however, it will be helpful to further review the concept of lethality along with selected empirical studies. Because of space limitations and the recent growth in research in this area, we will concentrate on factors related to lethality that in our viewpoint hold some potential for understanding violence in New Orleans.

Homicide and Lethality

While research focused specifically on murder is invaluable to our understanding of the crime, it is inherently limited in scope because, by definition, it only examines violent crimes that result in a death. This approach, though informative, misses an important part of the broader picture by ignoring other crimes that have the potential to result in a murder, namely aggravated assaults, but for various reasons do not. The primary goal of lethality research is to understand what characteristics of a violent incident or its aftermath increase the odds that one or more deaths will ensue.

Because lower death rates are the ultimate goal of policy interventions targeting homicide, lethality research can be a valuable tool for policy makers. Most interventions focus on efforts to reduce the level of violence in a neighborhood or city, and this approach should remain the most significant one for crime prevention. If policy makers can act to lower the lethality of violence in an area, however, lower homicide rates will naturally follow even if the level of violence remains unchanged. Thus, lethality research expands the range of tools available to law enforcement and other government agencies from asking only what can be done to change potential offenders to also considering what else may be done that may have the same intended result, that is the lowering of homicide rates. Briefly stated, lethality research identifies homicide as the outcome of a social process involving interaction between victims, offenders, and possibly an audience in a specific location at a specific time (see Luckenbill, 1977). Changes in any of these five elements, as well as the aftermath of a life-threatening injury, may reduce the odds of violence resulting in a death.

The concept of lethality is a relatively recent addition to criminology. First proposed in the late 1950s, lethality research has steadily increased during the past decade (Felson and Painter-Davis, 2012; Libby, 2009; Libby and Corzine, 2007; Weaver et al., 2004). Many of these studies have been done at the incident level, examining which variables associated with a violent encounter raise the likelihood of a lethal outcome. Factors consistently found to be associated with a rise in lethality include the involvement of drugs; the ages of the offender and victim; the use of a weapon; and the type of weapon used. In addition to factors directly tied to the violent encounter, researchers have also found that what happens after the violence ends affects the odds of a homicide. The type and quality of available medical resources, as well as the travel time for a seriously injured victim to reach a trauma center, are of major importance for preventing murder (Harris et al., 2002). In the following section, we define lethality and briefly discuss findings from past research on four factors — guns; drugs; medical resources, notably trauma centers; and road networks — that in our view are relevant for understanding twenty-first century homicide in New Orleans.

A Definition of Lethality

As many researchers, commentators, and police officers have long noted, the difference between a homicide and an aggravated assault may simply be a matter of luck. In a sense, if the offender's intent was to kill the victim, aggravated assaults are failed homicide attempts. Conversely, an offender may plan to punish, not kill, the victim, but an unintended death results. Lethal violence is defined as the number of homicides divided by the number of homicides plus aggravated assaults in a given jurisdiction for a given time period. The resulting number varies from "0" to "1," and is often multiplied by 100 to produce a rate-based measure. In this chapter we use the following formula to measure lethality:

Lethality Rate = (Murders/Murders +Aggravated Assaults) x 100

Using this formula, the U.S. Lethality Rate during the past several years has hovered around 2, meaning that there have been approximately 2 homicides per 100 violent assaults that potentially could have produced a death.

Firearms and Lethality

There is substantial agreement across studies that the presence of a firearm in a violent encounter increases the likelihood of a fatality. Furthermore, using incident-level data from the National Incident-Based Reporting System (NIBRS), Libby and Corzine (2007) found that firearms are the most lethal weapons used in violent encounters, with shotguns being the most deadly firearms. These findings are consistent with Weaver et al. (2004), who found that the mere presence of any weapon increased the lethality of violent encounters, but the risk of a death was highest when a firearm was present. Additionally, Libby and Wright (2008) established that the deployment of firearms with an automatic, as opposed to semi-automatic, firing capability raised the likelihood of multiple victims resulting from a single incident.

When applied to an aggregate level, these findings have implications for ecological factors, such as the availability of firearms within a population. A higher level of availability would likely increase both the quality of firearms being used in assaults, as well as the frequency of their use. There would, in turn, be an increased potential for an escalation in the lethality of assaults and robberies. Thus, an important question that is partially addressed below is whether firearms are more likely to be used in violent felonies in New Orleans than in comparable cities.

Drugs and Lethality

Several studies have noted the positive impact of illegal drug markets on crime, including murder and aggravated assault (e.g., Blumstein, 1995). Additionally, there is evidence that if violent encounters are connected to drugs, their lethality increases (Weaver et al., 2004).

Goldstein's (1985) tripartite model hypothesizes that there are three pathways linking drugs to violence: (1) psychopharmacological, (2) economic compulsive, and (3) systemic. The psychopharmacological connection operates through the drug's impact on the user's mental state. The economic compulsion link occurs because some users commit crimes to obtain resources for purchasing drugs. Systemic violence related to drugs occurs because illegal drug markets are unregulated and disputes among upper-level suppliers, street-level sellers, and users are often settled with violence. Recent studies show that the systemic link is by far the largest contributor to both a rise in the level of violence as well as an increase in its severity (Phillips, 2012). This implies that the daily operations of drug markets are the primary factors behind the links between drugs and violence. Because much of the violence related to drug markets arises in disputes among sellers, it follows that cities with disorganized drug markets, i.e., a higher number of smaller drug organizations, will have more drug-related violence than those with more organized markets.

Medical Resources and Lethality

Doerner and his associates were the first to examine the relationship between medical resources and lethality (Doerner 1983, 1988; Doerner and Speir, 1986). Although Doerner and Speir were the first to look at specific medical resources, the link between advances in medical resources and a decrease in lethality has been hypothesized by researchers since the late 1950s (Wolfgang, 1958). These advances include more rapid communication among citizens, police, and emergency services as well as an increase in medical beds and personnel per capita, and a rise in the number of emergency medical technicians (EMTs), who receive advanced life support rather than basic life support training (Harris et al., 2002). These studies indicate the importance of access to high quality medical resources in saving the lives of victims of interpersonal violence.

Researchers following Doerner and Speir examined the link between increasing medical resources and lowering lethality rates across various dimensions including rural contexts, time, and nations (Barlow and Barlow, 1988; Chon, 2010; Giacopassi, Sparger, and Stein, 1992). Most of these studies report that increased access to medical resources is the *primary key* to decreasing lethality.

In terms of increasing survivability of assaults in a given area, trauma centers have proven to be invaluable resources worthy of consideration apart from other medical assets (Nathens et al., 2000; O'Keefe et al., 1999; Regoeczi, 2003). A trauma center is a special medical center specifically organized to deal efficiently with life-threatening damage to multiple bodily systems. These centers are required to have a doctor on call at all times and certain resources available at any given moment for immediate treatment of emergency cases. Criminally-induced trauma that requires the care of a trauma center is largely due to penetrating wounds, which are usually inflicted with a gun or a knife.

The strategy for saving lives is to have victims of violence delivered to the trauma center as rapidly as possible. By keeping a trained staff and special equipment on hand, trauma centers enhance both access and quality of care provided to seriously injured patients. The closing of trauma centers has been hypothesized to increase lethality rates, though this relationship has proven somewhat difficult to isolate due to the simultaneous presence of other ecological elements in a community that could also explain changes in the lethality rate (Regoeczi, 2003).

Road Networks and Lethality

The relationship between road networks and the effectiveness of emergency responses to potentially lethal cases has recently come under scientific scrutiny (Sullivan et al., 2010; Taniguchi, Ferreira, and Nicholson, 2012). Although the research has been primarily concerned with disaster preparedness (Libby, 2009), studies of road networks hold implications for everyday emergency situations as well (Sullivan et al., 2010). These studies have reported that the more options a road network provides to get from point A to point B, the more reliably emergency medical services operate in emergency situations. Theoretically, a more reliable network would likely decrease the lethality rate in an area, as aggravated assaults are treated more rapidly and are less likely to become murders. For everyday emergency situations, slowdowns in road networks are most likely due to heavy traffic, construction projects, traffic accidents, and other mundane situations rather than natural disasters. Although, to our knowledge, the point has not received any attention in prior research it also follows that the location(s) of a city's trauma center(s) in relationship to neighborhoods with high concentrations of shootings and stabbings will impact lethality by affecting the average travel time of victims to medical services.

In the following section, we refocus our attention on New Orleans and its recent levels of lethal homicides. After providing data for the period from 2001 through 2010 (2012 for selected statistics), we review the possible implications of the topics discussed above—firearms; drugs; medical resources, including trauma centers; and roadways—for understanding the wave of lethal violence that has been a persistent problem for the Big Easy in the twenty-first century.

Lethal Violence in Twenty-First Century New Orleans

The demographics of homicide victims and offenders in New Orleans closely reflect those for most other large cities, with young African American and other minority males disproportionately involved in the transactions that lead to killings in the central cities of the Northeast, Midwest, and South. Wellford and his colleagues' (2011) recent analysis of two hundred New Orleans homicides occurring in 2009 and 2010 underscores the Big Easy's similarities and differences from other cities that annually register high homicide counts. Of the two hundred victims, 92 percent were black, 86 percent were men, and over half were under twenty-eight years old. Almost three-fourths, 73 percent, had a criminal record, with over two-thirds having a prior drug charge (Wellford et al., 2011: p. 11).

Overall, homicide offenders in New Orleans are drawn from the same segment of the population as the victims. Of the 102 known offenders, 97 percent were black, and 95 percent were male.[4] Eighty-three percent had a prior criminal record; 58 percent had at least one drug arrest. Offenders were somewhat younger than victims, with half under twenty-four years old at the time of the killing.

Of the two hundred homicide victims, 189 succumbed to "penetrating wounds," i.e., they were shot or stabbed. Only eleven victims died of some other cause, e.g., a blunt object or personal weapons (i.e., the offender's hands, fists, or feet.) Reflecting the patterns for other large cities and the U.S., 156 of 180 victims who died from being shot were killed with a handgun (Wellford et al., 2011). Overall, 90 percent of the victims were killed with firearms, a percentage that is somewhat higher than for other cities with a chronic homicide problem. In Baltimore, 367 of 464 homicide victims, or 79 percent, in 2009 and 2010 combined were shot.[5] On the other hand; the difference in the use of firearms between New Orleans and Baltimore is one of degree.

For two other characteristics of New Orleans homicides, however, the report by Wellford et al. (2011) is perplexing. There is a

4. Only 102 of the 200 homicides examined by Wellford and his colleagues (2011) were solved. This clearance rate may seem low to some readers, but it is not atypical for large central cities.

5. The homicide numbers for Baltimore were taken from the Baltimore Homicide Map maintained by the *Baltimore Sun* and based on records obtained from the Baltimore Police Department.

substantial literature showing that gang affiliation increases weapon carrying and the risk of becoming a homicide victim (Jensen and Thibodeaux, 2013; Melde, Esbenson, and Taylor, 2009), with McDaniel (2012) stating that 20 percent of homicides in large cities between 2002 and 2006 were gang-related. Wellford et al. (2011) identify only 2 of 200, or 1 percent, of the New Orleans victims as involved with a gang/crew. The recurrent difficulties in defining gang membership are well known (Ball and Curry, 1995; Gilbertson, 2009), but for only 1 in 100 homicide victims in a large U.S. city in the twenty-first century to be gang involved would appear to be a serious undercount. This is especially the case when the New Orleans Police Department (NOPD) has reported that they are aware of thirty-nine different groups, gangs, or crews selling drugs in the Crescent City. In all fairness, Wellford and his colleagues were limited by the material in the NOPD case files, and they discuss their own uneasiness with this statistic. In addition, the homicide statistics for New Orleans in 2012 show a very different picture. According to Christian Bolden, an academic researcher in New Orleans, 62 of 204 homicides, or 30.4 percent can be classified as having a gang member involved (Bolden, 2013).[6]

Second, as mentioned in the above paragraph, thirty-nine different groups selling drugs would indicate a disorganized drug market, one that is conducive to a high level of homicide, and estimates of the percentage of homicides that are drug-related in large cities like New Orleans range as high as 80 percent. Wellford et al. (2011) report that NOPD labeled 28.5 percent of the two hundred homicides as drug-related, and their separate analysis of case files reaches a similar conclusion with 27 percent being classified as drug-related. They report that both argument/conflict and revenge are more common motives than drugs. Again, the researchers had to rely on available data from the New Orleans Police Department, but the obvious questions are "What was the argument about?" and "Revenge for what?" Their summary conclusion that "(g)angs and organized drug markets appear to play less of a role in homicides in New Orleans..." requires further investigation. In the following section, we begin our attempt to understand the most important question about homicide in New Orleans: "Why are there so many of them?"

---

6. This classification is different than gang related.

Murder Rates for New Orleans
and Selected Other U.S. Cities

Figure 1 presents the 2010 murder rates for New Orleans and selected other large cities (250,000 + population). The comparison cities were chosen for different reasons. Along with New Orleans, Baltimore, Detroit, and St. Louis comprise the four cities that have consistently recorded homicide rates in the top five during the decade from 2000 to 2010. Of course, Orlando was chosen because it was Superintendent Serpas's primary point of comparison with New Orleans violent crime in Wellford et al., (2011). There has been significant media attention on Chicago homicides for the past two years, although the city's rates do not place it in the top ten deadliest cities during the decade. Finally, New York and Philadelphia are large East Coast cities. Although the rates for both cities have generally decreased in recent decades, the rate of decline for New York has been much steeper than that for Philadelphia.

It should not be surprising that New Orleans's murder rate of 49 per 100,000 is the highest for this group of cities. St. Louis, Baltimore, and Detroit are in the 2nd through 4th places, respectively, with each city having a rate above 30 per 100,000. New York has the lowest rate at 6 per 100,000 while Orlando's is slightly higher. The most important point from figure 1 is that the recent homicide rates in New Orleans are in fact very high, easily outpacing those from other cities with a chronic homicide problem. Although the data in figure 1 are from 2010, not much has changed in the last two years.

Figure 1: 2010 Murder Rates for Selected Cities

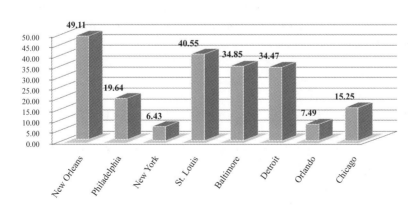

Figure 2: 2010 Assault Rates for Selected Cities

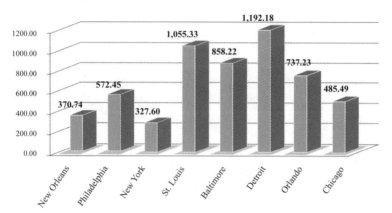

The murder rates in the Big Easy were 58 per 100,000 in 2011 and 53 per 100,000 in 2012. In the latter year, however, New Orleans was replaced as the city with the highest murder rate, being surpassed by two Michigan cities, Flint and Detroit (Federal Bureau of Investigation [FBI], 2013).

Figure 2 shows numbers for aggravated assaults, the second component of the Lethality Rate. In a reversal of the pattern for murder, the rate of 371 per 100,000 in New Orleans is the second lowest, with only New York City's rate of 328 per 100,000 being lower in 2010. Three cities with high homicide rates, Detroit, Baltimore, and St. Louis, also recorded elevated levels of aggravated assaults. Although it has a low murder rate, Orlando's aggravated assault rate of 737 is relatively high among these cities. New York represents the fourth logical pattern with low rates for both violent crimes.

Figure 3: 2010 Lethality Rates for Selected Cities

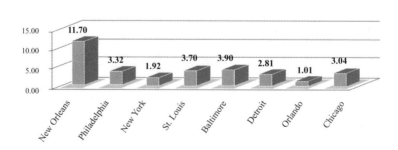

The lethality rates for 2010 in the eight cities chosen are displayed in figure 3. New Orleans's lethality rate of 11.70 is amazingly high both *sui generis* and in reference to the other cities. Remember that the lethality rate for the U.S. is typically close to 2, and note that Baltimore's lethality rate of 3.90, although second highest, is one third that of New Orleans. At the low end of the distribution, Orlando's rate of 1.01 is approximately one-half of that for the nation. These differences are important. An individual who was the victim of a serious violent assault was approximately twelve times more likely to die in New Orleans than in Orlando in 2010. The pattern for lethality rates displayed in figure 3 is not unusual; lethality rates for New Orleans in 2011 and 2012 were 13.11 and 10.99, respectively. For Baltimore, Detroit, and St. Louis, three other cities with chronically high homicide rates, the lethality rate of 4.48 for Baltimore in 2012 was the highest recorded (results not shown). The primary driver behind New Orleans's high homicide rate for 2010 is not the overall level of violent crime, but its atypically high lethality rate.

Figure 4: 1996-2010 New Orleans Lethality Rates

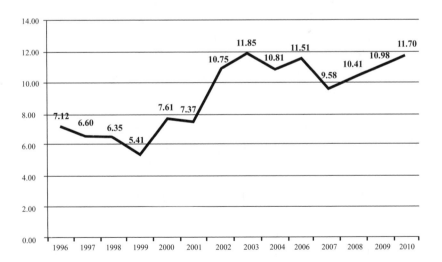

It is important to further investigate if New Orleans's lethality rate of 11.70 is a one-year anomaly, a long-term characteristic of violence in the city, or reflective of the changes brought about by Hurricane Katrina in 2005. Figure 4 presents the city's lethality rates for each year between 1996 and 2010 with the exception of 2005. The immediate effect of Katrina in that year makes it very difficult to calculate a lethality rate (or any other rate) that has much credibility because the true population figure is especially difficult to estimate.

The first important finding from figure 4 is that the 2010 lethality rate for New Orleans is not an outlier; the lowest recorded lethality rate, 5.41 in 1999, is significantly higher than the lowest rate recorded for any of the cities in figure 3. During the earlier years, the city's lethality rate varied within a narrow range of 5.41 in 1999 to 7.61 in 2000, and then rapidly spiked from 7.37 in 2001 to 10.75 in 2002. Except for a rate of 9.58 in 2007, it has remained above 10 for the past ten years, reaching a high of 13.11 in 2011.[7] Notably, the sharp increase in New Orleans's lethality rates occurred three years before Katrina. Thus, this tragedy can be ruled out as a cause for the high lethality rates in the Big Easy.

The consistently high lethality rates in New Orleans have not escaped prior notice. In 2003, Gordon Russell, a reporter for the *Times-Picayune*, published a story in the newspaper making this identical point; the city is characterized by a high number of homicides per capita but a relatively low rate of aggravated assaults in comparison to similar cities (Russell, 2013). Not much has changed during the ensuing decade.

It should be emphasized that the change in lethality rates in New Orleans before and after 2001 makes a significant difference. The mean lethality rate for the earlier period, 1996 to 2001, is 6.70. For the later period, 2002 to 2013, it is 11.69. If the lethality rate for the early years was in effect for 2012, the city would have experienced 118 homicides for a rate of 32.44. Viewed from a different perspective, seventy-five lives would not have been lost. Reducing the level of violence in New Orleans is obviously a very important policy goal, but as discussed in detail below, an explicit consideration of the unusual lethality of violence in the city expands the range of possible strategies for reducing its homicide rate.

7. Data for 2013 show that the lethality rate for New Orleans declined to .094.

Explaining the Lethality Rate in New Orleans[8]

First, it is possible that New Orleans's high lethality rate reflects reporting practices by the NOPD. It is unlikely that significant differences would exist in the classification of homicide between New Orleans and other large cities, but aggravated assaults are a more ambiguous crime. The line between simple assault (a misdemeanor that does not show up in the FBI Part I Crime Index) and an aggravated assault (a felony that is one of the seven Part I FBI Index offenses) can be blurry, but any classification scheme that would produce substantial differences in lethality rates across cities would have to be systemic. That is, they would need to be embedded in formal or informal department practices. Moreover, because New Orleans has recorded unusually high lethality rates for two decades, they would have had to be operative over numerous police administrations.

The NOPD has been under intense scrutiny for a number of internal and external problems, and a recent investigation by the U.S. Department of Justice found the department's Sex Crimes Unit adopted a pattern of behavior that classified a number of sexual assaults as miscellaneous complaints (United States Department of Justice, 2011: pp. 43-49). A more recent audit of NOPD cases by the Inspector General of New Orleans also reported a high percentage of forcible rape cases reviewed had been misclassified (Quatrevaux, 2014). The Department of Justice investigation does not raise any concern over the processing of assault cases by NOPD, however, and it is unlikely that assaults involving serious injuries, especially shootings, would be systematically downgraded to misdemeanor or non-criminal status. Admittedly, it is possible that a lower percentage of aggravated assaults are reported to the NOPD than to police departments in other cities. To our knowledge, the data to evaluate this possibility do not exist. At this time, we believe that the available evidence supports the validity of the reported differences in lethality rates between New Orleans and the comparison cities; they do not appear to be a statistical artifact resulting from a suppression of the number of aggravated assaults in the Crescent City.

8. Ideas expressed in this section have benefitted from personal communications with several individuals who have current or former ties to New Orleans, including newspaper reporters, academics, a former high-ranking NOPD officer, and other past and present residents of the city.

The Role of Firearms

As noted earlier, the presence of a firearm in a violent encounter enhances the odds of a murder (Weaver et al., 2004). The pivotal question is whether guns are more likely to be present in violent crimes in New Orleans than in other cities. FBI Return A data for 2007, 2008, and 2009 for New Orleans show that the weapon in 74 percent of robberies and 52 percent of aggravated assaults was a firearm.[9] In Orlando for the same years, 50 percent of robberies and 22 percent of aggravated assaults were committed with a firearm. Taken at face value, these numbers indicate that New Orleans has a substantially higher lethal violence rate than Orlando, in part, because a firearm is more likely to be present during violent crimes. There are two overlapping possibilities. The first is that there are simply many more guns in circulation in New Orleans than in Orlando, although both Florida and Louisiana are states with relatively few controls on gun purchases and carrying. The second is that the street culture in New Orleans is more violent than in Orlando, so potential offenders in New Orleans are more likely to be armed. Because a high percentage of individuals arrested for non-lethal, violent offences have a criminal record, their possession of a firearm is illegal *per se*.

New Orleans's current *NOLA for Life* campaign encompasses several initiatives, including Ceasefire, designed to reduce the motivation of potential offenders. Although a more systematic analysis of patterns of criminal gun use in New Orleans is needed, the presence of a firearm in 74 percent of robberies and 52 percent of aggravated assaults is a major concern. Enhancing police interventions to reduce the supply of firearms by removing guns from the streets and disrupting illegal gun markets in the city should be strongly considered.

The Role of Drugs

The estimate of 25 to 30 percent of New Orleans's homicides being defined as drug-related is very likely an undercount of the role of illegal drug markets in the city's violence. Structurally, or-

9. These data were provided to us by Laura Maggi, a reporter for the *Times-Pica-yune*.

ganized drug markets with a relatively small number of sellers are less conducive to violence than disorganized markets with many small organizations because of the increased chances for competition over market share (Goldstein, 1985).

The data are not available to gauge changes in the organization of a city's illegal drug markets over time, but significant population dislocations beginning before Katrina undoubtedly affected the territorial boundaries of drug markets in the Big Easy. In the 1990s, gangs in New Orleans were organized by political wards with housing projects serving as the focal points of their activities (McSeveney, 2012). Most of the buildings in the St. Thomas Project (Tenth Ward) were torn down by the end of 2001, and the Desire Project (Ninth Ward) was totally demolished by 2003. The likely result was that members of different gangs began living in closer proximity to one another causing a disruption in the established territories. The expected outcome would be an increase in drug-related violence that is more lethal than that stemming from other felonies (Weaver et al., 2004). Of course, these population dislocations were exacerbated by Hurricane Katrina, which also led to the abandonment of the Lafitte Projects (Seventh Ward). Furthermore, the aftermath of the storm changed the nature of the city's population, with a significant increase in the proportion of Hispanic residents and a corresponding decrease in the relative size of the African American population.

Although we suggest that the high number of drug organizations competing for market share of the illegal drug business in New Orleans contributes to the high lethality rate, policy recommendations are not straightforward. Almost all urban police departments place a high priority on disrupting outdoor drug markets as a matter of routine policy, but evaluations of these efforts have not shown a consistent benefit of reducing violent crime (Corsano et al., 2012).

The Role of Medical Resources

Several measures of medical resources have been used in lethality research. Many of these variables, the percent employed in medical professions for example, would not be expected to change very much over a short period of time or even across two decades in New Orleans or any other city. Although they may provide a partial explanation for the persistently high lethality rate in New Orleans, it is doubtful that they add any understanding for the sharp spike in lethality beginning in 2002. New Orleans is the home of two university medical schools, Louisiana State University and Tulane University, and has a noted medical complex located north of Interstate 10 near the Mercedes-Benz Superdome. There is little evidence to support the contention that an overall shortage of medical resources in New Orleans is behind its high rate of lethality.

Until 2005 when it suffered severe flooding damage from Katrina, the Level I trauma center for New Orleans was located in Charity Hospital at 1532 Tulane Avenue, on the other side of I-10 from the medical complex. After its closure, a trauma center opened in the Interim LSU Public Hospital at 2021 Perdido Street in the medical complex, approximately two-thirds of a mile from the old Charity Hospital Building.

One of the primary determinants of whether a seriously injured victim will live or die is thought to be the length of time between injury and arrival at a trauma center, and a crucial piece of data is the mean time between when an ambulance picks up a shooting or stabbing victim in the city and their arrival at the trauma center on Perdido Street. An analysis of four months of data from New Orleans Emergency Medical Services (NOEMS) showed no significant relationship between response times and the odds of a shooting resulting in a fatality, however. The authors are attempting to acquire comparable data for a longer time frame from both NOEMS and NOPD. A related research project would be to map the locations of homicide and aggravated assault incidents to determine if distance between the site of the injury and the trauma center affects a victim's chance of survival. It is noteworthy that the current trauma center is located in an area with little violent crime.

The Role of Road Networks

The bend of the Mississippi River that borders much of the city has contributed to New Orleans being referred to as the Crescent City as well as to a road network that differs from a traditional grid pattern. This is important as recent research has established a link between a more connected road network and a lowering in a city's lethality rate (Poole, 2013). Though the causal mechanism of this relationship is not yet concretely established, it is largely thought to be due to an increase in what Beland et al. (1998) called "locational accessibility" of emergency services, or the reduction in actual distance traveled between an incident and medical services. From this point of view, anything that disrupts a city's road network connectivity, such as a river or highway, could make travel through the network more time consuming and by extension decrease the accessibility of available medical resources.

In addition to the issue of road network connectivity, the secondary streets in New Orleans are in poor condition, and road repair is a recurrent political issue for the city. In fact, Mayor Landrieu (2012, p. 7) recently stated that "… our neighborhood interior streets are still in awful shape." The condition of streets does not directly contribute to the level of violence in a city, but has been shown to impact lethality (Poole, 2013). Poor streets increase the length of travel time to transport seriously injured residents to trauma centers, thereby increasing the odds of a death. We do not have access to data on street conditions as they relate to the locations of shootings and stabbings or the more heavily traveled routes ambulance drivers use to transport individuals to the trauma center. Again, this is an area that requires additional research.

Final Thoughts

The primary contributions of this chapter are twofold. First, we shed new light on the underlying social mechanisms producing the high homicide rates that have plagued New Orleans in the twenty-first century. Specifically, we show that the Big Easy's homicide problem is linked to an unusually high lethality rate that has characterized the city for at least the past two decades, predating the dislocations following Hurricane Katrina. Second, we identify a new puzzle. What aspects of New Orleans's social arrangements, culture, and infrastructure produce the atypically high lethality rate? Answering this question will require further research. Our assessment at this point is that investigations of New Orleans violence should focus on three areas:

- gun use in assaults and robberies,
- the (dis)organization of the illegal drug trade, and
- the provision of emergency medical services for violent crime victims.

During the past fifteen months, New Orleans has made significant progress in reducing the number of homicides, with reductions in both calendar year 2013 and the first quarter of 2014. The reasons for these reductions are being debated within New Orleans, with city officials pointing to Mayor Landrieu's *NOLA for Life* Campaign, a collection of anti-crime measures, as the primary trigger for homicide reductions (Martin, 2014). On the other hand, the introduction of new techniques for treating gunshot wounds, many of them developed by the military in Iraq and Afghanistan, by EMT and trauma center personnel increased the survival rate for shooting victims from 81 to 86 percent between 2012 and 2013 (Martin, 2014). Obviously, these explanations for the homicide decline are not mutually exclusive.

The overall recent trend in New Orleans violence is not positive, however. Shootings declined by a smaller rate than homicides in 2013 and, along with robberies and assaults, increased noticeably in the first quarter of 2014. The shooting of ten people, one of whom died, on Bourbon Street on June 29, 2014, brought the violence into the heart of the French Quarter and led local officials to call for state and federal assistance (Daley, 2014).

Turning to policy questions, the efforts to reduce homicide in New Orleans have focused on lowering the rate of violence, and these interventions should obviously be continued. An additional step would be implementing policies specifically designed to reduce the lethality rate. In some cases, this may involve placing more emphasis on specific violence reduction strategies. It may also require rearranging how emergency medical care is provided to the city's citizens who are victims of violence and repairing roads so that they can be more easily navigated. To implement a comprehensive strategy will require a significant investment in further research to unravel the sources of lethality in the Big Easy. A systematic research program will require more detailed data than are now available to develop a better understanding of lethality, however. For example, victims with multiple gunshot wounds and gunshots to the head and torso are more likely to die than those struck by a single bullet or whose wounds are in the limbs. Changes in the percentage of shooting victims with multiple wounds or head wounds in a city over time will impact its fatality rate, and the same logic applies to comparisons across cities.[10] There is some evidence that these types of potentially more fatal assaults are linked to drug-related shootings (Weaver et al., 2004), and their prevalence may be a barometer for what is happening on the street. Unfortunately, these data are not available in any published reports. A more nuanced understanding of homicide and lethality to develop effective interventions will depend on increased collaborations between researchers, law enforcement, and the medical establishment.

References

Ball, R.A., and G. David Curry. (1995). "The logic of definition in criminology: Purposes and methods for defining gangs." *Criminology* 33: 225-45.

Barlow, H., and L. Barlow. (1988). "More on the role of weapons in homicide violence." *Medicine and Law* 7: 347-58.

Beland, F., A.Lemay, and M. Boucher. (1998). "Patterns of visits to hospital-based emergency rooms." *Social Science & Medicine* 47: 165-79.

Bolden, C. (2013). Personal communication. October 8.

Blumstein, A. (1995). "Youth violence, guns, and the illicit-drug industry." *The Journal of Criminal Law and Criminology* 86: 10-36.

Chon, D.S. (2010). "Medical resources and national homicide rates: A cross-national assessment." *International Journal of Comparative and Applied Criminal Justice* 34: 97-118.

Corsano, N., E.D. Hunt, N.K. Hipple, and E.F. McGarrell. (2012). "The impact of drug market pulling levers policing on neighborhood violence: An evaluation of the High Point Drug Market Intervention." *Criminology & Public Policy* 11: 167-99.

Daley, Ken. (2014). "In wake of Bourbon Street shootings, Landrieu, Serpas ask for help." *Times Picayune*. Retrieved from http://www.nola.com/crime/index.ssf/2014/07/bourbon_street_shootings_landr.html

Doerner, W. (1983). "Why Does Johnny Reb die when shot? The impact of

---

10. We thank Dee Wood Harper for emphasizing this pivotal factor in explaining lethality.

medical resources upon lethality." *Sociological Inquiry* 53: 1-15.

Doerner, W.G. (1988). "The impact of medical resources on criminally induced lethality: A further examination." *Criminology* 36: 171-79.

Doerner, W., and J. Speir. (1986). "Stitch and sew: The impact of medical resources upon criminally induced lethality." *Criminology* 24: 319-30.

Federal Bureau of Investigation. (2013). *Crime in the United States 2012.* Retrieved from:http://www.fbigov/about-us/cjis/ucr/crime-in-the-u.s./2012.

Felson, R.B., and N. Painter-Davis. (2012). "Another cost of being a young Black male: Race, weaponry, and lethal outcomes in assaults." *Social Science Research* 41: 1241-53.

Gambino, R. (1977). *Vendetta.* New York: Doubleday.

Giacopassi, D., J. Sparger, and P. Stein. (1992). "The effects of emergency medical care on the homicide rate: Some additional evidence." *Journal of Criminal Justice* 20: 249-59.

Goldstein, P.J. (1985). "The drugs/violence nexus: A tripartite conceptual framework." *Journal of Drug Issues* 14: 493-506.

Gilbertson, D.C. (2009). "Are gangs a social problem?" *Journal of Gang Research* 16: 1-25.

Harris, A., S. Thomas, G. Fisher, and D. Hirsch. (2002). "Murder and medicine: The lethality of criminal assault 1960-1999." *Homicide Studies* 6: 128-66.

Jensen, G.F., and J. Thibodeaux. (2013). "The gang problem: Fabricated panics or real temporal patterns?" *Homicide Studies* 17: 275-90.

Landrieu, Mayor Mitchell J. (2012). State of the City Address.

Libby, N. (2009). "Predictors of firearm use and effects of weaponry on victim injury in violent crime: A criminal events approach." Unpublished doctoral dissertation, University of Central Florida.

Libby, N.E., and J. Corzine. (2007). "Lethal weapons: Effects of firearm types on the lethality of violent encounters." *Justice Research and Policy* 9: 113-37.

Libby, N.E., and J.D. Wright. (2009). "Influence of automatic firearms on the presence of multiple victims of violence: A research note." *Journal of Contemporary Criminal Justice* 25: 89-105.

Luckenbill, D. (1977). "Criminal homicide as a situated transaction." *Social Problems* 25: 176-86.

Maggi, L. (2011). Personal communication. April 25.

Martin, Naomi. (2014). "New Orleans murders fall again in 2013." *Times Picayune.* Retrieved from http://www.nola.com/crime/index.ssf /2014/01/2013_new_orleans_murder_rate_d.html.

McDaniel, Dawn Delfine. (2012). "Risk and protective factors associated with gang affiliation among high-risk youth: A public health approach." *Injury Prevention* 18: 253-58.

Melde, C., F.A. Esbensen, and T.T. Taylor. (2009). "'May piece be with you': A typological examination of the fear and victimization hypothesis of adolescent weapon carrying." *Justice Quarterly* 26: 348-76.

Nathens, A.B., G.J. Jurkovich, P. Cummings, F. Rivera, and R. Maier. (2000). "The Effect oforganized systems of trauma care on motor vehicle crash mortality." *Journal of the American Medical Association* 283: 1990-94.

O'Keefe, G.E., G.J. Jurkovich, M. Copass, and R. Maier. (1999). "Ten-year trend in survival and resource utilization at level I trauma center." *Annals of Surgery* 229: 409-15.

Phillips, M.D. (2012). "Assessing the impact of drug use and drug selling on violent offending in a panel of delinquent youth." *Journal of Drug Issues* 42: 298-316.

Poole, A.C. (2013). "Road networks, social disorganization, and lethality: An exploration of theory and an examination of covariates." Unpublished doctoral dissertation, University of Central Florida.

Quatrevaux, E.R. (2014). *A Performance Audit of the New Orleans Police Department's Uniform Crime Reporting of Forcible Rape A&R 13 PAU002.* The City of New Orleans: Office of Inspector General.

Regoeczi, W.C. (2003). "Studying the relationship between medical resources and homicide rates in an urban community." Paper presented at the annual meeting of the Homicide Research Working Group. Sacramento, CA.

Russell, G. (2013). Personal communication. March 12.

Sullivan, J.L., D.C. Novak, L. Aultman-Hall, and D.M. Scott. (2010). "Identifying critical road segments and measuring system-wide robustness in transportation networks with isolating links: A link-based capacity-reduction approach." *Transportation Research Part A* 44: 323-36.

United States Department of Justice. 2011. *Investigation of the New Orleans Police Department.* Washington, D.C.: United States Department of Justice, Civil Rights Division.

Taniguchi, E., F. Ferreira, and A. Nicholson. (2012). "A conceptual road network emergency model to aid emergency preparedness and response decision-making in the context of humanitarian logistics." *Social and Behavioral Sciences* 39: 307-20.

VanLandingham, M.J. (2007). "Murder rates in New Orleans, La, 2004-2006." *American Journal of Public Health* 97: 1614-16.

Weaver, G.S., J.E. Clifford Wittekind, L. Huff-Corzine, J. Corzine, T.A. Petee, and J.P. Jarvis. (2004). "Violent encounters: A criminal event analysis of lethal and nonlethal outcomes." *Journal of Contemporary Criminal Justice* 20: 348-68.

Wellford, C., B. Bond, and S. Goodison. (2011). *Crime in New Orleans: Analyzing crime trends and New Orleans' responses to crime.* Washington, D.C.: Bureau of Justice Statistics.

8 | The Importance of Communication, Coordination, and Context in Reducing Lethal Violence

Wendy Regoeczi

Although rates of homicide can fluctuate considerably from year to year, no law enforcement agency relishes having to be in the position of reporting high or increasing homicide rates. Some debate exists as to what role, if any, police can play in reducing crime and homicides. In this paper, I take the position that law enforcement can and should take an active role in contributing to efforts to reduce homicides in their community. I argue that this can be achieved through an emphasis on communication, coordination, and context. I begin by describing the general benefits to law enforcement agencies of addressing these three issues. I then apply them, where possible, to the current problem of lethal violence in New Orleans.

Context

Cities differ in their nature and structure of crime, crime trends, police-community relations, the character and prevalence of gangs, and other aspects of criminal activity. However, their differences extend to characteristics beyond the particular crime problems experienced within their jurisdiction. Cities also differ in their population demographics, geographical structure, race relations, and history, to name just a few. There is wide variation across urban areas, for example, in terms of their socio-economic characteristics (e.g., median income, percent living in poverty, unemployment rates), family structure (e.g., the proportion of households that are female-headed, the percent of the population that is single, married, or divorced), mobility (e.g. the percent of households that are rented vs. owned, how frequently people move in and out of residences), and demographic structure (e.g., the racial distribution of the population, the proportion of the population that are young males).

These differences can impact both the prevalence and nature of crime across cities. Existing research implies that some types of homicides have features that likely transcend geography. For example, a number of studies have shown that intimate partner homicides are largely driven by jealousy and the desire of men to have power and control over women (e.g., Belknap et al., 2012; Block and Block, 2012; Daly and Wilson, 1988). These patterns have emerged in studies across different cities (Belknap et al., 2012; Block and Block, 2012; Campbell, 1992) and countries (Daly and Wilson, 1988; Johnson and Hotton, 2003; Polk, 1994). Similarly, homicides of children are frequently the outcome of a pattern of physical abuse that goes too far, the inability of caregivers to cope with the stress of parenting, or Shaken Baby Syndrome (Christoffel, 1984; Smithey, 1998). It is unlikely that the dynamics of child homicides will vary much across geographical locations.

In contrast, other types of homicides tend to exhibit geographical variation in their nature and context (Hepburn and Voss, 1970). Circumstances preceding gang-related homicides, for example, vary among large U.S. cities (Center for Disease Control and Prevention, 2012). The contexts of homicides can also change over time, even within a single locality (Chauhan and Kois, 2012; Miethe and Regoeczi, 2004). For example, many urban areas across the United States experienced a notable shift in the nature of homicides towards gun-related shootings driven by drug market violence in the late 1980s and early 1990s. More recently, Chicago has experienced changes in the structure of gangs operating in the city, which has impacted lethal violence there (Davey, 2012). As a result, what is happening locally with respect to serious violent crime needs to be tracked and analyzed locally. Little local operational utility to respond to homicide trends can be found in aggregate analyses of the Federal Bureau of Investigation's Uniform Crime Reporting Program (UCR) data. While city-specific data are available through the UCR, the aggregate nature of the data, the lack of detail available about individual crime incidents, and the lag between the reporting and publication of the data are just a few of the reasons why.

Yet significant obstacles may exist at the local level to maintaining current assessments of crime patterns and trends on an ongoing basis. By the very nature of its work, law enforcement must devote its time and attention to addressing current crime problems in its jurisdiction. The demands placed on homicide units in large urban areas, for example, make it virtually impossible for the staff in those units to take time away from the constant flood of new cases to assess whether changes are occurring in the location and forms of homicides they are investigating. I believe that long term police-researcher partnerships are critical to an ongoing assessment of the current nature and patterns of serious violence within a given locality. The development of long term police-researcher partnerships can provide systematic means for continued analyses of what is happening locally with respect to crime patterns. While many law enforcement agencies have crime analysis capabilities, the types of analyses an academic partner can provide to the agency differs substantially from the daily functions of these units. In particular, an academic research partner can assess changes in multiple attributes of homicides simultaneously and can compare locally emerging trends and patterns with those occurring in comparable localities.

Academic researchers can also provide information to law enforcement partners on prevention and intervention strategies that have been demonstrated to be effective. It is a challenge for law enforcement executives to stay current in the field of criminal justice evaluation research; for academic researchers, in contrast, this work is part of their profession. While not all intervention strategies are likely to work equally well across cities given the variations previously discussed in terms of the nature and patterns of local crime problems, there are some that have been demonstrated to be effective across multiple jurisdictions (e.g. Operation Ceasefire, discussed in greater detail shortly). There is also a growing body of evaluation research showing what approaches are *not* effective in reducing violence. In order to effectively tackle serious violent crime problems at the local level, it is critical for law enforcement administrators to be armed with this body of information. Long term police-researcher partnerships are the most efficient means of ensuring that the identification and selection of violence prevention strategies at the local level are evidence based.

Finally, ongoing analyses of the local context of crime should not be limited to homicides. In spite of the attention they receive in the media, homicide is the rarest form of serious violence. Moreover, whether the outcome of an incident of serious violence is deemed an offense of aggravated assault or homicide can be influenced by factors beyond the primary intent of the perpetrator, including the speed at which medical attention is sought and the availability of trauma emergency medical care (Chon, 2010; Doerner and Speir, 1986). To know whether the context of violence within the city has shifted requires looking beyond homicide statistics to include at minimum aggravated assault, sexual assault, and robbery offenses.

To address the problem of lethal violence in New Orleans, a relatively simple but significant step that can be implemented by the New Orleans Police Department is to initiate the development of one or more police-researcher partnerships. There is no shortage of first-rate academic institutions in the New Orleans area whose faculty have expertise in both crime in general as well as violence and homicide more specifically.

Coordination

Cooperation and coordination among criminal justice and so-cial service agencies is critical when seeking to understand and ad-dress existing and emerging local crime problems. Coordination can achieve a number of goals. First, coordination can provide an improved ability to identify new and emerging trends. When agen-cies work together instead of in isolation or in competition, their anecdotal sense of changes in the nature and patterns of local crime trends take on greater reliability. Second, when agencies maintain an ongoing, open, and cooperative dialogue with each other they are better positioned to identify gaps in existing policies and pro-cedures and implement solutions to address them. Third, coordi-nation helps facilitate a greater understanding of the roles of each individual agency within the criminal justice process, including the limitations and obstacles experienced by persons working within those agencies. This can facilitate more positive working relation-ships among agencies, reduce finger pointing between them, and help create a united front in the war against violent crime.

One means of improving coordination is through the use of fa-tality review teams. All states in the U.S. have created review teams to examine child fatalities, the majority of which are state mandated (Bunting and Reid, 2005). Somewhat fewer require an in-depth examination of deaths resulting from domestic violence. I am aware of only one city that currently uses a review system for *all* homicides committed in their jurisdiction. Grounded in a public health approach, the Milwaukee Homicide Review Commission engages in a review of all homicides in the city using a multi-level, multi-agency system (O'Brien, Woods, and Cisler, 2007). The goals of this commission are three-fold: "(1) to gain a better understanding of homicide through strategic problem analysis, (2) to develop innovative, effective responses, and (3) to focus limited enforcement and intervention activities on identifiable risks" (O'Brien, Woods, and Cisler, 2007: p. 385).

One aspect of the review process in Milwaukee is to bring together all criminal justice professionals on a monthly basis to share information on cases, assess whether and how homicides could have been prevented, and identify ways of improving existing practices and create novel approaches to preventing further violence. The pilot test of the Milwaukee Homicide Review Commission, which was implemented initially in three of seven Milwaukee police districts, revealed that improved communication among local, state, and federal criminal justice agencies was a significant benefit of the process (O'Brien, Woods, and Cisler, 2007).

Under the leadership of Ronal Serpas, authorization was approved for New Orleans to be one of the first cities in the U.S. to implement and replicate the Milwaukee Homicide Review Commission. Through the years 2011-2014 the NOPD operated and staffed the replication and expansion of this program under the Mayor's Strategic Plan to Reduce Murders.

Communication

For many years now in the United States, deterrence has been a prevailing strategy relied upon for reducing crime. Born out of the Classical School of criminology and the writings of Cesare Beccaria and Jeremy Bentham, deterrence theory assumes that crime can be deterred by making punishments severe, swift, and certain (Akers and Sellers, 2004). Examples of current criminal justice policy rooted in a deterrence philosophy are plentiful, including the use of the death penalty, the development of three strikes laws, the implementation of mandatory minimum sentences, and the increase in eligibility for transferring youths to adult court. However, efforts to increase the severity of punishment have shown only limited success in reducing serious violent crime (Tonry, 2008).

Studies on the death penalty, for example, generally find that capital punishment is not a more effective deterrent than life without parole (Dölling, Entorf, Hermann, and Rupp, 2009; Sorenson, Wrinkle, Brewer, and Marquart, 1999; Tonry, 2008). Evaluations of the impacts of mandatory minimum sentences for deterring offending have produced mixed findings with respect to expected reductions in violent crime. There is also evidence to suggest that reductions produced by implementing mandatory minimum sentences for some forms of violent crime are negated by displacements into other related offenses (Pennsylvania Commission on Crime and Delinquency, 1984). Research on the ability of three strikes laws to deter individuals from committing serious violent crimes generally finds little to no immediate impact from the implementation of these laws on violent crime (e.g., Ramirez and Crano, 2003). Furthermore, in several studies the use of three strikes laws has even been found to *increase* homicide rates (Kovandzic, Sloan, and Vieraitis, 2002; Marvell and Moody, 2001).

In contrast, efforts seeking to increase the certainty of punishment have shown greater promise. Successful programs such as Boston's Operation Ceasefire are grounded on this premise. They place a strong emphasis on a combination of certainty and swiftness of punishment, with communication of such followed by action. For example, Operation Ceasefire relied on a strategy of "pulling levers," where attention was focused on a small group of individuals driving much of the crime. These chronic gang members were given a message of no tolerance for violence and every available legal "lever" was used to respond to violence when it took place in order to produce a swift and intense response (Braga, Kennedy, Waring, and Piehl, 2001). Evaluations of this approach find that when offenders are provided with the message that any legal infraction committed *will* result in consequences, groups of offenders begin to police themselves (Kennedy, 2012).

Increasing clearance rates for serious violent crimes constitutes another means of increasing the certainty of punishment. Solving a higher proportion of homicides in New Orleans (and elsewhere) would achieve several things. Justice for victims and families is an obvious benefit. Prevention of opportunities for unrestrained retaliation is another. The recent study of crime in New Orleans funded by the Bureau of Justice Assistance revealed that approximately one quarter of homicides in the city are revenge killings (Wellford, Bond, and Goodison, 2011). Increased clearance rates could also function as a deterrent to those with a propensity for violence. From a deterrence perspective, homicide rates and solvability rates may represent two sides of the same problem, so improving solve rates may be one avenue for reducing homicides.

With respect to the situation in New Orleans, it will be important for law enforcement administrators to view the high rates of homicide incidents and low rates of homicide clearances as sharing some of the same underlying causes. For example, trust in the police and informal social control are likely key factors influencing both types of rates. In cities that have experienced massive natural disasters, social control can become unstable. Residents will be more apt to take the law into their own hands, producing a greater reliance on self-help (Anderson, 1999; Black, 1976). In turn, this may reduce reliance on and trust in the police (Riedel and Jarvis, 1998). The disruption to neighborhoods caused by disasters such as hurricanes and tornadoes can cause significant damage to levels of collective efficacy within those neighborhoods. A number of negative consequences may result, including feelings of despair and alienation. Residents may lack feelings of empowerment to address local crime problems (Sampson, Raudenbush, and Earls, 1997).

In a forthcoming paper in *Justice Quarterly*, John Jarvis and I develop and partially test a theoretical model in which we apply concepts of social disorganization theory to explain homicide outcomes (figure 1) (Regoeczi and Jarvis, forthcoming). Contemporary versions of social disorganization theory posit that neighborhoods with high levels of concentrated disadvantage and residential instability are characterized by low levels of collective efficacy (Sampson, Raudenbush, and Earls, 1997). In particular, these types of neighborhood conditions are believed to weaken social institutions and the ability of residents to exercise informal social control by regulating the behavior of individuals in the neighborhood, thereby reducing social cohesion and mutual trust (Bursik and Grasmick, 1993; Kornhauser, 1978; Sampson 2002; Sampson and Groves, 1989; Sampson, Raudenbush, and Earls, 1997; Simcha-Fagan and

Schwartz, 1986; Warner, 2007). Prior research establishes links between these mechanisms and neighborhood rates of homicide and
serious violent crime (e.g., Sampson, Raudenbush, and Earls 1997).
In the forthcoming article, we find support for our argument that
these same mechanisms may influence the outcomes of homicide
cases, including whether the incidents result in the arrest and conviction of one or more suspects.

Figure 1*
**Theoretical Model Displaying Mechanisms through which Social
Disorganization Impacts Homicide Outcomes**

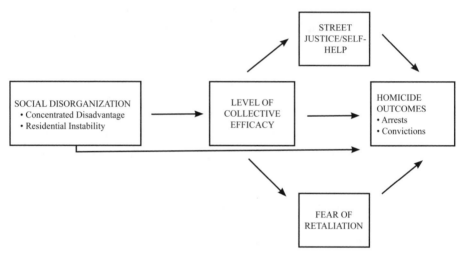

*from Regoeczi and Jarvis (forthcoming). "Beyond the social production of homicide rates: Extended
social disorganization theory to explain homicide case outcomes." *Justice Quarterly*

We tested the model by conducting both qualitative and multilevel analyses on data collected from homicide cases occurring
in Cleveland between 1998 and 2002 (N=495 offenders). Through
the qualitative analysis of the homicide narratives we were able
to identify support for the intervening mechanisms we theorized
were impacting homicide arrests and convictions, including reduced motivation to cooperate with law enforcement investigations, residents not knowing the identity of suspects, reliance on
street justice and self-help in resolving disputes, and fear of retaliation. The multilevel analyses of variation in the likelihood of arrest

and conviction in homicide cases across Cleveland neighborhoods uncovered a somewhat complex set of relationships in the sense that the influence of neighborhood characteristics interacted with the victim's race and incident characteristics in predicting these homicide outcomes.

New Orleans would benefit from a similar assessment of its homicide data in order to give some important context to its current homicide clearance rate, which hovers around the 50 percent mark (Wellford, Bond, and Goodison, 2011). An in-depth, qualitative assessment of homicide case files for a sample of open and closed cases will be necessary to shed some light on the specific obstacles faced by New Orleans police officers investigating homicides occurring in the city. By determining to what extent our proposed theoretical model holds in New Orleans, the New Orleans Police Department will be able to identify what specific issues should be targeted for improving its homicide clearance rate.

This is another area where police-researcher partnerships can be mutually beneficial. Pulling such detailed information from homicide case files will be too time-consuming for homicide detectives juggling on-going investigations, but researchers are specifically trained for this type of data collection and analysis and can assist law enforcement agencies with both tasks. At the same time, researchers benefit from the ability to replicate studies testing theoretical models that have been supported by research conducted in one or a handful of other urban areas. This is critical to assessing the generalizability of such models.

I believe the model we present in the forthcoming paper that applies concepts from social disorganization theory to understanding homicide outcomes could be further extended to explain both the production of homicide incidents and homicide outcomes simultaneously. In other words, it is very possible that (1) homicide incidents and homicide outcomes (arrests and convictions) are both influenced by the same kinds of neighborhood dynamics and (2) that levels of homicide incidents influence levels of homicide outcomes at the neighborhood level. Below I present a revised theoretical model that incorporates these points (figure 2).

Figure 2:
Theoretical Model Displaying Mechanisms through which Social
Disorganization Impacts Rates and Outcomes Outcomes

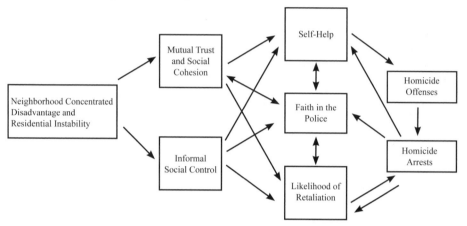

In the proposed model, levels of concentrated disadvantage (e.g., poverty, unemployment, family disruption) and residential instability (e.g. few homeowners, frequent population turnover) have a negative impact on the level of mutual trust, social cohesion, and informal social control occurring among residents in those neighborhoods. This in turn produces a number of undesirable consequences, including an increased reliance on self-help, reduced faith in the police, and an increased likelihood of retaliation. Rates of homicide and serious violent crime will be amplified under these conditions. These same factors can also interfere with the ability of law enforcement to successfully investigate these incidents through their erosion of deterrence.

Where trust in the police is lacking or hampered, residents are more likely to feel the need to resolve their own disputes by relying on either informal or alternative methods for resolving conflicts that are often violent in nature rather than seeking assistance from formal authorities (Anderson, 1999; Cooney, 2009; Kubrin and Weitzer, 2003). This lack of legitimacy of police results not only in increased violence, but reduces the willingness of residents to cooperate with police (Kane, 2005; Riedel and Jarvis, 1998; Warner, 2007), which in turn can impact the ability of police to successfully investigate violent crimes and the ability of prosecutors to put together strong enough cases to secure convictions. Where a greater number of residents engage in self-help in response to victimization, rates of homicide and other forms of serious violent crime (e.g., aggravated assault, robbery) will be higher, and solve rates for these crimes will likely be lower. Furthermore, recent research outside of the United States suggests that higher levels of police legitimacy, in turn, are related to increased levels of collective efficacy (Kochel, 2012), reflected in the bi-directional arrow between mutual trust and social cohesion and faith in the police in figure 2.

Law enforcement can intervene in this cycle at various points. If done effectively, this could reduce the rate of homicide while also improving the homicide clearance rate. One place this can be accomplished is with respect to faith in the police. Research indicates that trust in police can be improved through a variety of means, some of which target more positive interactions between police and citizens (e.g., Becton et al., 2005; Pope, Jones, Cook, and Waltrip, 2007) and others which focus on police communication with the public more generally (e.g., Hohl, Bradford, and Stanko, 2010). The implementation of Transparent Internal Affairs processes are another means through which trust between the community and law enforcement can be improved and maintained (International Association of Chiefs of Police, 2010).

A second means of intervention is through the development of a homicide commission, as described previously. Incorporating a model such as that used in Milwaukee could accomplish a variety of things related to this cycle. First, the Milwaukee model is unique to the extent that it provides community members an explicit role in the process. More specifically, the fourth level of the process involves semi-annual meetings with community members during which information generated from the reviews is shared with these individuals, who in turn may provide additional information about the cases. Community members are also afforded the opportunity to provide their feedback on proposed and existing approaches for violence prevention and to provide suggestions for other strategies. By openly seeking participation and feedback from community members, faith in the police could and should improve.

Implementing a multi-level, multi-agency review of all homicide cases in New Orleans could also intervene in the cycle by simply producing a reduction in lethal and near-lethal violence within the city. O'Brien, Woods, and Cisler's (2007) pilot study of the Mil-

waukee Homicide Review Commission revealed a significant reduction in tavern-related homicides and shootings following the
implementation of a recommendation generated by the Commission's work. They also noted a decline in homicide counts in general in the targeted districts whereas counts were increasing in the
other districts.

Finally, the development of a Homicide Review Commission in
New Orleans may also improve the solvability rate of homicides in
the city, thus providing another point of intervention in the cycle.
The improved communication among criminal justice agencies —
and between criminal justice agencies and the community — should
improve information sharing and possibly generate new leads in
homicide investigations.

Conclusion

Law enforcement can and should play a role in reducing homicides. The offense category of homicide includes a diverse array of
incidents and circumstances that share a common ending — death.
Different types of homicides will lend themselves to different types
of violence reduction strategies. For example, the types of policies
that need to be implemented to reduce homicides of children or intimate partner homicides will differ from those that seek to reduce
lethal violence among individuals involved in illegal drug markets.
More attention needs to be paid to the contexts surrounding homicide incidents. These will vary by place, but also can change over
time. For law enforcement to be effective in reducing and preventing homicide, an on-going assessment of the context in which homicides are occurring is necessary. Police-researcher partnerships
can be extremely valuable in this on-going effort to be vigilant in
analyzing the changing dynamics of homicide in New Orleans and
other cities across the country.

References

Akers, Ronald L., and Christine S. Sellers. (2004). *Criminological Theories:
    Introduction, Evaluation, and Application.* 4th edition. Los Angeles, CA:
    Roxbury Publishing.

Anderson, Elijah. (1999). *Code of the Street*. New York: W.W. Norton.

Becton, J., Leslie Meadows, Rachel Tears, Michael Charles, and Ralph Ioimo. (2005). "Can citizen police academies influence citizens' beliefs and perceptions?" *Public Management* (May): 20-23.

Belknap, Joanne, Dora-Lee Larson, Margaret L. Abrams, Christine Garcia, and Kelly Anderson-Block. (2012). "Types of intimate partner homicides committed by women: Self-defense, proxy/retaliation, and sexual proprietariness." *Homicide Studies* 16: 359-79.

Black, Donald J. (1976). *The Behavior of Law*. New York: Academic Press.

Block, Carolyn Rebecca, and Richard Block. (2012). "Margo Wilson's contribution to the Chicago Homicide Dataset: Sexual rivalry and sexual jealousy." *Homicide Studies* 16: 404-27.

Braga, Anthony A., David M. Kennedy, Elin J. Waring, and Anne Morrison Piehl. (2001). "Problem-oriented policing, deterrence, and youth violence: An evaluation of Boston's Operation Ceasefire." *Journal of Research in Crime & Delinquency* 38: 195-226.

Bunting, Lisa, and Colin Reid. (2005). "Reviewing child deaths: Learning from the American experience." *Child Abuse Review* 14: 82-96.

Bursik, Robert J. Jr., and Harold G. Grasmick. (1993). *Neighborhoods and Crime*. New York: Lexington Books.

Campbell, Jacqueline C. (1992). "If I can't have you, no one can: Issues of power and control in homicide of female partners." In Jill Radford and Diana E. H. Russell (Eds.), *Femicide: The Politics of Woman Killing*. New York: Twayne.

Center for Disease Control and Prevention. (2012). "Gang homicides – Five U.S. cities, 2003-2008." *Morbidity and Mortality Weekly Report* 61: 46-51.

Chauhan, Preeti, and Lauren Kois. (2012). *Homicide by Neighborhood: Mapping New York City's Violent Crime Drop*. New York: Research and Evaluation Center, John Jay College of Criminal Justice, City University of New York.

Christoffel, Katherine K. (1984). "Homicide in childhood: A public health problem in need of attention." *American Journal of Public Health* 74: 68-70.

Chon, Don Soo. (2010). "Medical resources and national homicide rates: A cross-national assessment." *International Journal of Comparative and Applied Criminal Justice* 34: 97-118.

International Association of Chiefs of Police. (2010). *Building Trust between the Police and the Citizens They Serve: An Internal Affairs Promising Practices Guide for Local Law Enforcement*. Washington, D.C.: U.S. Department of Justice Office of Community Oriented Policing Services.

Cooney, Mark. (2009). *Is Killing Wrong*. Charlottesville, VA: University of Virginia Press.

Daly, Martin, and Margo Wilson. (1988). *Homicide*. New York: Aldine de Gruyter.

Davey, Monica. (2012, June 26). "Rate of killings rises 38 percent in Chicago in '12." *New York Times*. A1.

Doerner, William G., and John C. Speir. (1986). "Stitch and sew: The impact of medical resources upon criminally induced lethality." *Criminology* 24 (2): 319-30.

Dölling, Dieter, Horst Entorf, Dieter Hermann, and Thomas Rupp. (2009). "Is deterrence effective? Results of a meta-analysis of punishment." *European Journal on Criminal Policy & Research* 15: 201-24.

Hepburn, John, and Harwin L. Voss. (1970). "Patterns of criminal homicide: A comparison of Chicago and Philadelphia." *Criminology* 8: 21-45.

Hohl, Katrin, Ben Bradford, and Elizabeth A. Stanko. (2010). "Influencing trust and confidence in the London Metropolitan Police." *British Journal of Criminology* 50: 491-513.

Johnson, Holly, and Tina Hotton. (2003). "Losing control: Homicide risk in estranged and intact intimate relationships." *Homicide Studies* 7: 58-84.

Kane, Robert J. (2005). "Compromised police legitimacy as a predictor of violence crime in structurally disadvantaged communities." *Criminology* 43: 469-98.

Kennedy, David. (2012). Stopping the killing in New Orleans: Focus, legitimacy, and common ground. Preventing Lethal Violence in New Orleans Symposium. October 26. Loyola University, New Orleans.

Kochel, Tammy Rinehart. (2012). "Can police legitimacy promote collective efficacy?" *Justice Quarterly* 29 (3): 384-419.

Kornhauser, Ruth R. (1978). *Social Sources of Delinquency: An Appraisal of Analytic Methods*. Chicago: University of Chicago Press.

Kovandzic, Tomislav V., John J. Sloan, III, and Lynne M. Vieraitis. (2002). "Unintended consequences of politically popular sentencing policy: The homicide promoting effects of 'three strikes' in U.S. cities (1980-1999)." *Criminology & Public Policy* 1: 399-424.

Kubrin, Charis, and Ronald Weitzer. (2003). "Retaliatory homicide: Concentrated disadvantage and neighborhood culture." *Social Problems* 50: 157-80.

Marvell, Thomas B., and Carlisle E. Moody. (2001). "The lethal effects of three strikes laws." *The Journal of Legal Studies* 30: 89-106.

Miethe, Terance D., and Wendy C. Regoeczi. (2004). *Rethinking Homicide: Exploring the Structure and Process Underlying Deadly Situations.* New York: Cambridge University Press.

O'Brien, Mallory, Laurie Woods, and Ron Cisler. (2007). "The Milwaukee Homicide Review Commission: An interagency collaborative process to reduce homicide." *Wisconsin Medical Journal* 106: 385-89.

Pennsylvania Commission on Crime and Delinquency. (1984.) *Preliminary Assessment of the Deterrent Effects of Mandatory Sentencing – Robbery, Aggravated Assault, and Driving Under the Influence.* Harrisburg, PA.

Polk, Kenneth. (1994). *When Men Kill: Scenarios of Masculine Violence.* New York: Cambridge University Press.

Pope, Jacqueline, Tena Jones, Shannon Cook, and Bill Waltrip. (2007). "Citizen's police academies: Beliefs and perceptions regarding the program." *Applied Psychology in Criminal Justice* 3: 42-53.

Ramirez, Juan R., and William D. Crano. (2003). "Deterrence and incapacitation: An interrupted time-series analysis of California's three-strikes law." *Journal of Applied Social Psychology* 33: 110-44.

Regoeczi, Wendy C., and John P. Jarvis. (Forthcoming). "Beyond the social production of homicide rates: Extending social disorganization theory to explain homicide case outcomes." *Justice Quarterly.*

Riedel, Marc, and John Jarvis. (1998). "The decline of arrest clearances for criminal homicide: Causes, correlates, and third parties." *Criminal Justice Policy Review* 9: 279-306.

Sampson, Robert J. (2002). "Organized for what? Recasting theories of social (dis)organization." In E. Waring and D. Weisburd (Eds.), *Advances in Criminological Theory.* Vol. 10. pp. 95-110.

Sampson, Robert J., and W. Byron Groves. (1989). "Community structure and crime: Testing social-disorganization theory." *American Journal of Sociology* 94: 774-802.

Sampson, Robert J., Stephen W. Raudenbush, and Felton Earls. (1997). "Neighborhoods and violent crime: A multilevel study of collective efficacy." *Science* 277 (August 15): 918-24.

Simcha-Fagan, Ora and Joseph Schwartz. (1986). "Neighborhood and delinquency: An assessment of contextual effects." *Criminology* 24: 667-704.

Smithey, Martha. (1998). "Infant homicide: Victim/offender relationship and causes of death." *Journal of Family Violence* 13: 285-97.

Sorenson, Jon, Robert Wrinkle, Victoria Brewer, and James Marquart. (1999). "Capital punishment and deterrence: Examining the effect of executions on murder in Texas." *Crime and Delinquency* 45: 481-93.

Tonry, Michael. (2008). "Learning from the limitations of deterrence research." *Crime & Justice* 37: 279-311.

Warner, Barbara D. (2007). "Directly intervene or call the authorities? A study of forms of neighborhood social control within a social disorganization framework." *Criminology* 45: 99-130.

Wellford, Charles, Brenda J. Bond, and Sean Goodison. (2011). "Crime in New Orleans: Analyzing Crime Trends and New Orleans' Responses to Crime." Bureau of Justice Assistance Report. U.S. Department of Justice. [media.nola.crime_impact/other/BJA Crime in New Orleans Report March 2011.pdf.].

9 The Future of Lethal Violence Abatement in New Orleans

Ronal Serpas

Nearly three hundred years old, New Orleans is one of America's most unique and historic places. For centuries New Orleans has been a city steeped in the history of how American cities grew and prospered. Starting as a walking city in the historic French Quarter, falling under the rule of Spanish and French governments before being purchased by the United States, the city grew to become an anchor for national and international shipping at the Port of New Orleans. As important, New Orleans thrived as a city that embraced different cultures, music . . . and of course, food. New Orleans reached its most populous period in the 1960s with more than 600,000 residents; however, for the following four decades or more New Orleans would fall dramatically in population, as nearby cities with direct access to the Gulf of Mexico shipping lanes chipped away at the preeminence of the Port of New Orleans. Beginning in the mid-1980s, the city witnessed an explosion in violence, particularly murder, among young African American men.

As with many phenomenona, there can be multiple causes to explain the effect. In many police circles, the explosion of "crack" cocaine in the mid-1980s in American cities fueled the subsequent skyrocketing rates of violence, and most particularly murder, in our cities. The crack cocaine drug market was viewed as a key culprit. New Orleans was no exception. Between the mid-1980s and 1994 the New Orleans murder rate became increasingly more alarming—both to the people of New Orleans and as a comparison to other cities in America. Capped with 421[1] murders in 1994, the city of New Orleans was virtually at the precipice of a complete collapse, on the issue of murder and its prevalence in New Orleans, as

---

1. Throughout this document, the numbers of murders in New Orleans in any given year was sourced from New Orleans Police Department records.

a place believed to be a First World city.

In October 1996 the New Orleans Police Department, under reform by then-Mayor Marc Morial and Richard Pennington, an out-of-town Police Superintendent appointed in 1994, adopted and implemented a new policing strategy originating in New York City called *Compstat*. This style of policing relied on timely and accurate data, effective tactics, rapid deployment, and relentless follow-up through the use of weekly "accountability" meetings of police field commanders. Between 1997 and 2000, the New Orleans Police Department recorded dramatic decreases in murder, violent crime, and overall crime. It is widely suggested that during the years 1994 through 1999 the number of murders in New Orleans were cut in half. It is not the purpose of this chapter to dismiss the various, and often sound arguments, about what is the extent to which a police department can reduce crime, or murder specifically. This recap of events is just meant to set the stage for changing winds that were clearly going to impact the city and the efforts that were undertaken from May 2010 forward to reorient the New Orleans Police Department and the city of New Orleans to engage in the fight to make New Orleans a City of Peace.

There were ominous signs of slippage in the fight to reduce murder by the end of the year 2000, and questions began to circulate as to what part of the dramatic decline of murder in New Orleans followed a national trend that was witnessed during the same years. It has been widely reported that during the years 1994-2000 the nation witnessed a sustained and dramatic decline in murder, perhaps as much as a 40 percent reduction in murder. While New Orleans surpassed a 40 percent reduction with just over a 61 percent reduction during the period 1994 (421 murders) through 1999 (162 murders), in the year 2000 there were 205 murders recorded, an increase of 26 percent compared to 1999. Unquestionably from the year 2000 forward, murder began a slow but steady rise. This change occurred as the New Orleans Police Department reached its highest level of officer staffing in its history and as the city of New Orleans saw very little change in some of the typical social disorganization variables (single female head of household, under eighteen age cohort, poverty at the family level, school achievement, etc.) that might offer explanation.

All that was known about New Orleans and its continuing fight to reduce murder was laid to waste with the landfall of Hurricane Katrina on August 28-29, 2005. In the immediate days following the storm significant disorder prevailed in the city. And as has been evidenced by numerous criminal civil rights violation cases tried in the Federal Court, significant disorder within the New Orleans Police Department hindered its ability to function. The police department and the city were virtually laid to waste in the aftermath of the storm. In the years following Hurricane Katrina, the New Orleans Police Department slowly, but inevitably, fell into an advanced state of stagnation in its operation and into isolation from the very people the department was sworn to protect and serve —the people of New Orleans. This state would continue until the election of a new mayoral administration and the appointment of a new police superintendent in May of 2010.

The first decisions related to the New Orleans Police Department and what to do regarding its apparent disconnect from the community, its disconnect from a coherent strategy to implement community policing and the numerous federal civil rights trials in the days preceding and following Hurricane Katrina that were imminent, was to request a full investigation by the U. S. Department of Justice Civil Rights Team and to appoint new leadership in the New Orleans Police Department. Newly-elected Mayor Mitchell Landrieu undertook both steps with deliberate dispatch. By May 2010, new police leadership was in place, and by the summer of 2010 the civil rights investigation by the Department of Justice was underway. These two factors were critical in laying the subsequent ground work for planning and implementing the future abatement of lethal violence in New Orleans. In this chapter, although not exhaustive of all the strategies designed, implemented, and realigned as appropriate over time, four strategies will be discussed that bare directly on the central question—reducing lethal violence in one of America's grandest cities. New Orleans. These four strategies are: (1) The rebuilding of the New Orleans Police Department—First Steps, issued August 23, 2010; (2) the Multi-Agency Gang Task Force and Street Gangs Unit implemented in November 2012 as a component of Mayor Landrieu's *NOLA for Life* initiative (*NOLA for Life*, 2012); (3) the use of advanced social network analysis; and, (4) the use of sophisticated citizen satisfaction surveys of the New Orleans Police Department's performance and public perceptions of that performance.

Rebuilding the New Orleans Police Department
— First Steps: A 65 Point Plan to Reform the Department

In the summer of 2010 the Department of Justice civil rights investigation was not the only assessment being made of the New Orleans Police Department. Also being identified were the immediate, mid-range, and long-range changes that must be made to bring the department back into at least the mainstream of police leadership, crime fighting, and implementing Community Policing in earnest. The new superintendent issued a comprehensive plan in August of 2010 entitled *Rebuilding the New Orleans Police Department — First Steps* (see appendix A), which has often been referred to as the "65 Point Plan" to rebuild the New Orleans Police Department.

The plan at its release noted areas that had already been acted upon in the first ninety days of the new police administration's time in office, and it outlined new steps that would be implemented in the months and years ahead. The 65 Point Plan to reform the department begins with ten principled statements to inform and guide the document as well as to inform and guide the cultural changes desired within the New Orleans Police Department. As stated in the plan, these ten guiding principles were:

> The New Orleans Police Department will no longer tell neighborhoods what their problems are; instead, the NOPD will listen, collaborate and respond proactively. We will do that by:
>
> 1.   Respecting the spectacular diversity of our community and our employees, as well as respecting the value of our most important resource – the men and women of the NOPD.
> 2.   Maintaining a zero tolerance for untruthful, unprofessional, unethical or illegal behavior of any employee.
> 3.   Embracing the philosophy of Community Policing to inform and prioritize our crime fighting and quality of life initiatives throughout the City of New Orleans.
> 4.   Using the weekly accountability meeting known as Compstat to hold all commands accountable to this philosophy to ensure department-wide implementation.
> 5.   Employing decentralized assignment of personnel to district commands, as a first choice, to provide district commanders au-

thority, autonomy, resources and accountability to take the initiative in meeting demands for service from New Orleans' neighborhoods and communities.

6.   Engaging each neighborhood in collaborative problem solving, prioritize our response, apply the response with relentless follow up, and evaluate results.

7.   Auditing crime reporting mechanisms vigorously to ensure accuracy and confidence and work tirelessly to encourage the community to report all crime that is known.

8.   Focusing on proactive policing as our first priority to interrupt crime before it happens while ensuring the timeliest response to emergency calls for service as possible.

9.   Producing the highest quality investigations and stand ready to contribute in securing convictions of those who have made choices harmful to public safety.

10. Working collaboratively with local, state and federal law enforcement and prosecutorial offices to leverage any and all resources to advance public safety in New Orleans.

These ten principles will guide how the New Orleans Police Department will implement the 65 point plan for reform and the philosophy of Community Policing. The following sections on crime fighting, community outreach and transparency, integrity and accountability and hiring, training and labor relations detail 65 specific points which are the 'First Steps' of rebuilding the New Orleans Police Department" (p.1).

Just as the title suggests, when released in August of 2010, these first steps began the long process of reform of the New Orleans Police Department that would also include the work done during the Department of Justice civil rights investigations, the Consent Decree negotiation process, the final U.S. District Court approval of the Consent Decree itself in January 2013, and the implementation of the approved Consent Decree.

The first component, *crime fighting*, included twenty-three specific action items to realign the existing NOPD focus on crime fighting to a more modern and data driven approach. In fact, the hallmark of the NOPD's crime fighting effort was the use of Compstat practices;[2] however, the Compstat data analysis sets, and the week-ly "Compstat book" that was created to advise and hold District Commanders accountable was substantially unchanged from the "Compstat book" that was used to lead NOPD weekly accountabil-ity meetings in July of 2001. In other words, by the summer of 2010 the NOPD had not updated its key accountability tool in nearly nine years to adapt to and accommodate changing policing techniques (e.g., Data Driven Approaches to Crime and Traffic Safety), nor had the NOPD successfully completed a nascent project of installing and using twenty-first century crime analytic software tools such as *Omega CrimeView*, or even considered purchasing deployment soft-ware packages such as *Corona Ops Force Deploy* so that rationale and logically based spatial and temporal deployment of first responder police officers could be made.

It was also evident and clear in the summer of 2010 that the New Orleans Police Department's centralized investigative units—homicide, sex crimes, firearms examinations, etc.—were woefully underprepared to produce effective, reliable, and timely investiga-tive outcomes. The 65 Point Plan called for a major overhaul of these three units, and specific assistance was requested from state and national experts to assess these units and give advice on best prac-tices to adopt as they were realigned to meet more current trends.

In all, the twenty-three specific steps were just a beginning in making fundamental and dramatic changes in the day-to-day op-erations of the New Orleans Police Department's crime fighting ef-forts.

The next component, community outreach and transparency, included nineteen specific steps to be taken to reverse what had become a very insular New Orleans Police Department with dete-riorating support among the public at large and the local media in specific. For example, the standard response from the New Orleans

---

2. The NOPD has been widely reported as the first police agency in the United States to adopt the New York Police Department Compstat Model of policing, holding its first regularly scheduled weekly Compstat meeting on October 18, 1996. Then Deputy Superintendent and Chief of Operations Ronal Serpas was responsible for leading this meeting and incorporating the Compstat style of accountability into the daily management of the NOPD. Serpas retired from the NOPD in July of 2001, and was appointed the Chief of the Washington State Patrol in July 2001 where he served until being appointed Chief of the Metropolitan Nashville Police Department in January 2004, serving in Nashville until appointed Superintendent of the NOPD in May 2010.

Police Department's Public Affairs Office was "no comment" to virtually all media related requests for information. The department's public crime mapping software was antiquated, not timely, and generally perceived to be inaccurate. Essentially, the New Orleans Police Department had cut off normal and expected communication with the "outside" world . . . unquestionably the most fundamental precept of community policing that a department must embrace is transparency. Several of the specific steps put into place were specifically tailored to reverse this position: (1) opening to the public weekly Compstat meetings at the department and patrol district level; (2) creating a logical process for responding to media inquiries and making available for comment members of the department with expertise or specific knowledge to inquiries being made; (3) utilizing new and innovative technology such as *Omega CrimeView* to provide for publicly released crime mapping that was timely and accurate; and (4) initiating a citizens call back system by supervisors to ensure that victims of crime received a call after the crime event so that police leadership could assess the quality of the police service provided by officers and accuracy of crime reporting. These were all clear actions necessary to enhance the transparency of the department.

By the summer of 2010 the New Orleans Police Department's outreach efforts to the community had atrophied. The 65 Point Plan called for expanding the use of the existing district-based quality of life officers[3] with a new position, staffed by a police sergeant, called the Community Coordinating Sergeant. This position, which was known to be very successful in the Metropolitan Nashville Police Department, provided a focal point in each district to begin the process of implementing community policing. They would come to be known as the "Co-Co Sergeants," and these leaders were charged with supervising the efforts of the quality of life officers and were given specific and ongoing training in topics such as: community policing; crime prevention through environmental design; build-

---

3. The New Orleans Police Department implemented a Quality of Life Officer program in the late 1990s. This program, a first of its kind in the department at that time, assigned specific officers to work closely with district commanders and the public to craft a police response, or more accurately police collaboration with other city agencies, to issues such as: abandoned vehicles, illegal trash dumping, public health issues, etc. These Quality of Life issues, to this day and in many departments in the nation, remain the most prolific source for complaints from neighborhood residents.

ing neighborhood watch groups; and the SARA model of problem identification and solution strategies, for example. Over the ensuing years these Co-Co Sergeants led thousands of meetings with residents and business owners sharing the messages of the New Orleans Police Department's community policing and crime prevention methods with more than 75,000 attendees. Undoubtedly, over time these meetings and professional police leaders made a difference in public perception of the New Orleans Police Department as evidenced in more than one independently collected scientific survey of citizen satisfaction (which will be discussed in more detail below).

Taken together, these nineteen specific steps began the process of realigning the New Orleans Police Department in to a modern day organization that had well-structured community outreach efforts and communicated effectively with the public at large about the issues of crime fighting, community policing, and quality of life issues. A modern police department must have a professional and meaningful relationship with the media so that the department can have some influence as appropriate on messaging, and inform the public at large of noteworthy events that occur in the community.

The next component, integrity and accountability, included thirteen specific steps aimed at dealing with the omni-present perceptions that the New Orleans Police Department was essentially unable to hold its employees, and the department itself, in conformance with law and any resemblance of professionally led or disciplined work force. Immediate steps had to be taken to regain control of the internal disciplinary process so that there could be faith and confidence by the public at large, but equally as important to the officers themselves, that there could be professional and competent investigations of officer misconduct allegations. The department appointed, for the first time in its history, in July 2010 of a licensed attorney, experienced in trial litigation, civil rights litigation, and the rules of the New Orleans Civil Service Commission to be a Deputy Superintendent of Police in charge of the Public Integrity Bureau (i.e., Internal Affairs). In addition he was a full peer of the Deputy Superintendents who were career police officers overseeing the uniformed and investigative functions of the department, crucial to any and all future efforts in this component of the 65 Point Plan. It is very likely that in the summer of 2010 there were only three such appointed Internal Affairs leaders in large police agencies who were not career police officers: Nashville, Tennessee, Seattle, Washington, and New Orleans, Louisiana. Many police agencies in the country have moved to appointing trained professional experts, in lieu of career police officers, to run large organizational units at the Deputy Chief level and rank for functions such as management and budget services. The use of professionally trained and experienced lawyers (specifically with litigation) must be strongly considered as a desired appointment among the Deputy Chief level of police agencies. The benefits of this type of appointment far outweighs to external audiences and internal audiences any criticism that the Internal Affairs function should be, and can only be, led by a police officer.

Another critical issue the New Orleans Police Department faced in the summer of 2010 was the numerous on-going federal civil rights criminal investigations of police officer conduct immediately preceding and in the aftermath of Hurricane Katrina. It was imperative at that time (and continues to be in police service in general) that there must be a non-negotiable expectation of truthfulness in the answers to job related questions asked properly of police officers, and that the submission of a false or inaccurate report (oral or in writing) must be met with termination as the presumptive discipline without the benefit of progressive disciplinary steps. Simply put, American police officers provide the strength of their truthfulness, without compromise to the fidelity of their statements, in the performance of their duties and in the conduct of arrests and investigations.[4] The New Orleans Police Department policy in the summer of 2010 did not call for presumptive termination to either of these two principles. The 65 Point Plan clearly changed the expectations to that of unwavering truthfulness in response to questions about the work performed and in the written or spoken report of any duties performed. This policy shift had immediate impact in the police department, and more importantly the public. There was significant media coverage of this policy change,

4. For more information on the evolution of such policies see: Ronal Serpas, Superintendent, New Orleans, Louisiana, Police Department; and Michael Hagar, Captain, Metropolitan Nashville, Tennessee, Police Department, "The Untruthful Employee: Is Termination the Only Response?," *The Police Chief* 77 (August 2010): 114-20.

as was expected and by design, but on balance the people of New
Orleans were very supportive. In fact, it is not uncommon for officers themselves to support such a strict policy—for they too know
that a commonly held belief and expectation that officers always
tell the truth is valuable when they testify in the performance of
their duty, as well as to seek support when occasionally there are
those who testify falsely against them. Taken together the thirteen steps to realign the department's policies and procedures to
foster a workplace environment of integrity and accountability is
the lynchpin to bring to success the changes brought about to advance crime fighting and community policing as found in the 65
Point Plan.

The final component, "hiring-training-labor relations," included ten specific steps to advance the New Orleans Police Department's internal mechanisms of hiring and training of new
officers, new procedures in working with the three established
labor organizations,[5] and direct employee feedback opportunities
to the Superintendent. The New Orleans Police Department in the
early 2000s had successfully petitioned the Civil Service Department and Commission to implement rule changes on promotions
of police sergeants, lieutenants, and captains. Over a ten year
period, requirements to be eligible to take promotional examinations included specific totals of accredited college credits, and/
or degrees, which must be held by the candidate to be eligible.
However, there had been no change in the ensuing years to the
requirement that upon hire, police officer candidates must have in
possession a specific number of accredited college hours of training. The 65 Point Plan called for working with Civil Service to
update the hiring minimum qualifications of police recruits. In
the fall of 2010 the Civil Service Commission approved a New Orleans Police Department request that all police recruit candidates
must have at least sixty hours of earned accredited college credit.
The only substitution at that time was any candidate who had
two years of successful United States armed forces military service. This type of requirement, earned college credit or successful
military experience, served a valuable goal in that police recruit

---

5. There are three labor organizations within the New Orleans Police Department: the
Fraternal Order of Police (the largest); the Police Association of New Orleans; and, the
Black Order of Police. There is no collective barging agreements, nor are there meet and
confer requirements in the department.

candidates are likely to be more successful in training if they have been exposed to either of these experiences. Further, it is also in the best interest of the department, given that promotions to sergeant, lieutenant, and captain require threshold educational levels, that the department would be requiring upon original appointment, ensuring that future candidate pools for promotion are more robust.

As critical as the decisions on hiring officers are, the original training that new officers receive and the yearly in-service training required of all officers is paramount to the success of a police agency. More importantly, during yearly in-service training police leadership can introduce new and evolving concepts of policing styles and strategies to be implemented in a concerted and predictable fashion.

The 65 Point Plan called for an evaluation and update of all New Orleans Police Department recruit training, to include a broader approach to utilizing local experts to offer more timely and effective training. As an example, United States and local prosecutors were given more time to offer training to recruits on the importance of court room demeanor, trial preparation, and the laws that routinely play a part in the day-to-day lives of police officers. At the release of the 65 Point Plan, the New Orleans Police Department's yearly in-service training of officers was approximately twenty-six hours, and there was great flexibility in if, or how, the officers received this training. The only real structured requirement was annual firearms qualification. There was no separation of in-service training for supervisors, and there was little to no evidence of any specific supervisory training to assist in developing leadership, mentoring, or decision making skills of departmental supervisors. To remedy these deficiencies, the yearly in-service training was expanded to a mandated forty hours per year. Over the ensuing years, a supervisor-specific yearly in-service program was created. In both officer and supervisor yearly in-services the department implemented procedures to require annual planning and review and developed weekly lesson plans in each future year to ensure that the in-service training was timely and flexible to adapt to changing needs in training.

One example of how critical continual learning is for police officers is the use of training and day-to-day leadership to instill new and evolving police strategies and theories of policing. It is the specific intent of the New Orleans Police Department—and it was in the summer of 2010—to embrace the theories of Police Legitimacy and Procedural Justice. It is the goal of the New Orleans Police Department to pursue these concepts in the day-to-day delivery of service as noted recently by Fischer (2014) as, "Legitimacy and procedural justice are measurements of the extent to which members of the public trust and have confidence in the police, believe that the police are honest and competent, think that the police treat people fairly and with respect, and are willing to defer to the law and to police authority" (p. 3).

The 65 Point Plan was intended, and remains, the first steps of reforming the New Orleans Police Department. The criticality of the plan can be seen as it became clear that significant portions of the 65 Point Plan would eventually be mirrored in the final negotiated Consent Decree between the city of New Orleans and the Department of Justice that was completed in July 2012—nearly two full years after the issuance of the 65 Point Plan. For example, forty-four (or 68 percent) of the initial 65 Point Plan specific items released in August of 2010, in some form or fashion, were incorporated into the final Consent Decree submitted to the U. S. District Court in July 2012.

In further direct support of the 65 Point Plan, during the summer of 2010 while the plan was being created, the New Orleans Police Department sought from the Bureau of Justice Assistance (BJA) two Technical Assistance projects for BJA funding. The request was twofold: First, to assess the current crime condition in New Orleans and the New Orleans Police Department's response, and second, to review and assess the current performance, structure, policies, and procedures of the New Orleans Police Department Homicide Unit. The BJA agreed to fund these two Technical Assistance grants and reports were issued publicly.

In December 2010 the BJA Technical Assistance Project titled "An Assessment of the New Orleans Police Department Homicide Section: Recommendations for Best Practices" was released with eighty-two specific recommendations to be used as a guide to rebuilding the Homicide Section (Medaris and Sigworth, 2010). The department implemented 98 percent of all the recommendations by February of 2012.[6]

6. The 2 percent of outstanding items are related to budget issues that have not yet

In March of 2011, the BJA Technical Assistance Project titled, "Crime in New Orleans: Analyzing Crime Trends and New Orleans' Response to Crime" was released. This project reflected very positively on the 65 Point Plan and the efforts being made at that time to reform the New Orleans Police Department and noted that the crime fighting efforts identified as being successful in other cities and subsequent actions of the New Orleans Police Department added new specificity to this impressive plan (Wellford, Bond, and Goodison, 2011). More specifically, the report noted, "on August 23, 2010, the Superintendent released a 65-point plan to rebuild the NOPD. Included in that plan was a series of steps that were aimed at reducing violent crime. These initiatives included most of what we would have recommended to the department if they had not already been adopted. . . . These include (1) Project Safe Neighborhood, (2) Code 6, (3) Violent Crime Abatement Teams, (4) knock and talk, (5) crime laboratory enhancements, and (6) staffing and deployment" (p. 23).

By June of 2012, the New Orleans Police Department had implemented the elements of the 65 Point Plan. In February 2013 the New Orleans Police Department released a "Reform Status Report—May 2010 Through December 2012 (32 Months)" (see appendix B) that chronicles how many of the original specific actions items in the 65 Point Plan were implemented and/or evolved, as well as adding new reform measures that were implemented after the release of the 65 Point Plan.

Multi-Agency Gang Unit

In early 2011, the New Orleans Police Department and the city of New Orleans began identifying successful programs for interrupting the cycle of violence and death of young men in the city. In its past, the New Orleans Police Department had adopted strategies found to be successful in other cities to fight crime, violence, and murder—most notably the adoption of the Compstat model of policing in October 1996 as well as the adoption of Community Policing in 1994. However, what was clear in early 2011 is that the

---

been resolved within the department, or other minor items (i.e., aligning Intel analyst to homicide, whereas the department has aligned an Intel analyst to the Multi-Agency Gang Unit, which then provides actionable intelligence across several investigative units including homicide).

New Orleans Police Department had not in the years following Katrina been active in analyzing and adopting evolving trends in crime fighting and murder reduction strategies.

For example, the New Orleans Police Department had not analyzed and or implemented several current successful national model strategies: (1)Data-Driven Approaches to Crime and Traffic Safety (Data-Driven Approaches to Crime and Traffic Safety, 2014); (2) The Milwaukee Homicide Review Commission (O'Brien, Woods, and Cisler, 2007); or, (3) any of the evolving strategies of Professor David M. Kennedy, such as Operation Cease Fire, Drug Market Intervention, or Group Violence Reduction Strategies (Kennedy, 2011). It is important to note that the devastation of Katrina was far and wide in the New Orleans Police Department. But by the summer of 2010, it was clear that the storm's effects in the fall of 2005 had largely been ameliorated, at least as it related to the functionality of day-to-day policing and criminal investigation. There were still significant infrastructure needs, no question; but, by the summer of 2010 the New Orleans Police Department did have the capacity to police the city of New Orleans sufficiently enough to have had at least undertaken an examination of new and evolving trends and implement those trends. As the department moved forward into 2011 and 2012, with essentially the same infrastructure in place as found in the summer of 2010, and following a dramatic fiscal collapse of the city of New Orleans in having a significant impact on the budgeting of city services into 2012 and 2013, the New Orleans Police Department in the first quarter of 2011 began the process of assessing and adopting new and innovative police strategies from around the nation.

During 2011 the New Orleans Police Department set about to invest in significant technologies to provide the basis to implement crime fighting strategies that have shown significant promise. Reordering the direction of the New Orleans Police Department with the goal of reducing crime and murder in the community by using new and evolving technologies of crime mapping and officer deployment software was a critical first step. During this year, software purchases and installations such as *Omega CrimeView* (CrimeView, 2014) and *Corona Ops Force Deploy* (Ops Force—One Step Ahead, 2014) allowed the New Orleans Police Department to implement the Data-Driven Approaches to Crime and Traffic Safety strategies and realign patrol district boundaries and deployment patterns of officers (which had not been significantly changed in more than thirty years) using a rational and data driven approach in January of 2012.

As a result of a Department of Justice Grant, Dr. Mallory O'Brien's work creating *The Milwaukee Homicide Review Commission* was being brought to cities in the nation to implement and replicate. Serendipitously, while New Orleans Superintendent of Police Ronal Serpas was the Chief of Police in Nashville, Tennessee, he served on the International Association of Chiefs of Police Research Advisory Committee. Dr. O'Brien also served on this committee, and in a meeting in late 2009 Dr. O'Brien announced that the grant funding to export her project was approved for implementing in 2010 and beyond. After being appointed Superintendent in New Orleans in May of 2010, Serpas requested of O'Brien (and authorization was approved) for New Orleans to be one of the first, if not the first, city in the nation to implement and replicate the *Milwaukee Homicide Review Commission*. Through the years 2011 to 2014 the New Orleans Police Department and the city of New Orleans operated and staffed the replication and expansion of this program under *The Mayor's Strategic Command to Reduce Murders*.

As the department continued to move forward with deployment strategies, resource allocation strategies, and managing several years of staggering budget shortfalls inherited by the prior administration, 2011 and 2012 were years where fundamental investments were made in revolutionizing the department's ability to respond to and interdict crime. The use of *The Mayor's Strategic Command to Reduce Murder, Data-Driven Approaches to Crime and Traffic Safety, Omega CrimeView,* and *Corona Ops Force Deploy* stabilized the day-to-day crime fighting decision making by departmental leaders. The New Orleans Police Department, like many agencies, uses software and deployment strategies like these to provide a base upon which to build. All police departments must be nimble and ready to respond decisively and effectively to emerging trends, and to meet this demand. The New Orleans Police Department continues to use the weekly Compstat Accountability meeting strategy (first started in October 1996) to align the department to the demands it faces.

For decades New Orleans has experienced a significantly

higher per capita murder rate than all cities. Early in 2011 the New Orleans Police Department was observing, as were many other cities in America, that young men were associating more loosely in "groups" as opposed to the historical understanding of gangs. This was not to say that New Orleans did not have gangs — to the contrary, intelligence was informing departmental leaders that both groups and gangs existed. A significant and obvious area where the New Orleans Police Department had to invest considerable time and resources was inventorying the number of young men who were involved in groups or gangs, how many of those groups or gangs existed in the city, where did these groups or gangs operate, and what was the lethality of these groups or gangs. It was clear from the analysis of crime in New Orleans (Wellford, Bond, and Goodison, 2011), that young African American men were committing murders and less-than-lethal shootings primarily among one-another at a rate far exceeded the per capita average murder rate of any city in America.

In response, in early 2012, the New Orleans Police Department set out to inventory and document group and gang membership, location of activity, among other things. By early 2012, New Orleans Police Specialized Investigation Division, working with District Patrol commands had identified fifty-three groups or gangs with an estimated 576 members. The groups or gangs were also identified to specific patrol districts (or neighborhoods within the city).

By June of 2012 the city of New Orleans and the New Orleans Police Department, under the auspices of the *NOLA for Life* strategic plan (*NOLA for Life*, 2012) had contracted with Dr. Robin Engel of the Cincinnati Violence Reduction Initiative to assist in refining group or gang identification techniques and to begin the process of implementing a focused deterrence model (Engel, Tillyer, and Corsaro, 2011). Professor David M. Kennedy was consulted with as the lead on this work so that the refined data developed could be used to meld with the emerging *Group Violence Reduction Strategy*. The purpose of these partnerships was to assist the police department in identifying and categorizing group or gang behavior of violent individuals. In June of 2012, working together with Dr. Engel's team and Professor Kennedy's strategies, the group and gang membership estimates of New Orleans had been refined and tentatively identified as thirty-nine violent street gangs with 649 potential members. This identification process resulted in an ongoing strategy of detectives using a score sheet entitled "Gang Member Involved" (GMI) for each non-lethal, or lethal shooting. Detectives utilize this form to notify and inform the work of the Multi-Agency Gang Unit, homicide detectives, and patrol district based detectives.

Once the analysis had been done to identify groups or gangs, their membership, their geographic locations, their criminality, and their lethality, the New Orleans Police Department in November 2012 created a Multi-Agency Gang Unit (MAG) so that long term investigations could begin to dismantle these groups or gangs and bring them to indictment and conviction for criminal enterprises at either the state or federal level. The MAG is under the leadership of the New Orleans Police Department and brings together through a Cooperative Endeavor Agreement the following agencies to be co-located in the same facility, sharing resources and collaboratively managing investigations with state and federal prosecutors:

New Orleans Police Department (NOPD)
Bureau of Alcohol, Tobacco, Firearms, and Explosives (ATF)
Drug Enforcement Administration (DEA)
Federal Bureau of Investigations (FBI)
Orleans Parish District Attorney's Office (DA)
Orleans Parish Sheriff's Office (OPSO)
United States Attorney's Office (USAO)
United States Marshal's Service (USMS)
Louisiana State Police (LSP)
Louisiana Division of Probation & Parole/Adult
Jefferson Parish Sheriff's Office (JPSO)

The MAG is also supported internally by the New Orleans Police Department through the assignment of a Street Gang Unit (SGU), under the direction of the MAG. Whereas the MAG conducts long-term complex investigations that lead to significant and extensive indictments (federal or state), the SGU provides for a fast acting unit that can saturate areas of the city where immediate group or gang violence has erupted. The purpose of this chapter is to describe the MAG, not necessarily the use of Focused Deterrence, Group Violence Reduction Strategies, "Call-Ins" of offenders believed to be Gang Member Involved (GMI).[7] However, as an integral part of the work of the MAG unit, the SGU can provide a focused law enforcement response to lethal or non-lethal shootings of GMI-identified actors in furtherance of MAG investigations and the Group Violence Reduction Strategy-specific component of swift and certain law enforcement follow up to the next group or gang that causes injury or death following a Call In.

Since the formation of the MAG, this unit has produced investigations and indictments at the state and federal level that have dismantled eight identified violent groups or gangs, with more than ninety individuals indicted as members of these criminal conspiracies. These types of investigations and subsequent prosecutions were new to New Orleans and were clearly a game changer. The young men who became targets of these criminal conspiracy investigations, based upon their actions and collaborations with others, were laid bare before the conspirators themselves and the community at large. The impact of a coordinated investigative and prosecutorial plan was far reaching in its scope. The message to the public was clear: real results in dismantling dangerous groups and gangs could be achieved. Many of these cases have resulted in negotiated guilty pleas resulting in lengthy and even life prison sentences. The MAG maintains an inventory of cases that averages between four and six cases being actively investigated.

The MAG, SGU, and retooled Homicide Unit are three key law enforcement units that may have some direct impact on the number of murders a community experiences. Since the summer of 2010, the New Orleans Police Department has adopted, implemented, refined, and advanced several well documented strategies to interdict violent groups or gangs and conduct homicide investigations with greater clarity and potential success. It would be jejune to suggest that the substantial drop in murders in New Orleans for 2013 and the continuation of that through June 30, 2014, is directly or solely linked to the work of the MAG, SGU, and Homicide Unit (see table 1). Likewise, it would be a superficial conclusion to discount that the work of these units has not

---

7. See generally the work of Professor Kennedy and Dr. Engel

had some impact on the change in murder in New Orleans. New Orleans, as with many American cities, experiences the tragedy of an over populated count of murderers or their victims among African American men, who are undereducated, often times addicted to drugs or alcohol, over represented in prior criminal behavior experiencing significant rates of recidivism and associated with groups or gangs that use violence purposefully to advance their criminal enterprises, or sadly, use the ultimate act of violence in response to the slightest provocations.

Table 1:
Social Network Analysis

Homicide Comparisons

Murder Comparisons Last Five Years
Year to Date through 6/30/14

	2013	2014	# Differential	% Change
Murders	76	70	-6	-8%

	2012	2014	# Differential	% Change
Murders	97	70	-27	-28%

	2011	2014	# Differential	% Change
Murders	105	70	-35	-33%

	2010	2014	# Differential	% Change
Murders	105	70	-35	-33%

	2009	2014	# Differential	% Change
Murders	97	70	-27	-28%

As noted, New Orleans has experienced a per capita murder rate that has been substantially higher than the national averages for American cities for decades. Despite some abatement of the murder rate in the late 1990s, as was likewise observed nationally, New Orleans still had a significantly higher murder rate. Clearly, traditionally known and accepted concepts of social disorganization, rates of intra-racial violence, predicting factors of high rates of under achievement academically and economically, coupled with extraordinarily high rates of recidivism have all been used to attempt to explain or understand the murder rates of New Orleans. All of these ideas however look to large scale institutional and structural factors to understand and observe trends of murder. Recently there have been new and innovative research findings that suggest social network analysis of identifiable individuals can give greater clarity in understanding this violent behavior. The expanding work of social network analysis has been published widely by Andrew Papachristos of Yale University, who in a recent article postulated, "Risk of homicide in urban areas is even more highly concentrated than previously thought. We found that most of the risk of gun violence was concentrated in networks of identifiable individuals. Understanding these networks may improve prediction of individual homicide victimization within disadvantaged communities" (Papachristos and Wildeman, 2013).

With the implementation of the Multi-Agency Gang Unit within the New Orleans Police Department, and the completion and continual update of the "gang member involved" data bases, the New Orleans Police Department has recently been able to conduct social network analysis (SNA) on each non-fatal shooting and fatal shooting. Over the last year, using the SNA of each shooting event and the expanding knowledge of the gang member data sets, the New Orleans Police Department's Criminal Intelligence analytic capacity has soared. Following many of the ideas of Papachristos, the New Orleans Police Department has created an analytic process that has now identified just over 2,600 known individuals who are at high risk due to their involvement in shooting events, either as a victim or a suspected shooter. This new analysis and its precision have become more robust by the day.

The New Olreans Police Department's daily use of SNA of all shooting events, fatal or not, also explores the criminal relationships of these known individuals and continues to make this data set identified as high risk more accurate and up-to-date. From this point of view, the concepts of "degrees of separation" as outlined by Papachristos and others are reinforced by these analytic techniques that link person(s) to criminal events and groups or gangs in ways never before seen at the local level of law enforcement. Specifically as these relationships between those who shoot and those who are shot, and their linkages to one another, provides a more precise data set to use when aligning police and prosecutorial resources. Clearly the greater clarity of relationships brought to light through SNA advances investigations exponentially, including—advancing traditional detective work, use of confidential informants, and co-operating defendants.

Criminal investigations of shooting events in the city have been significantly advanced through the use of SNA. Relationships previously unknown to investigators have now been made clearer resulting in new investigative leads to follow. Often new leads developed by studying the SNA produced for each victim provides leads and potential closure of other crimes not related to the shooting that initiated the analysis.

Criminal prosecutions, by either state or federal authorities, through the Multi-Agency Gang Task Force have been undoubtedly advanced by the use of the SNA technique, and other traditional techniques, to identify with more clarity and in some cases certainty, those groups or gangs that should be the focus of a Mutli-Agency Gang Task Force investigation. Between November 2012 and July 2014 there have been at least eight groups and/or gangs dismantled with more than ninety defendants indicted at the state or federal level. These investigations benefited greatly and were informed by the SNA techniques. There is a high probability that the effect of these investigations, and the use of SNA to help further refine and identify those engaged in groups or gangs, has brought a chilling effect to those who choose murder as a way to operate their nefarious trade in the city of New Orleans.

It is the intention of the New Orleans Police Department to continue to expand upon the analytic skills and tools necessary to refine this list of known individuals and to share this information as appropriate with other members of the criminal justice system. Just as critical as it is to criminal investigations to know who these 2,600 known individuals are, so too is it that this information can be shared with social service providers. The criminal justice system has very clear responses to acts of violence in the community; however, virtually all of these responses are just that—a response to a criminal event that has occurred. The use of SNA and other such analytics that can identify individuals with more precision due to their known past criminal indices who could benefit greatly to tailored outreach programs aimed at reducing their chances of victimizing others or becoming a victim must be one of the department's highest priorities.

Citizen Satisfaction Surveys

For decades one of the most used and cited tools to assess the level of crime in the nation, and by design or happenstance the success of local law enforcement, has been the Federal Bureau of Investigation (FBI) annual Uniform Crime Report (UCR) released annually under the title *Crime in the United States*. The UCR was developed in the 1920s by committee action of the International Association of Chiefs of Police to accomplish the goal of having a nationalized view of crime statistics, and the UCR has been managed by the FBI since 1930.[8] The UCR is an index system that separates crimes into two major categories, UCR Part I and UCR Part II, and participation in the UCR is voluntary by law enforcement agencies in the nation. Crimes are those events that are reported or discovered and then classified and scored by law enforcement following the UCR guidelines of reporting. UCR Part I crimes are the serious personal and property crimes of: murder, rape, robbery, aggravated assault, burglary, theft, auto theft, and arson. UCR Part II crimes are essentially the remaining crimes that are defined by legislation as criminal acts. To be counted as a UCR crime (Part I or II) the event must be first classified as a UCR crime and then the numbers of classified crimes are scored. It is, however, the UCR Part I crime that is cited in media reports, grant requests, and comparative analysis of cities (despite strong warning from the FBI to not do such comparisons[9]).

Over the last few years, many police chiefs have sought to find more useful data to assess the success or challenges of their departments. The UCR, while a longitudinal data set of exceptional importance, has limitations that are known and expected. Recently researchers have found an estimated 4 percent misclassification rate of UCR Part I index crimes, and more startling for the crimes of aggravated assault, burglary, larceny, and robbery there was a statisti-

8.   http://www.fbi.gov/about-us/cjis/ucr/crime-in-the-u.s/2011/crime-in-the-u.s.-2011/aboutucrmain.

9.   http://www.fbi.gov/about-us/cjis/ucr/crime-in-the-u.s/2011/crime-in-the-u.s.-2011/caution-against-ranking.

cally significant classification error rate in an analysis of more than 31,000 UCR Part I reports randomly drawn from reporting agencies in the state of West Virginia (Nolan, Haas, Lester, Kirby, and Jira, 2006). Nolan et al., are even more direct in providing a potential explanation as to error:

> These findings suggest that, perhaps, law enforcement officers have some difficulty in making the fine distinctions that are necessary for accurately classifying crimes that are conceptually close in nature. Thus, while officers were often correct in determining that an assault had occurred in this study, the error occurred when making the decision of whether the particular incident should be classified as an aggravated versus simple assault" (p. 16).

More recently, and along the same line in acknowledging known and or expected error in UCR reporting, the Office of Inspector General for the City of Chicago stated in an April 2014 audit, "Chicago Police Department Assault-Related Crime Statistics Classification and Reporting Audit:" "… misclassification rate is under the 10% rate that the FBI/CJIS Training & Advisory Process Unit states is acceptable for agencies participating in the UCR program" (p. 13), and at footnote 47, "OIG did not evaluate whether the 10% error rate deemed acceptable by the FBI for participating agencies constitutes and acceptable error rate for other users." (Chicago, 2014). What is important to note here is that in both of these reports it is clear and unequivocal that the UCR reporting system has inherent and expected error, and that in the case of the FBI UCR, up to a 10 percent threshold of error in classifications and scoring can be expected and is tolerable. Police chiefs are aware, generally, of these issues and must juxtapose the mixed value (longitudinal data tool versus use as a measure of current police success) of the UCR in their day-to-day interactions with the public, elected leaders, and of course, media inquiries.

Another significant and longitudinal research project that further undermines the efficacy of relying on the FBI UCR reports as a measure of police success is the Bureau of Justice Assistance National Crime Victimization Survey (NCVS). Started in 1973, the NCVS is the primary source of information on criminal victimization and utilizes data obtained from representative sampling of about 90,000 households, interviewing nearly 160,000 persons.[10] For police chiefs, one of the most significant findings is the rates at which respondents to the NCVS who acknowledge that they have been the victim of crime state that they *actually* report that criminal event to local police. For example, the most recent release of the NCVS, "Criminal Victimizations, 2012" (Truman, Langton, and Planty, 2013) at table 4, clearly demonstrates a significant percentage of crime is not reported to local police. The findings in the 2012 NCVS released on this point have generally remained the same for decades.

Table 4: Percent of victimization reported to police, by type of crime, 2003, 2011, and 2012

Type of crime	2003	2011	2012
Violent crime[a]	**48%**	**49%**	**44%**
Rape/sexual assault	56	27	28
Robbery	64	66	56
Assault	45	48	44
Aggravated assault	56	67	62
Simple assault	43	43	40
Domestic violence[b]	57	59	55
Intimate partner violence[c]	60	60	53
Violent crime involving injury	56	61	59
Serious violent crime[d]	**58%**	**61%**	**54%**
Serious domestic violence[b]	61	58	61
Serious intimate partner violence[c]	63	59	55
Serious violent crime involving weapons	59	67	56 †
Serious violent crime involving injury	64	66	56
Property crime[e]	**38%**	**37%**	**34% †**
Burglary	54	52	55
Motor vehicle theft	77	83	79
Theft	31	30	26 †

Note: See appendix table 6 for standard errors.
† Significant changes from 2011 to 2012 at the 95% confidence level.
[a] Includes rape or sexual assault, robbery, aggravated assault, and simple assault.
[b] Includes victimization committed by intimate partners (current or former spouses, boyfriends, or girlfriends) and family members.
[c] Includes victimization committed by current or former spouses, boyfriends, or girlfriends.
[d] Includes rape or sexual assault, robbery, and aggravated assault.
[e] Includes household burglary, motor vehicle theft, and theft.
Source: Bureau of Justice Statistics, National Crime Victimization Survey, 2003, 2011, and 2012.

10. http://www.bjs.gov/index.cfm?ty=dcdetail&iid=245.

Taken together with the errors known and expected in the FBI UCR reports, and the clear and compelling data reported by the NCVS, police chiefs are well advised to look to more robust measures of success, not only on the crime front, but on the delivery of police service as well.

For decades the presumption has been (and chiefs of police and other public officials have clearly been responsible for adding to this concern) to trumpet declining crime rates as evidence of successful police work (ignoring that the entire criminal justice system must have an impact on the rates of crime and victimization) or in the alternative when crime rates rise, then there must be a failing in the police. These discussions occur daily and with great vigor on either side; but, what is not answered by any of these measures is how the public perceives police service, crime, and fear of crime.

In the middle of the last decade, it became apparent that police chiefs needed a more thorough and thoughtful way to assess their success or challenges in the communities that they serve. Police chiefs needed the value of quality citizen satisfaction survey research that had been done from time to time through partnerships with local universities, but they needed the timeliness of professionally provided citizen satisfaction, or opinion polls, not unlike the data that political leaders use to craft positions or gauge support. Beyond the clear need for timely and actionable satisfaction or opinion surveys, police chiefs could use these types of tools to test concepts much larger than just changes in crime rates. Questions can be crafted that assess, or have been asked and surveyed by other institutions, on topics such as professionalism of officers, cooperation with the public, fear of crime, sense of safety in one's neighborhood, or that mimic *Gallup* poll questions such as "have you or a member of your household been the victim of a crime in the last twelve months" to assess or compare a community, procedural justice and police legitimacy.

The results of these types of surveys can be used to help manage a modern day police department in many ways. Although not an exhaustive list, first, the results can help the chief understand more globally the depth of the public's support, or non-support, for the department and share this with the officers and leaders of the department. Second, the results can help craft a thoughtful external and internal communications plan. Third, the results can be shared with, and used as a learning tool for commanders throughout the department to help mold and shape the police response to the community. Fourth, depending upon issues confronting the department at the time, the survey can be amended to include new and evolving issues and test how those issues are being perceived by the public. Fifth, an area that a police chief can be successful in, but must be cautious with, is using the results of the surveys to build political support to advance the needs of the department.

In the March 2011 Harvard Kennedy School Program in Criminal Justice publication, "Toward a New Professionalism in Policing," support for the expanding use of citizen surveys can be found (Stone and Travis, 2011). It states, "On crime, for example, we expect to see more police agencies conducting their own routine public surveys, as many do now, holding themselves accountable not only for reducing reported crime, but also for reducing fear and the perception that crime is a problem in particular neighborhoods or for especially vulnerable residents" (p. 13). As has been discussed earlier in this chapter, the New Orleans Police Department embraced the adoption of strategies to advance the concepts of procedural justice and police legitimacy as a core component of increasing citizen support of the efforts of the department (Fischer, 2014). As Stone and Travis put clearly, "The legitimacy of policing under the New Professionalism embraces...wining the trust and confidence of the people policed..." (p. 14). The use of citizen satisfaction surveys that include questions that flesh out officer behavior which advances procedural justice and police legitimacy, as well as citizens' perceptions of professionalism, confidence, cooperation, and crime gives a police chief a real guide to altering the internal culture of the department to meet the external expectations of the diverse citizenry served. By using surveys to reach outside of the department, in addition to the internal mechanism of accountability and management, police chiefs can attach their departments to the new professionalism: "As the New Professionalism develops...departments will be able to use better surveys than are common today... In 2007, then-Senator Barack Obama underscored the importance of this pillar of the New Professionalism when he promised that, as president, he would work for a criminal justice system that enjoyed the trust and confidence of citizens of every race, ethnicity and age....Public surveys that capture the satisfaction of people in these discrete groups...can help measure progress..." (p. 15).

The use of twice per year (June and December) surveys of citizen satisfaction in the city of Nashville began in June 2005. The Nashville Police Department procured the services of a professional survey firm to complete these surveys and to create and modify the questions. It is likely that in 2005, Nashville, a city of more than 600,000 residents, was the largest police department in the nation to routinely use citizen satisfaction surveys obtained this way. These results, over time, demonstrated a significant and continuing level of support for the police department and its service. The results were critical in being used to advance support for expanding the size of the police department and the addition of two new patrol precincts facilities. Another example of the strength of these routine surveys was the ability to seek authorization and funding to build a new state-of-the-art crime laboratory with full DNA analytic capacity. What makes this notable is that the State of Tennessee, through the Tennessee Bureau of Investigation, provided as a cost free service to local law enforcement DNA testing and analytics. During 2008 and 2009 when the Nashville Police Department was building public momentum to fund and build these two new precinct patrol facilities and a full service crime lab and DNA laboratory that would cost millions of dollars to build and operate, it was the citizen surveys that were used repeatedly by supporters internal and external to the department to make the argument for these costly investments. During these same years, Nashville, like many cities in the nation, was suffering from the 2008 collapse of the national economy. Despite these difficult financial times, the city of Nashville, its mayor, and its council, ultimately supported and funded the costly new infrastructure investments and has now completed all of the projects requested.

In New Orleans, unlike Nashville, a private group of citizens, the New Orleans Crime Coalition (NOCC),[11] provided the initiative

---

11. The New Orleans Crime Coalition (NOCC) includes nearly twenty community organizations working together to reform our local criminal justice system for the benefit of all. Since its founding in 2007, the NOCC has played a key role in obtaining an additional $5.7 million in federal funding for local criminal justice agencies and monitoring the expenditure of those funds; seeking improved cooperation between the District Attorney's office and NOPD; supporting the creation of an independent NOPD monitor; obtaining city funding for the Orleans Public Defenders Office for the first time; and creating one integrated computer-based information management system for the local criminal justice

and funding to begin citizen satisfaction surveys of this type. The NOCC independently procured professional surveying services and fielded the first citizen satisfaction survey of this kind in New Orleans in August of 2009 (see appendix C), almost one full year before the new mayor and police administrations would take office in May 2010. The timeliness of this survey to serve as a baseline for the incoming police administration proved to be a valuable resource. As part of its mission, the NOCC agreed to continue to provide the funding and support of the citizen satisfaction survey, and agreed with the police department's request to conduct the survey twice per year. The NOCC fielded the August 2010 survey, and has done so twice per year, with the latest survey being released in March 2014 (see appendix C).

In the case of New Orleans, and many other cities, the constant attention, superficial coverage, and very often highly negative and critical stories of police issues, crime, and criminal justice by local media can be daunting. Valid and timely citizen satisfaction surveys can serve as a counter balance to these media forces. Police officers, like anyone else, read media reports. Often times, without a contravening force, officers themselves can lose sight of how much support the department really does have (or, worse, does not have). Police leaders must and can use these satisfaction surveys to help motivate the officers under their charge. The surveys can be used to help define areas for improvement and then be used as a guide for officers to alter their behavior as appropriate. Moreover, it is completely acceptable to use these surveys when police leaders are participating in community meetings. It is always a mistake to allow a survey or data to drown out or talk over the specific complaints that affect individuals — however, in a community meeting or a room full of people, having the data or survey available to give the "big picture" can and will be successful. As can be seen in the NOCC survey results (see appendix C), the New Orleans Police Department has made steady and demonstrable success in turning the many negative opinions of New Orleanians found in the August 2009 survey, to more positive opinions. The department's leadership in New Orleans, and Nashville (during the period of June 2005-December 2009), utilizes the survey to educate leaders and officers inside the department and to share the findings with

system. http://www.crimecoalitionnola.com/.

the public at large.

For example, in August of 2009 when asked to assess the professionalism of New Orleans Police Officers, the NOCC survey found that 48 percent of respondents had a favorable perception. The desire of leadership to advance the perceptions of professional behavior was one of the many behaviors measured in the NOCC survey that could be addressed by constant attention at daily roll call briefings, in-service training for officers and supervisors, the use of disciplinary actions when necessary, and the media relations managed by the department's Public Affairs Office to the message that professional behavior in the delivery of police service was expected, unconditionally. When looking at the longitudinal change in the public's perception of this one behavioral trait, a slow and steady rise in approval can be seen, ending with the latest measure in March 2014 of a 68 percent (the highest rating of the series) favorability response to this question.

New Orleans presents an interesting question in regards to the different ways in which a police department is perceived to be successful in delivering services. For example, in the fifty months before and after May 2010, the start of the new police and mayoral administration, Part I Violent Crime, Part I Property Crime, and overall Part I crimes fell about 5 percent, each. At the same time the New Orleans Police Department lost, without replacement, approximately 22 percent (or more than three hundred) of its police officer staff and subsequently arrest activity (state, narcotics, municipal, or juvenile charges) fell approximately 41percent. These measures, standing alone, would tend to be viewed as positive indication that fewer officers using better training, technology, crime analytics, and deployment decisions, making fewer arrests could still have the impact of lowering the major crime rates. In other words, the 65 Point Plan served as a basis for advancing the department and traditional police measures tended to suggest just that. A perusal of local media reports during this time would suggest that crime was not lowered[12] and that the New Orleans Police Depart-

---

12. As has been noted, there is an expected and known error rate in UCR reporting. This has a deleterious effect upon the perceptions of the public and media when audits of police reporting mechanisms do find error. In the NOPD there were several independent audits (non-randomized samples) that reported errors in some reporting systems .The NOPD embraced the findings of error found in reporting systems and made the necessary corrections. Equally as important, there was no evidence found in any of the several audits

ment was not advancing in its service delivery or professional status. However, what gives greater depth to the experience of New Orleans in the years and months between May 2010 and June 2014 are not just these data points. The consistent and demonstrable increases found in citizen satisfaction with the New Orleans Police Department on a host of issues monitored by the NOCC Citizen Satisfaction Survey, coupled with similar findings of the University of New Orleans Quality of Life Survey (Chervenak, Dai, and Juhasz, 2013) in key areas such as overall quality of police protection, perceptions of safety around one's home, and the rate at which respondents reported a crime committed against them or a family member, provide balance, insight, and in no small way support for the proposition that the citizens of New Orleans were changing their opinion of the New Orleans Police Department in meaningful and long term ways. In New Orleans, overall crime reduction did occur, and notably murder declined significantly in 2013 and remained on a downward trajectory through the first half of 2014, as noted; but, what was as important and meaningful was the Citizen Satisfaction survey data from more than one source that demonstrated independently that the people of New Orleans sensed a change...a change to the positive in their perceptions of the New Orleans Police Department.

For police chiefs of today, it is all about measuring progress. As our nation's cities continue to streamline cost, fight deficits, consider the challenges of recruiting new and diverse work forces of police officers, and confront recidivism rates that drain resources and energy by their very nature, it is the police chief that is most "in tune" with the community that will have the better chance of success. It is the police department that is "in tune" with the diverse community it serves that will be able to generate enough public support to persuade political capital to be used in complex and often times limited financial resource allocation decisions to advance the department. Public opinion surveys are used by many different institutions, both public and private, to help identify messages, and to craft solutions and strategies to advance the goals and objectives of the institution — this has been going on for years. For police departments to adopt the same techniques is unquestionably timely, intelligent, and desirable. In the face of overwhelming evidence

conducted of any scheme or purposeful effort to under report crime in the city.

that UCR reports have inherent and known error, that UCR reports capture about half of the UCR Part I major crimes that occur in the country according to long standing findings of the NCVS, it makes sense that police chiefs purposefully and forcefully add citizen satisfaction survey data as the most vigorous, if not the primary, tool of measuring police success.

Conclusion

The reformation of the New Orleans Police Department will understandably take many years. The fundamental steps of the 65 Point Plan, many of the additional items of reform that are reported in the Reform Status Report (see appendix B), and the continuing and encouraging trends of the NOCC Citizen Satisfaction Surveys (see appendix C), give solid reason to believe that the department will advance and succeed. Beyond these steps, the department and the city are working daily to meet the terms and the conditions of the Consent Decree that resulted from the Department of Justice investigation issued in March of 2011.

The city of New Orleans and the police department have unfortunately been battered by dramatic budget restrictions that essentially stopped all hiring from June 2010 through the years 2011 and 2012. However, as a result of a stabilizing city budget, the department initiated a police officer hiring campaign in the summer of 2013 that continues. Given the number of years of no significant hiring to offset normal and expected yearly separations of personnel,[13] the impact on the department has been stark: between May 2010 and June of 2014 the New Orleans Police Department saw its commissioned strength fall from 1,448 to 1,123 or a 22.44 percent reduction. What is also remarkable is that during these years of dramatic staffing declines, the New Orleans Police Department continued to demonstrate, time and time again, that it is unparalleled in its ability to manage large crowds and assist the city of New Orleans in being the venue of choice for some of the largest attended sporting events in the world. Despite this dramatic reduction in personnel, there have been notable successes that set the stage for the future of continuing violence abatement in New Orleans.

13. For the twenty year period ending in 2013, the NOPD averaged 137 separations of police officers of any rank per year

The 65 Point Plan offered that smarter policing and crime fighting, coupled with an expanded Community Policing effort through the use of Community Coordinating Sergeants[14] specifically created, trained, and deployed to help reduce crime and enhance public confidence in the New Orleans Police Department. Early signs indicate that the 65 Point Plan may have achieved, at least partially, these goals. At the release of the 65 Point Plan it was not expected or suspected that the department would experience significant staffing reductions as noted above; however, despite these challenges there have been some demonstrable positive outcomes.

For example, accepting the known and expected error that can be found in the Uniform Crime Report (UCR) (Chicago, 2014) (Nolan, Haas, Lester, Kirby, and Jira, 2006), when reviewing the Part I UCR in New Orleans for the period of May 2010 through June 2014, compared to April 2010 through March 2006, according to New Orleans Police Department monthly submissions of UCR crimes to state and federal officials, overall UCR Part I crimes declined by 5 percent. Violent UCR Part I crimes declined by 4.9 percent. And, property UCR Part I crimes declined by 5 percent.

As has been argued in this chapter, the use of the UCR to be the primary gauge of the success or challenges of a police department is not robust. When reviewing the New Orleans Crime Coalition survey of citizen satisfaction in New Orleans (see appendix C), there are unquestionable signs that the people of New Orleans are more supportive of the department, particularly in comparison with the August 2009 findings to the March 2014 findings. Moreover, the University of New Orleans Quality of Life Series released in October of 2013 finds similar results (Chervenak, Dai, and Juhasz, 2013). Taken together, the multi-year findings of continued growth in support of the NOCC survey and the findings of the University of New Orleans survey provide burgeoning evidence that the New Orleans Police Department has begun the long term process of reconnecting with the community it serves—a dramatic difference from the summer of 2009.

The clear and compelling outcome of a significant reduction of murders in 2013 and the continuation of murder reduction in 2014

---

14. The NOPD uses the Community Coordinating Sergeants as a basis and starting point for implementing Community Policing throughout the department as staffing levels increase to allow for patrol officers to become more engaged in Community Policing.

bode well for the continued support of and staffing of the Multi-Agency Gang Task Force and Street Gang Unit. More compelling is the comparative reduction of murders over the preceding five years that gives indication that there is a tangible change in the community of those who belong to groups or gangs engaging in criminal enterprise. It is clear that this one unit is not solely responsible for the change in the numbers of murders in New Orleans. It is also without contradiction that a unit such as this, narrowly focused on investigating and prosecuting groups and gangs that ply their trade of death, can have an impact on these types of crimes and criminal enterprises. It is not the purpose of the chapter to analyze, or dismiss, the *NOLA for Life* initiative, of which the reforming of the New Orleans Police Department (including the formation of the MAG) is a critical component. *NOLA for Life* is a multi-faceted plan, and policing and prosecution is just one part.

American policing cannot be static. New and evolving technologies have revolutionized American policing in just the last decade. The expansion and use of DNA technology, the dramatic advancements in Digital Forensic technology, the continuing advancements in ballistics examination, and the powerful crime analytic tools that daily get closer to providing true predictive policing will continue to shape and mold how police departments operate. These technologies offer new and bold opportunities for success in policing. But, police departments must hold as their highest goal, their most sought after approach, the ability to be connected to the public they serve. Advancing toward a new professionalism in policing (Stone and Travis, 2011), fully embracing and integrating the concepts of procedural justice and police legitimacy (Fischer, 2014) in the day-to-day interactions of officers and detectives are the very cornerstones upon which the next generation of policing must be built. A professional police department that has the support of its community can solve crimes, can solve problems, and can be successful. If the New Orleans Police Department can continue to combine these ideas, we can have greater confidence in future violence abatement in the City of New Orleans.

References

Chervenak, E., S. Dai, and E. Juhasz. (2013, October). *University of New Orleans.* Retrieved July 11, 2014, from University of New Orleans: http:// poli.uno.edu/unopoll/studies/docs/2013QOL%20Report.pdf.

Chicago, O. o. (2014). *Chicago Police Department Assault-Related Crime Statistics Classification and Reporting Audit.* Chicago: Office of Inspector General.

City of new Orleans. (2012). *NOLA for Life: A Comprehensive Murder Reduction Strategy.* Retrieved July 10, 2014, from http://www.nolaforlife. org/campaign.

CrimeView. (2014, July 19). Retrieved from The Omega Group: http:// www.theomegagroup.com/police/crimeview_desktop.html.

Data-Driven Approaches to Crime and Traffic Safety. (2014, March 18). Retrieved July 19, 2014, from National Institute of Justice Office of Justice Programs: http://www.nij.gov/topics/law-enforcement/operations/traffic/Pages/ddacts.aspx.

Engel, R., M. Tillyer, and N. Corsaro. (2011). "Reducing Gang Violence Using Focused Deterrence: Evaluating the Cincinnati Initiative to Reduce Violence (CIRV)." *Justice Quarterly*: 1-37.

Fischer, C., ed. (2014, March). *Legitimacy and Procedural Justice: The New Orleans Case Study.* Retrieved July 13, 2014, from Police Executive Research Forum: http://www.policeforum.org/assets/docs/Free_Online_Documents/Leadership/legitimacy%20and%20procedural%20 justice%20-%20the%20new%20orleans%20case%20study.pdf.

Kennedy, D. M. (2011). *Don't Shoot: One Man, A Street Fellowship, and the End of Violence in Inner-City America.* New York: Bloomsbury.

Medaris, M., and C. Sigworth. (2010). *An Assessment of the New Orleans Police Department Homicide Section: Recommendations for Best Practices.* Washington D.C.: Bureau of Justice Assistance US Departement of Justice.

New Orleans Crime Coalition. (2014, March). *New Orleans Crime Coalition.* Retrieved July 10, 2014, from http://www.crimecoalitionnola. com/213.

Nolan, J., S. Haas, T. Lester, J. Kirby, and C. Jira. (2006). *Establishing the "Statistical Accuracy" of Uniform Crime Reports (UCR) in West Virginia.* Charleston: State of West Virginia Criminal Justice Statistical Analysis Center-Division of Criminal Justice Services.

O'Brien, M., L. Woods, and R. Cisler. (2007). "The Milwaukee Homicide Review Commission: An Interagency Collaborative Process to Reduce Homicide." *Wisconsin Medical Journal* 106 (7): 385-88.

Ops Force – One Step Ahead. (2014, July 19). Retrieved from Corona Solutions: http://www.coronasolutions.com/.

Papachristos, A., and C. Wildeman. (2014). "Network Exposure and Homicide Victimization in an African American Community." *American Journal of Public Health* 104 (1): 143-50. doi:10.2105/AJPH.2013.301441.

Stone, C., and J. Travis. (2011, March). *Harvard Kennedy School.* Retrieved July 11, 2014, from http://www.hks.harvard.edu/var/ezp_site/storage/fckeditor/file/pdfs/centers-programs/programs/criminal-justice/ExecSessionPolicing/NPIP-TowardsaNewProfessionalisminPolicing-03-11.pdf.

Truman, J., L. Langton, and M. Planty. (2013, October). *Criminal Victimization, 2012.* Retrieved July 19, 2014, from Office of Justice Programs - Bureau of Justice Statistics: http://www.bjs.gov/content/pub/pdf/cv12.pdf.

Wellford, C., B. Bond, and S. Goodison. (2011). *Crime In New Orleans: Analyzing Crime Trends and New Orleans' Response to Crime.* Washington, D.C.: Bureau of Justice Assistance, Office of Justice Programs (2008-DD-BX-K675).

E

Epilogue
New Orleans: A Great American City

Lydia Voigt, Dee W. Harper, and
William E. Thornton Jr.
—October 2015

The city of New Orleans and the Gulf region commemorated the tenth anniversary of Hurricane Katrina in August 2015. Activities surrounding this anniversary paid special attention on the city's progress in recovery. The city is also preparing for a celebration of the three hundredth anniversary of its establishment in 2018. Together these events are drawing public attention to the question of the future of New Orleans. Despite many positive signs and progress both with respect to the city's recent recovery from Katrina and its more distant past history, citizens remain concerned about many problems that plagued the city even hundreds of years prior to Katrina and that have continued unabated in the post-Katrina era. Among the top concerns of residents, city leaders, and observers of New Orleans is the city's intractably high murder rate (The Future of New Orleans, 2015: A-1, 5).

Beginning with the publication of *The Katrina Index* in December 2005, the Brookings Institute's Metropolitan Policy Program has been tracking the recovery of the New Orleans metropolitan area using indicators that measure changes in population, economy, housing, and infrastructure. In 2007 the institute partnered with the Greater New Orleans Data Center to track an expanded list of indicators, adding indicators related to social inclusion, quality of life, and sustainability. In commemoration of the fifth anniversary of Katrina, *The New Orleans Index at Five* was released in August 2010. This report represents a shift from assessing disaster recovery to documenting progress and transition of the city—"the remaking of a great American city and region" (Greater New Orleans Data Center, 2010: 4). A more recent report, *The New Orleans Index at Eight: Measuring Greater New Orleans' Progress toward Prosperity* continues to offer measures of progress as the city of New

Orleans moves forward (Greater New Orleans Data Center, 2013). This report includes comparisons of New Orleans's performance on the indicators of both the ten-parish region and the nation. While progress may be noted in many of the key indicators, there are still economic, social, and environmental metrics suggesting that New Orleans is not performing as well as the nation. For example, according to the report, on the positive side, by 2012 New Orleans has rebounded from the 2008 recession compared to national metrics. The city has also been experiencing growth in its knowledge-based industries, and entrepreneurship continues to increase as well (501 new business startups per 100,000 adults in 2012, which exceeds the national rate, 56 per 100,000). Moreover, the expansion of arts and culture nonprofits (34 organizations per 100,000 residents) exceeds the national rate (13 per 100,000) (Voigt and Thornton, 2015).

However, the report underscores that there are still important challenges facing the city. For instance, the adult educational attainment level has not been sufficiently advancing in comparison to national benchmarks (e.g., the percent of black men obtaining bachelor's degrees has not increased since 2000). The percentage of growth in minority-owned businesses also lags behind the national average. According to *The New Orleans Index at Eight*, the problem of crime and criminal justice is a particularly important area to address.

While crime rates have declined over the years and are currently lower than pre-Katrina levels, the city's crime rates are still significantly greater than for other cities of comparable size or the national average. Of increasing concern is the incarceration rate in New Orleans, which is among the highest in the state and also in the nation. The report suggests that for New Orleans to truly realize its potential, it must continue its commitment not only to enhance its assets, but to seriously work to solve its problems. In that spirit, *The New Orleans Index at Eight* concludes with the following statement:

> Despite all the shocks it has endured, New Orleans may be on a path toward long-term success. But to fulfill its potential, leaders must look to bolster current strengths and add to them by addressing persistent challenges (Greater New Orleans Community Data Center, 2013: 8).

For example, long-term problems in the New Orleans Police Department (NOPD), including a serious shortage of police officers, have been coming to a head in the last couple of years. The NOPD has lost over 30 percent of its officers consistently over the past five years, down from 1,600 commissioned officers to 1,146 as of April 3, 2015. The city has not had the money to replace officers lost to retirement, termination, or other reasons for these five years (Daley, April 3, 2015: A-1, 8). Additionally, the department is down to twenty-two homicide detectives, a loss of about 25 percent of the staff since 2014 when the division had twenty-nine officers. Hiring new police officers came to a stop when Mayor Mitch Landrieu inherited a $79 million city budget deficit from the Ray Nagin administration (Rising Murders, Falling Ranks, 2015: E-2). Despite requests and admonitions from past and current NOPD administration and the Police Association of New Orleans, new and replacement hires have not been forthcoming until recently with several new recruit classes. It takes, however, a significant amount of time for the training of new officers and their subsequent time on the streets before they are experienced enough to be effective in their duties. The current goal of the mayor and chief of police is to get the number of NOPD officers back up to 1,600, although there is some debate about the possibility or need for this given the reduced population in the city post-Katrina. And, in terms of murder reduction in relation to the number of officers on the streets, and effectiveness of homicide investigations, immediate impacts on murders are unlikely. However, as noted by Rafael Goyeneche, President of the Metropolitan Crime Commission, "an unsolved murder could allow a killer to target more victims or could spark revenge killings…that could put entire neighborhoods at greater risk." (Rising Murders, Falling Ranks, 2015: E-2). And, common wisdom by police leaders and city administrators receiving criticism from residents and business owners (in light of increases in crimes in areas such as the French Quarter) is that more visible police officers are needed now more than ever. Many people believe that there are simply not enough police officers to protect the city and that criminals recognize this weakness and may be taking advantage of the situation. A case in point is a recent proposal by Mayor Landrieu for a new French Quarter sales tax increase to pay for long term deployment of Louisiana State Police troopers in the Quarter, a tourist hub (Daley, April 3, 2015: A-8).

There were 156 murders in New Orleans in 2013 and 150 in 2014, down by about 4 percent. We note, however that there was a double digit percent increase in all categories of major crimes from 2013 to 2014 except murder; the biggest jumps were in rapes and armed robberies, up 39 percent and 37 percent, respectively, over the totals reported for 2013. Nonfatal shooting increased by 20 percent. Reported violent crimes against persons in the city increased by 27 percent from 2013 to 2014 (Daley, Feb. 8, 2015:A-1, 10; Martin, 2015: A-7).

While New Orleans was in eighth place on the list of U.S. Cities with the highest *volume* of murder, it came in second in the nation with respect to the *rate* of murder, which controls for population size (in 2014 the rate was 42 per 100,000 population). The murder rate in New Orleans following the Katrina disaster peaked in at about 77 percent per 100,000 and then began to decline in subsequent years. Although still on the decline, New Orleans's murder rate appears to have stabilized over the last couple of years; however, it remains among the highest in the country. The graph below displays the rates of murder for the cities with the highest volume of murders in the United States As can be observed, in 2014 New Orleans follows Detroit, Michigan (which has the highest rate standing at 45 per 100,000). By way of comparison New York City with its 328 homicides, which is the second highest recorded volume of murders for 2014 (following Chicago's 407 homicides), when adjusted by population size only has a rate of approximately 4 murders per 100,000 population (see graph below).

The small drop in murders for 2014 has been attributed to the *NOLA for Life Murder Reduction Strategy* by city officials, including Mayor Mitch Landrieu, New Orleans Police Department Superintendent Michael Harrison, and Charles West, who heads the team that helped create the plan (City of New Orleans, 2013). Despite this small success in murder reduction, as of the writing of this, three months into 2015, there have been forty-two murders in the city, on average a murder every two or three days, which represents "a significant spike over the same period in 2014." City officials are quick to note that this may not be a trend or foretelling of things to come: "There are always fluctuations throughout the year," said Charles West (Rising Murders, Falling Ranks, 2015: E-2). While it

Murder Rates

Source: FBI, Census, Police Departments

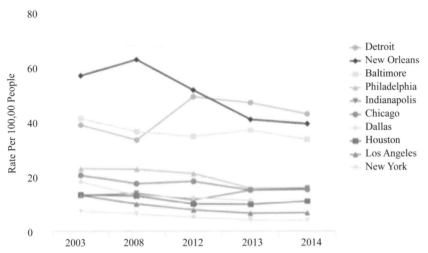

(Source: http://www.thedailybeast.com/article/2015/01/03/america-s-2014murder-capital.html.)

may be too early to know what the final counts of homicide will be for 2015, it is clear that for New Orleans to truly realize its future potential, it must address its root problems before it can solve its crime problem. *NOLA for Life* represents an important step in the right direction.

As the history of New Orleans clearly demonstrates, the city will not be able to solve its crime problem with arrests so long as social inequality or social injustice prevents some its citizens from reaping the full benefits of this great city. In order for the city of New Orleans to maximally achieve its potential as a truly "Great American City," it must value all of its citizens ensuring that young people and families have the opportunities to succeed.

Reference List

City of New Orleans. (2013, September). *NOLA for Life: A Comprehensive Murder Reduction Strategy.* New Orleans, LA: City of New Orleans.

Daily, K. (2015, April 3). "NOPD's Ranks Decrease Again, Despite Recruits." *Times-Picayune.* A-1, 8.

Greater New Orleans Community Data Center. (2010, August). *The New Orleans Index at Five*. New Orleans, LA: Greater New Orleans Community Data Center.

Greater New Orleans Community Data Center. (2013, August). *The New Orleans Index at Eight*. New Orleans, LA: Greater New Orleans Community Data Center.

Martin, N. "Murder Rate Falls in N.O." (2015, January 7). *Times-Picayune*. A-1, 7.

"Rising Murders, Falling Ranks." (2015, March 29). *Times-Picayune*. E-2.

"The Future of New Orleans." (2015, March 4). *Times-Picayune*. A-1, 5.

Voigt, L., and W. E. Thornton. (2016). "Disaster-Related Crime Mitigation and Recovery." In D.W. Harper and K. Frailing (Eds.),*Crime and Criminal Justice in Disaster*. Durham, NC: Carolina Academic Press.

Appendix A

REBUILDING THE NEW ORLEANS POLICE DEPARTMENT – FIRST STEPS
Superintendent Ronal W. Serpas
August 23, 2010

Community policing is a philosophy and an organizational strategy that promotes new partnerships between people and the police. It is based on the premise that both the police and the community must work together to identify, prioritize, and solve contemporary problems such as crime, drugs, fear of crime, social and physical disorder, and overall neighborhood decay, with the goal of improving the overall quality of life in the area.[1]

The New Orleans Police Department will no longer tell neighborhoods what their problems are; instead, the NOPD will listen, collaborate and respond proactively. We will do that by:

1. Respecting the spectacular diversity of our community and our employees, as well as respecting the value of our most important resource – the men and women of the NOPD.

2. Maintaining a zero tolerance for untruthful, unprofessional, unethical or illegal behavior of any employee.

3. Embracing the philosophy of Community Policing to inform and prioritize our crime fighting and quality of life initiatives throughout the City of New Orleans.

4. Using the weekly accountability meeting known as Comstat to hold all commands accountable to this philosophy to ensure department-wide implementation.

5. Employing decentralized assignment of personnel to district commands, as a first choice, to provide district commanders authority, autonomy, resources and accountability to take the initiative in meeting demands for service from New Orleans' neighborhoods and communities.

6. Engaging each neighborhood in collaborative problem solving, prioritize our response, apply the response with relentless follow up, and evaluate results.

---

[1] Trojanowicz, Robert, and Bonnie Bucqueroux. Community Policing: How to get Started. Cincinnati: Anderson Publishing Co., 1994

Superintendent Ronal Serpas
August 23, 2010 Page: 1

7. Auditing crime reporting mechanisms vigorously to ensure accuracy and confidence and work tirelessly to encourage the community to report all crime that is known.

8. Focusing on proactive policing as our first priority to interrupt crime before it happens while ensuring the timeliest response to emergency calls for service as possible.

9. Producing the highest quality investigations and stand ready to contribute in securing convictions of those who have made choices harmful to public safety.

10. Working collaboratively with local, state and federal law enforcement and prosecutorial offices to leverage any and all resources to advance public safety in New Orleans.

These ten principles will guide how the New Orleans Police Department will implement the philosophy of Community Policing. The following sections on crime fighting, community outreach and transparency, integrity and accountability and hiring, training and labor relations detail 65 specific points which are the "First Steps" of rebuilding the New Orleans Police Department.

CRIME FIGHTING

1. The NOPD instituted major reforms on June 25, 2010 to streamline senior leadership positions and reduce what was clearly an inflated and inefficient command structure. Not only did these decisions reduce cost and unnecessary fractures of accountability, the new organizational structure has created more coherent lines of authority, responsibility and clarity of mission. It will be our first duty to continually assess the NOPD for further efficiencies in organizational structure to achieve the maximum effectiveness. *COMPLETED*

2. The NOPD in May 2010 replaced all existing leadership in the Central Evidence and Property Division and initiated an exhaustive analysis of facility and security needs. *COMPLETED*

3. The NOPD, on June 10, 2010, created and staffed a Project Safe Neighborhood (PSN) detective in each of the eight districts and one in the Special Operations Division, a first for the NOPD. The PSN detectives, in collaboration with an ATF Agent assigned to each, are responsible for conducting extensive follow up investigation on every firearms related arrest in the City. Each week, the PSN Detective, ATF Agents, District Attorneys and United States Attorneys meet to go

over each case in exacting detail to determine the most appropriate venue for prosecution. *COMPLETED*

4. The NOPD in <u>June 2010 assigned each District PSN Detectives as the point of contact for Criminal Intelligence information sharing with the NOPD's Specialized Investigations Division (SID) and their District.</u> SID is the unit that participates in state and federal investigative partnerships as well as internal NOPD programs such as the Violent Criminal Abatement Team, Code 6, Narcotics, Vice and Intelligence units. *COMPLETED*

5. The NOPD is <u>making significant changes in and expansion of the Crime Lab's ability to process firearms-related evidence.</u> With the assistance of ATF, the NOPD is now utilizing federally funded grant overtime to hire Firearms Examiners from outside the Department to process some of our backlogged cases. At present, ATF has contracted one examiner from the St. Tammany Parish Sheriff's Office and is in negotiation with other experts. The NOPD is currently exploring ideas with the Jefferson Parish Sheriff's Office to provide another resource to analyze backlogged firearm related cases. The NOPD has successfully secured training for two additional members of the Crime Lab for NIBIN (placing firearms related evidence into computerized systems) entry. These employees have completed the training and are currently undergoing a brief internship, and upon completion will double our staffing in this position from two to four NIBIN entry specialists. The NOPD currently has one full time Firearms Examiner. The NOPD has already identified and assigned an officer to become a full time examiner – this officer is nearing the completion of the academic portion of the two-year training program offered by the ATF to become a Firearms Examiner. In the first quarter of 2011, this employee will begin the 12-18 month field apprentice portion of training. The NOPD has recently identified two additional officers to be sent for ATF training to become Firearms Examiners. The goal is for the NOPD to have 4-5 fully certified ATF-trained Firearms Examiners working full-time with a zero case backlog. *IN PROGRESS*

6. The NOPD has <u>made significant changes to the Crime Lab's ability to process and analyze DNA evidence.</u> Working in conjunction with the Louisiana State Police Crime Lab, the NOPD will secure staffing to begin working under a Memorandum of Understanding with the LSP Crime Lab on NOPD DNA cases. Our personnel will be working at the LSP Crime Lab while we await the construction and certification of the new NOPD DNA Lab. This MOU will serve several valuable purposes: 1) begin working NOPD cases; 2) ensure excellent training and experience that will enable our DNA Lab, once constructed, to have scientists certified, experienced and ready to perform examinations in the NOPD DNA Lab; 3) reduce the need and cost of outsourcing DNA cases to private labs;

and 4) reduce the time between the recovery of the evidence and test result identifications, thereby speeding potential prosecutions. The NOPD is currently interviewing for a new DNA Lab Director. *IN PROGRESS*

7. The NOPD is <u>committed to rebuilding and establishing a fully functional, fully accredited, Crime Lab</u> capable of providing state-of-the-art services to departmental investigators so that timely and quality prosecutions can be achieved. *IN PROGRESS*

8. The NOPD in June 2010 <u>requested the assistance of the U.S. Department of Justice - Bureau of Justice Assistance, to conduct a review of the homicide investigation function</u> within the Department and will make recommendations to the Department in terms of policy, procedure and training improvements that will expectantly lead to an improved clearance (closure) rates. This analysis will also assist in setting the appropriate staffing level. The BJA begins their review August 23, 2010. The NOPD added additional homicide detectives in late May 2010. *IN PLACE*

9. The NOPD is negotiating with U.S. Department of Justice to provide <u>onsite technical expert analysis of Domestic Violence and Sexual Assault investigations.</u> *IN PROGRESS*

10. The NOPD in July 2010 <u>realigned the Sex Crimes Section and placed it under a new commander tasked to conduct a review of the existing policy and procedures of the unit.</u> *COMPLETED*

11. The NOPD in August 2010 <u>requested The Louisiana Commission on Law Enforcement (LCLE) to perform an audit to determine the status and accuracy of NOPD classification protocols in the Sex Crimes Section.</u> Subject to the requested audit and other review(s), additional investigations may be required and conducted. *IN PROGRESS*

12. The NOPD in July 2010 <u>established two District-Based Task Forces</u> for each District. The Task Forces are staffed by one sergeant and six officers in each Task Force Unit, providing the flexible units District Commanders need to immediately respond to crime patterns and trends identified by community and neighborhood groups and NOPD analysis. *COMPLETED*

13. The NOPD in July 2010 <u>established a District Based Narcotics Team</u> of one sergeant and six detectives in each District to conduct street level investigations and follow up on Crime Stoppers Narcotics Hotline Complaints (phone 822-1111). The District Narcotics Teams are linked with the Specialized

Investigations Division Narcotics Unit to ensure consistency of investigations, sharing of critical information, equipment and training. Likewise, District-Based Narcotics Teams are also routinely sharing information with District Detectives to advance our crime fighting mission. ***COMPLETED***

14. The NOPD in June 2010 <u>decentralized and reassigned the Traffic Division Motorcycle Officers to the eight Districts</u> to provide another resource under the control of District Commanders to respond effectively and timely to problems identified and prioritized with neighborhood and community groups. ***COMPLETED***

15. The NOPD in June 2010 <u>decentralized and reassigned the Mounted Unit</u> from the Special Operations Division to the Eighth District to streamline and make accountable this resource to the area of the City wherein it performs the majority of its duties. ***COMPLETED***

16. The NOPD in July 2010 <u>created a Violent Criminal Abatement Team</u> assigned to the Specialized Investigations Division. This team of ten detectives and supervisors is specifically tasked with identifying and conducting extensive and thorough follow up investigations on the 25 most violent criminals in New Orleans. This team works closely with the Orleans Parish District Attorney's Office and other local, state and federal investigative agencies to ensure a narrow and relentless focus on these criminals. ***COMPLETED***

17. The NOPD in July 2010 <u>revitalized its Code 6 Program</u>. This is a program modeled after a very successful initiative of the Jefferson Parish Sheriff's Office. These detectives conduct a detailed analysis of career criminals. A pre-determined numerical value is assessed to each crime for which the suspect has been arrested. The value is commensurate to the violence associated with the crime. Once a pre-determined threshold has been reached the suspect is designated as a Code 6 offender. Once established, the designation allows for closer scrutiny by the NOPD and other criminal justice agencies in an effort to establish multiple bill offender status and ensure lengthier sentences post-conviction. It also establishes a basis to argue for higher bonds or no bond. Moreover, the NOPD has requested and received a cooperative assignment of two Orleans Parish Sheriff's Deputies to this team. ***COMPLETED***

18. The NOPD in July of 2010 <u>revived its Criminal Intelligence Unit.</u> The Intelligence Unit traditionally has monitored subversive groups both electronically and physically and provided dignitary protection. The mission has expanded to include documenting organized violent individuals and groups responsible for drug trafficking, murder, shootings, kidnappings, armed robberies,

home invasion burglaries, and serial theft. The Intelligence Unit now coordinates information across district/parish boundaries in an effort to reduce violent crime resulting from "turf" battles and retaliatory acts. *COMPLETED*

19. The NOPD, working closely with the District Attorney and US Attorney, will create and deliver <u>new training to all officers on the topics of: Report Writing, Courtroom Testimony; obtaining Search Warrants, Arrest Warrants, etc</u>. Holding accountable and successfully prosecuting those who have created victims in our community requires a competent, professional and thorough police investigation, as well as proficient participation in the courtroom phase of the Criminal Justice System. *IN PROGRESS*

20. The NOPD Special Operations Division (SOD) has been <u>tasked with identifying and following up on residents of New Orleans who have been convicted of a firearms crime.</u> SOD will be working in collaboration with Louisiana Probation and Parole officials. The NOPD has submitted for consideration a "Gun Offender Registry" ordinance following a successful ordinance and police strategy on this plan from the City of Baltimore. *COMPLETED*

21. The NOPD has <u>immediately begun a renewed focus on enforcing Curfew and Truancy ordinances</u>. Ensuring that children are off the streets during curfew has the dual benefit of reducing their risk of being the victims of crime and/or being the perpetrator of a crime. Ensuring that children are attending school reduces the rates of their victimization, rates as perpetrators, as well as provides an opportunity for the school systems to engage these children in a positive way. In the areas of Curfew and Truancy, the preferred course of action will be to return children to families and/or a school. *COMPLETED*

22. The NOPD in August 2010 is <u>purchasing Fingerprint Kits, supplies and is providing training for District Platoon personnel</u> to be able to search for and collect fingerprints on the scenes of crimes they are called to investigate. *Police Officers on the Patrol Platoons are police investigators, not simply report writers.* It is in the best interest of the NOPD and the citizens of our community to utilize, as much as possible, the power of collecting fingerprints on any and all crimes in our community. By training and equipping Patrol personnel with this resource, the duty of Crime Lab staff to respond to these calls will be greatly reduced, allowing the Crime Lab to further refine and utilize its specialty crime scene skills while, at the same time, advancing those skills through training. *COMPLETED*

23. The NOPD <u>in 2011, for the first time in modern history, will conduct a comprehensive and exhaustive analysis of staffing and deployment.</u> Unfortunately there has been no sound analysis of NOPD staffing models or

District boundary configurations in generations. The NOPD will take advantage of utilizing the most sophisticated and proven analytic tools to make these determinations and is in the process of obtaining these tools. *IN PROGRESS*

COMMUNITY OUTREACH AND TRANSPARENCY

24. The NOPD in May 2010 opened all Comstat Meetings (Department and Districts) to the public. The purpose of this is to demonstrate openness and transparency in the day to day functions of the Department, including accountability of its commanders, as it serves the citizens of New Orleans. *COMPLETED*

25. The NOPD in May 2010 created new practices for "opening up" the process for interviews and responses to media requests regarding NOPD activities, actions and employees. *COMPLETED*

26. The NOPD in July 2010, in consultation with the Office of Inspector General, created a methodologically sound Citizen Callback System. Each month, a list of randomly selected victims of violent and non-violent Part I crime are contacted by the Superintendent's Office of Compliance. The call serves five purposes: 1) provides for confirmation on the accuracy of the report; 2) allows the complainant to provide any additional information he/she may have; 3) provides for an opportunity to assess the delivery of police service and the professionalism of the officer; 4) provides positive feedback to employees who have performed well; and 5) provides feedback for remediation or discipline of employees who have failed to perform as expected. The NOPD is expanding these callbacks with the same methodologically sound format by phoning victims of Part II crimes. Finally, the NOPD is initiating another audit procedure wherein field supervisors will randomly visit the scenes of calls to NOPD where the original officer recorded the disposition as Necessary Action Taken, Unfounded or Gone on Arrival. The accuracy of the reporting of crime[2] is critical, and these audits will help that both the NOPD and the citizens of New Orleans can have confidence in crime reporting. *COMPLETED*

27. The NOPD in June 2010 opened for public and media review the crime reporting mechanisms of the NOPD. *COMPLETED*

---

[2]National Crime Victimization Data generally shows less than a 50% report rate of violent and property crime in U.S. for the period 1999 – 2008, see Figure 3, page 7:
http://bjs.ojp.usdoj.gov/content/pub/pdf/cvo8.pdf
A recent survey, August 2009, conducted by the New Orleans Crime Coalition of New Orleans residents, found that of those persons who responded yes to the question (#23) that they or any member of their family had been the victim of crime in the last 12 months, only 59% (Question #24) responded yes to the question, "…did you call 911 to report the crime?"

28. The NOPD in June 2010 <u>requested and received assistance from a local university that will conduct an independent analysis of NOPD's automated crime reporting systems.</u> *IN PLACE*

29. The NOPD in June 2010, in response to community requests, <u>revamped the public crime mapping web site and information to make the maps timelier and more useful.</u> *COMPLETED*

30. The NOPD in June of 2010 <u>created and staffed the new position - Community Coordinating Sergeant</u> (the "CoCo") in each District. The CoCo Sergeant has the specific duty of following up on the status and expansion of Neighborhood and Business Watch Programs. CoCo Sergeants are also responsible for supervising the Quality of Life Officers in each District, as well as serving as the main conduit for the coordination/communication of community requests to their District Commanders. CoCo Sergeants actively engage the community in crime prevention strategies, and, in the near future, will receive training in the area of Crime Prevention Through Environmental Design, Problem Oriented Policing and Crime Analysis and Neighborhood Watch development training. CoCo Sergeants report directly to their District Commanders to ensure a seamless and immediate response to neighborhood and community concerns by NOPD Districts. *COMPLETED*

31. The NOPD in September 2010 <u>has partnered with Dr. Michael Cowan, Loyola University, to provide Collaborative Community Problem Solving training for all CoCo Sergeants, Quality of Life Officers and Crime Prevention Unit officers.</u> Dr. Cowan has been involved in interfaith and interracial community organizing in New Orleans since 1992, and is a noted academic and practitioner in this field. This training will include two, two hour orientation sessions with follow on monthly sessions to increase the likelihood of success of the CoCo program. *IN PLACE*

32. The NOPD has <u>created and will implement before the end of 2010 a "Cops, Clergy and Community Coalition"</u> (CCCC). The CCCC is a Faith-Based Community Coalition which serves as a uniting force and catalyst to rebuild faith, restore citizen trust, and enhance quality of life services, while also serving as a resource clearinghouse for community policing, crime prevention, problem solving and collaboration strategies. *IN PROGRESS*

33. The NOPD will <u>offer an expanded and revitalized Citizen Police Academy</u> (CPA) in the Fourth Quarter of 2010. The CPA is a well-known, successful program that provides a unique opportunity for citizens to learn about the inner-workings of the

NOPD. For the first time, the NOPD will routinely offer the CPA on a continuing basis, no less than once per calendar year. *IN PLACE*

34. The NOPD in June 2010 dramatically expanded the Crime Prevention Unit's (CPU) mission to include "cold calls" on businesses (653 visits since inception), community groups and Faith based institutions throughout New Orleans. In partnership with Crime Stoppers, CPU personnel make visits to businesses that the NOPD with which the NOPD does not currently have a relationship. In these contacts, CPU personnel share the message of the NOPD Crime Prevention program, Crime Stoppers, and then link these business owners or community members with their District Commanders and CoCo Sergeants. CoCo Sergeants then conduct follow up calls to provide additional contact and linkage to District services. *COMPLETED*

35. The NOPD will create a Citizens Advisory Panel (CAP) in the first quarter of 2011. The CAP will provide input and assist the department with identifying and resolving community issues and concerns. The goal is to create a diverse advisory group made up of the communities/neighborhoods we serve, and to educate and inform the Department about the challenging issues and concerns within these specific communities. *IN PROGRESS*

36. The NOPD in July 2010 initiated monthly Crime Walks. The purpose of Crime Walks is to engage the senior leadership of each District, NOPD senior leadership and members of the NOPD to walk among the people of our community to hear first-hand about community needs/issues while, at the same time, creating personal and responsive relationships. *COMPLETED*

37. The NOPD has expanded in the fall of 2010 walk throughs and lunch meetings in Elementary and Middle Schools. This is a very positive activity, not unlike the Officer Friendly Program of years ago. District Commanders will identify time in the week to assign officers to Elementary and Middle Schools throughout our community and allow Patrol Officers time to engage and meet children. Over time, the NOPD will seek partners to help fund and produce appropriate literature to share with these school aged children. *COMPLETED*

38. The NOPD in July 2010 began a partnership with Nolan Rollins, President and CEO of the Urban League of Greater New Orleans to have NOPD CoCo Sergeants make brief presentations to Urban League job skills programs, as well as educate CoCo Sergeants on Urban League programs and training. By educating them on these important opportunities, CoCo Sergeants can incorporate this information into their community presentations. Issues of joblessness and the need for job training are discussed at many community meetings attended by the

NOPD. CoCo Sergeants will be briefed on, and can discuss, the City of New Orleans' JOB One Office which provides assistance in developing resumes, computer labs, interviewing tools, along with a list of job openings and availability of employment in the Greater New Orleans Area. *IN PROGRESS*

39. The NOPD in the First Quarter of 2011 will establish an El Protector Program to engage its Hispanic/Latino community. The El Protector Program originated in the California Highway Patrol and was initiated in the Washington State Patrol in 2002, and the Nashville Police Department in 2005. Nashville's El Protector Program, in February 2009, received national recognition from the Vera Institute of Justice as a "best practice" in reaching across the language divide. El Protector-type programs will enhance the NOPD's ability to serve the ever changing diversity of our community. The NOPD will also analyze the need for this or a similar program in our Vietnamese community, as well as others that may have language differences. *IN PROGRESS*

40. The NOPD in August 2010 implemented new policy directing the Victim / Witness Assistance Unit of the Investigation & Support Bureau to oversee identification and processing of U Visa's for non-citizen crime victims. NOPD staff will work closely with the District Attorney to ensure that non-citizen crime victims receive the assistance they need through this process. The U Visa is designed for non-citizen crime victims who have suffered substantial physical or mental abuse flowing from criminal activity, and cooperated with law enforcement officials investigating/prosecuting such criminal activity. *COMPLETED*

41. The NOPD in 2011 will field Bicycle Units and an expanded Mounted Officer program in the eight Districts. It is well established in Community Policing literature that programs such as these serve to put officers closer to the communities they assist, thus creating better relationships, communication and information sharing. *IN PROGRESS*

42. The NOPD Reserve Division has been directed to create for 2011 a "volunteer" program for members of our community who wish to work with the NOPD. This program will mirror a very successful program in the Phoenix Police Department. *IN PROGRESS*

INTEGRITY - ACCOUNTABILITY

43. The NOPD in June 2010 dramatically altered the Public Integrity Bureau (PIB) by appointing for the first time a civilian Deputy Superintendent to lead this unit. Arlinda Pierce Westbrook, Esq., was appointed on June 25, 2010, and brings 13

years of experience as a licensed attorney in the New Orleans' City Attorney's Office. Chief Westbrook's experience includes defending Police Administration decisions in employee misconduct matter and providing complex legal opinion and advice through research. *COMPLETED*

44. The NOPD on September 1, 2010 <u>will implement a revised Honesty and Truthfulness policy that will call for presumptive termination, without progressive discipline,</u> for any employee who makes a materially false statement with the intent to deceive. *IN PLACE*

45. The NOPD on September 1, 2010 <u>will implement a revised False or Inaccurate Reports policy that will call for presumptive termination, without progressive discipline,</u> when an employee knowingly makes, allows or causes to be made, a false or inaccurate oral or written report of an official nature. *IN PLACE*

46. The NOPD on September 1, 2010 <u>will implement a new Failure to Report Misconduct policy.</u> Any department employee who observes or becomes aware of any act of misconduct by another employee of the government shall immediately report the incident to their immediate supervisor or the most appropriate New Orleans Police Department supervisor (Violation of this provision may be charged up to and including the category of the underlying offense not reported). *IN PLACE*

47. The NOPD on September 1, 2010 <u>will implement a new Failure to Cooperate/Withhold Information policy.</u> In accordance with established rights under law, employees shall not withhold any information, acts, or omissions known to the employee that purposefully interfere or disrupt an authorized investigation, whether internally or externally, investigated by any official entity. Additionally, any employee who withholds information or fails to cooperate with any internal investigation may be disciplined in addition to any other disciplinary action based upon conduct disclosed by the primary investigation. *IN PLACE*

48. The NOPD in the Third and Fourth Quarter 2010 <u>will undertake a complete and exhaustive analysis of the "Early Warning System" and the "Professional Performance Enhancement Program"</u> (PPEP). Once thought to be national models, the NOPD Early Warning System and PPEP have not maintained the necessary level of excellence and will be fundamentally restructured. *IN PROGRESS*

49. The NOPD will <u>continue and expand the use of "integrity" checks</u> of officers and employees to ensure the community can expect and receive the highest quality of service and professionalism from NOPD employees. *COMPLETED*

Superintendent Ronal Serpas
August 23, 2010 Page: 11

50. The NOPD-PIB will dedicate full cooperation and collaboration with the Independent Police Monitor. The mutually respectful relationship between the NOPD-PIB and the IPM will serve the community and the NOPD well. *COMPLETED*

51. The NOPD, effective September 1, 2010, will prohibit the practice of accepting "cash" payments for off-duty paid details. *IN PLACE*

52. The NOPD by October 1, 2010, will implement procedures that will track and document every off–duty paid detail hour worked by every officer, ensuring compliance with existing and future regulations. *IN PLACE*

53. The NOPD is currently expanding the use of its existing in-car video system to include installation in District Task Force Units. These Mobile Video Units (MVU's) are currently installed in marked patrol cars and document officer/citizen interaction, especially during traffic incidents and pedestrian stops. The video/audio records created ensure accountability and provide supervisors with an important training and/or disciplinary tool. Grant applications have been submitted to purchase additional units. *IN PROGRESS*

54. The NOPD in June 2010 activated a previously unused feature of its Automatic Vehicle Location (AVL) system in patrol vehicles. This new activation, combined with recently developed software, captures the previous locations of patrol vehicles equipped with the system, providing supervisors with an important tool in ensuring the most effective and efficient use of their patrol resource. *COMPLETED*

55. The NOPD in August 2010 created a Use of Force Investigations team, comprised of all Integrity Control Officers (Lieutenants) and PIB Supervisors who are tasked with creating a modern and best practice Use of Force Investigations Manual. This first of its kind manual in the NOPD will create a guideline and expectations of all Use of Force Investigations conducted by NOPD supervisors. This project will be completed no later than December 1, 2010. *IN PROGRESS*

HIRING – TRAINING – LABOR RELATIONS

56. The NOPD will in the Third Quarter of 2010 work collaboratively with the Civil Service Department to revitalize the hiring standards of NOPD Recruit candidates. The hiring of new officers is one of the most critical actions of a police department. The NOPD will not be the employer of last resort; instead, the NOPD will seek to identify the very best applicants, and only offer employment

to those candidates that meet the highest standards of education, experience and potential success as a Police Officer. *IN PROGRESS*

57. The NOPD, before the next Recruit Class is in place, will completely and exhaustively analyze and reorganize the entire Recruit Training Program and curricula. By partnering with the Louisiana State Police, local and state prosecutorial offices, as well as other police training professional associations, the NOPD will put in place a Training Academy that espouses and utilizes the best practices in modern police training. *IN PROGRESS*

58. The NOPD will dramatically expand and alter the existing annual in-service training program. The existing annual in-service training fails at providing any meaningful or useful information to further the professionalism of NOPD Officers. In 2011, the in-service training program will be expanded to a mandatory 40 hours per employee, up from the existing 26 hours (all of which have not been mandatory), and will ensure that the annual in-service meets industry best practices. *IN PROGRESS*

59. The NOPD and the Louisiana Army National Guard have agreed to provide Leadership Training to all Police Sergeants and Police Lieutenants. This valuable on-site training will cover core areas of supervision, leadership, accountability, mentoring, counseling, etc. *IN PLACE*

60. The NOPD beginning in November 2010 will partner with the Police Executive Research Forum to provide advanced training for senior NOPD leadership in the, *Leadership in Action: Developing the Next Generation of Leaders* project funded by the US Department Justice – Bureau of Justice Assistance. Over 18 months, three departments, two from the United States and one from Great Britain, will be the recipients of this valuable and insightful leadership development training. *IN PLACE*

61. The NOPD during the months of June, July and August 2010 received advanced training in Mediation (40 hour block of instruction) for all senior leadership. In addition, all sergeants and lieutenants received the Responding to Allegations of Racial Profiling course. This training was provided by the U.S. Department of Justice – Community Relations Service. *COMPLETED*

62. The NOPD in August 2010 will implement a new Job Performance Improvement Plan (JPIP) policy. The JPIP is a written plan designed to address unsatisfactory, and/or below standard employee performance, and/or behavior, with clearly defined performance objectives and established timelines for improvement to assist the employee in obtaining acceptable performance. Failure of an employee

to successfully complete the terms and conditions of a JPIP will be grounds for corrective and/or disciplinary action. ***IN PLACE***

63. The NOPD in September 2010 <u>will implement a new Transfer Selection Process policy</u>. The purpose of the selection process is to promote the fair, equitable and transparent selection of applicants for positions within the Department. The policy will provide applicants with a defined set of standards so that an applicant can prepare himself/herself with the qualifications for a preferred position as well as provide for feedback to candidates not selected so that they may improve their Knowledge, Skills and Abilities for future position announcements. ***IN PLACE***

64. The NOPD in June 2010 <u>initiated monthly meetings with formal labor organizations of the Department</u>. Working together with labor allows for the on-going assessment and requisite realignment of resources and directives, which will enhance policy and procedure. ***COMPLETED***

65. The NOPD in June 2010 <u>established an "In Touch" anonymous communication system that allows employees to communicate directly with the Superintendent</u>. This modern day "suggestion" box provides an outstanding opportunity to communicate messages, ideas, etc. ***COMPLETED***

UPDATED INFORMATION – RELATIONSHIP NOPD AND DA'S OFFICE[3]

A coordinated effort to expedite the receipt of police reports by the DA and the expedited dispositions of cases has been a success. There has been a mutual realignment of infrastructure to better coordinate the timely completion of reports and the smooth transmission of these reports between the NOPD and the DA. Soon there will be a substantially automated report filing and receiving system that will represent a philosophical and technological breakthrough of considerable value.

DA Office efforts to develop training and management feedback on the conduct of investigations for the purpose of improving the quality of investigations and improving the likelihood of case prosecution and favorable court outcomes has resulted in increased acceptance rate in all range of cases while the successful disposition of cases has increased.

NOPD and DA's Office have established a joint case review process for Homicides, Sex Crimes and other Major Offenses that improves the quality of investigations, raises the rate of institution of prosecutions, improves the pre-trial preparation of the cases and has begun to show results in the timely conviction of serious offenders.

---

[3] This information is jointly provided by the NOPD and the DA's Office

NOPD and the DA in cooperation with the Municipal Court Judges, the Municipal Court Clerk and the Sheriff's office have designed a program to transfer certain non-violent misdemeanors from Criminal Court or to institute prosecutions in Municipal Court of non-violent state law misdemeanor violations. Preliminary findings suggest a significant reduction in the amount of Police Officers out of service for court appearances, reduced the time from arrest to disposition from approximately 5 months to 10 days, has improved the rate of favorable court dispositions and has resulted in a substantial reduction in pretrial detention jail population.

CLOSING

In building on these First Steps, the New Orleans Police Department will routinely assess its performance, structure and use of technology, and will immediately alter course to ensure continuous improvement toward the highest level of efficient, effective and respectful service.

The New Orleans Police Department is but one agency in the City of New Orleans governmental structure and recognizes its duty and responsibility to collaborate and cooperate with all agencies within the government. More specifically, the NOPD is aligned closely with the City of New Orleans Public Safety agencies: New Orleans Fire Department, the New Orleans Emergency Medical Services and Homeland Security agencies.

The New Orleans Police Department fully embraces its duty and responsibility to manage effectively and efficiently its resources, both human and capital, and also the criticality of operating within budget allocations received.

The New Orleans Police Department will continue to work collaboratively with the U.S. Department of Justice Civil Rights Division to advance the agency and utilize best practices, technical assistance and other relevant assistance.

The men and women of the New Orleans Police Department appreciate the support of Mayor Mitch Landrieu, the City Council and the community we serve, and we dedicate our service daily to expanding and increasing the public safety and quality of life of this great city.

# # # #

Superintendent Ronal Serpas
August 23, 2010 Page: 15

Appendix B

Reform Status Report
May 2010 – December 2012
(*32 Months*)

RONAL W. SERPAS
Superintendent of Police

Contents

Reform Status Report
May 2010 – December 2012
(*32 Months*)

INTRODUCTION

By the end of December 2012, a total of thirty-two months have passed since Mayor Mitchell J. Landrieu took office. One of the first orders of business for the Mayor was to remake a crumbling police department.

In May 2010, Mayor Landrieu appointed Ronal W. Serpas as Superintendent of the New Orleans Police Department and tasked him with restoring accountability and public confidence in the department. After a comprehensive assessment, in August 2010 Chief Serpas released a detailed 65 point plan entitled "*Rebuilding the New Orleans Police Department – The First Steps.*" This 15 page road map for reform seeks to create a department built on the philosophy of community policing and accountability. The initiatives outlined in this plan were designed to build on NOPD's capacity to fight crime; ensure transparency and accountability at all times; expand community outreach; and improve hiring, training & labor relations.

As we move forward into 2013 the following is meant to provide an overview of the work done thus far and update the public on our progress. We remain committed to our efforts to reform the NOPD and will ensure continuous improvement in our performance.

CRIME FIGHTING

- **Sexual Assault Investigations:** In the summer of 2010, new leadership was assigned to the Rape Investigation Section. Rather quickly, it became evident that the section was in extreme disarray. Rape investigations were not being fully investigated; sexual assault kits were not being processed and tested; and victims were not receiving the appropriate service, or resources. While a complete overhaul of the section was undertaken, the following initiatives were critical to the turnaround:

    a. LCLE Audit – By invitation of the newly appointed Rape Investigations Commander, the Louisiana Commission on Law Enforcement conducted an audit of sexual assault classifications. The audit confirmed the suspicions of the new Rape Investigations Commander and revealed that sexual assaults were being downgraded and under reported. In response, sweeping reforms of the unit were implemented. Additionally, dozens of downgraded cases were re-investigated.

    b. Marshall Project - Through a collaborative effort between the New Orleans Police Department, the National Institute of Justice, the Louisiana State Police and the Marshall University Forensic Science Center, a backlog of **833** sexual assault kits were tested in a 1-year period between January 2011 and January 2012. The project yielded **78** hits in the Combined DNA Index System ("*CODIS*"). By the end of 2012, all **78** cases were investigated by the Special Victims Section. Of the total cases investigated thus far, **nine** have been cleared by arrests and **one** has been referred to the District Attorney's Office for a grand jury indictment.

    c. *CODIS* Section – Prior to May 2010, nothing was being done with *CODIS* (or Combined DNA Index System), information / hits resulting from Sexual Assault Kit examinations. In the summer of 2010 a *CODIS* Section was created in the Rape Investigation Section. A detective was assigned to manage and investigate *CODIS* hits, which remained untouched for years. The renewed investigative follow-up effort targeting *CODIS* hits has brought numerous cases of sexual assault to a valuable conclusion for victims of these crimes.

- **Domestic Violence Investigations:** While the Domestic Violence Unit existed prior to May 2010, they did little more than direct victims to applicable resources. A change in the unit commander was made in the summer of 2010. Additionally, Domestic Violence detectives were provided with a new mission and operational direction. Detectives were charged with conducting follow-up investigations on all felony domestic violence cases, to include strangulation cases. New protocols were developed in collaboration with the District Attorney and the New Orleans Family Justice Center. Moreover, the following initiatives were instituted:

4

a. Consistent staffing levels were developed to provide follow-up investigation on all felony domestic violence cases.

b. In collaboration with the Orleans Parish District Attorney's Office and the New Orleans Family Justice Center, a comprehensive New Orleans Integrated Domestic Violence Protocol was completed and implemented in May 2011.

c. In addition to the Integrated Protocol, the Domestic Violence Unit collaborated with the city's Blueprint for Public Safety Coordinator and developed new policies and procedures in the New Orleans Police Department's response to Domestic Violence. A subsequent new DV policy and procedural guideline were established for the DV response by all New Orleans Police Officers.

d. The Domestic Violence Unit collaborated with the New Orleans Child Advocacy Center in developing a protocol for children of domestic violence. For the first time, all children present within the residence of felony domestic violence case are part of the forensic interview process during follow up investigations.

e. In the fall of 2011, the NOPD Police Academy provided mandatory on-line Victim/Witness Assistance and Domestic Violence training to all police department members. In addition, outside training was conducted by the U.S. Attorney's Office and the La. Attorney General's Office who co-sponsored a series of domestic violence training seminars for over 300 officers. The NOPD personnel were also provided training through the Louisiana Commission on Law Enforcement, relative to the Louisiana Protective Order Registry. Finally, Sex Crimes, Child Abuse and Domestic Violence detectives received victim focused training provided by Tulane University.

f. In the fall of 2011, the Investigations and Support Bureau ("ISB") provided over **60** roll call training sessions to district personnel on the new domestic violence policy and the new Orleans Integrated Domestic Violence Protocol.

g. ISB personnel were instrumental in developing curriculum on revised domestic violence procedures and the Integrated Domestic Violence Protocol. This curriculum was used throughout the 2012 In-Service Training. Every police officer and supervisor on the police department received this training in 2012.

h. The Domestic Violence Unit participated in numerous specialized training courses, which were incorporated into police officer in-service training. More specifically an Elder Abuse Seminar was sponsored in 2011 and the National Family Justice Conference was sponsored in 2012. Both of these training opportunities were sponsored by the Taylor Foundation. Additionally, the Domestic Violence Unit regularly sponsors training on teen dating violence and domestic violence prevention to students at the local high schools and universities.

- ***Project Safe Neighborhood:*** In July 2010, Superintendent Serpas directed that each of the eight districts and the Special Operations Division staff and assign a Project Safe Neighborhood ("*PSN*") detective. This brought from one to nine the total number of PSN detectives in the NOPD. The PSN detectives are charged with follow-up investigation of any arrest involving a firearm. Then each week, since July 2010, a PSN meeting is held at NOPD Headquarters where the PSN Detective, specialized Orleans Parish District Attorneys, U.S. Attorneys and members of the ATF meet to review each case to determine the best prosecutorial course and if there is any additional investigation required or desired to enhance the case. Since its formation, more than 790 cases have been processed under this initiative.

- ***Homicide Investigations:*** Like many other sections of the ISB, the Homicide Section was totally re-engineered in 2011. The transformation began with the collaboration between the Bureau of Justice Assistance and the police department. In June 2010, Superintendent Serpas met with senior leaders of the BJA to seek technical assistance in assessing how the NOPD conducts homicide investigations. In March 2011, the BJA delivered a report outlining eighty-two recommendations. The recommendations covered many areas of needed reform to include staffing, training, revised protocols and collaboration. Currently, of the eighty-two recommendations all but four have been implemented. Remaining items (e.g. – eliminating compensatory time and take home vehicle use fee) will be further reviewed. Highlights of the re-engineered Homicide Section include:

  a. Increased Staffing – The staffing of Homicide was increased from 16 detectives to **32** detectives. Most of these detectives received specially developed Crime Scene Preservation and Homicide Investigation training, which was delivered through BJA.

  b. Training – A focus on training enabled Homicide detectives to receive instruction in Homicide Investigations, Crime Scene Preservation & Evidence Collection, Interview & Interrogation, DNA & Forensics, Computerized Voice Stress Analysis, and more.

  c. Docu-Share Scanning – Protocols have been established to scan all homicide case files, so that they can be maintained in a digital format. To date, 4 years of homicide case files have been scanned (2009 – 2012).

  d. Community Policing - Acting specifically with the effort to implement the BJA's recommendation to "make a proactive effort and establish trusted and two-way communication sharing with the families of homicide victims", the Homicide Section implemented several community policing initiatives. Beginning in 2012, Homicide detectives participated in monthly City Crime

Walks and attended monthly NONPACC meetings (i.e., monthly meetings held in each patrol district between police and community members). The Homicide Section also implemented the "Next of Kin" program, holding three community meetings in 2011, and quarterly meetings in 2012 and thereafter. The "Next of Kin" meeting give the families of homicide victims the opportunity to meet with detectives one-on-one and discuss the case investigation. Additionally, the Homicide Section began a program known as *RESET*, or Rapid Engagement of Support in the Event of Trauma. *RESET* provides support to the community by immediately connecting the families to available resources. In 2012, the *RESET* team was activated a total of **34** times. Members met and spoke with **551** persons, who were offered a variety of social services. The *RESET* program also generated 7 investigative leads, which were forwarded to the Homicide Section.

- *Scientific Criminal Investigations Division – Firearms Unit:* In September of 2010, the Firearms Unit consisted of one Bureau of Alcohol, Tobacco and Firearms ("*ATF*") trained Firearms Examiner (who was to retire), two ATF trained technicians working on the National Integrated Ballistic Identification Network (NIBIN), two officers conducting weapon test fires and one officer doing serial number restorations. It was soon discovered that there was a **backlog** of potential NIBIN "hits" (where casings from two or more shooting cases may be related) numbering almost **500**. Additionally, weapons (handgun, rifles and shotguns) requiring test firing (to generate casings to be entered into NIBIN) numbered over **1000**. Firearms examination cases were being done at the rate of five per month and only immediately prior to prosecution, not for investigative leads. A complete overhaul of the unit was undertaken. Highlights of that overhaul include:

  a. Equipment Upgrades – The NIBIN equipment provided by the ATF in 2010 was the oldest in the nationwide system. With the assistance of the local Special Agent in Charge for ATF, this equipment was replaced with the latest version of Brass Trax 3-D and MatchPoint Plus. We are also in the final stages of purchasing a "data compressor" that will significantly speed up the transmission of the image files used by NIBIN and allow a near instantaneous return on possible matches rather than the 4 plus hours (or overnight) we currently experience.

  b. Staffing - The Firearms Unit staffing was increased from one (10 to three (3) ATF trained Firearms Examiners. Two examiners have graduated from the National Firearms Academy hosted by the ATF with one additional member currently attending this training which is scheduled for completion in May 2013. In order to graduate from the national ATF Firearms Academy, candidates must complete four (4) months of preliminary preparation work; four (4) months of classroom training in Maryland; and four (4) months of research project and presentation. In addition, there are now six (6) fully trained NIBIN technicians in the Firearms Unit and tow (2) alternates who are fully trained NIBIN technicians. The training for these individuals was also accomplished through the assistance of ATF, which virtually required a commitment from them in providing a one-on-one / instructor-to-student ratio. ATF has additionally provided technical training to three NOPD members in use of new '*Brass Trax 3D*' equipment and has dedicated two ATF agents to work alongside our personnel.

c. Backlogs Cleared – Over the past 2.5 years, the test fire backlog for handguns has been cleared. Moreover, the enormous list of "potential NIBIN HITS" has also been eliminated, as well as, the backlog of firearms needing serial number restoration (over 100). The multi-year backlog of Firearms Examination cases on shootings and murders is nearly eliminated. Projections are that ALL back logs of test fires and shooting cases will be completed by the end of 2013. The national average for the number of firearms examinations one Examiner will do in a month is five (5). Our Firearms Unit has done **812** examinations in 2012 alone. Since the change in command in 2010 and the restructure of the unit, **1,795** Firearms Examinations have been conducted (an average of more than 64 a month). **This is _13 times_ the national average.** Over **12,000** entries have been made into NIBIN and over **3800** weapons test fired. The Unit is near the **1,000** mark for confirmed NIBIN "HITS". (A "HIT" is a link between two or more cases involving the same weapon.) Investigative units like Homicide, the Gang Unit, Intelligence and District Investigative Units routinely receive Firearms Examination Reports and HIT Reports now to aid in furthering investigations.

- **Evidence Processing:** The handling and processing of evidence is critical to an effective prosecution. In May 2010, the Central Evidence & Property Section was still reeling from the aftermath of Hurricane Katrina. The facility was crammed with an ever increasing amount of property; DNA evidence was scattered throughout the warehouse; and large amounts of money remained on the premises. While numerous initiatives were taken to improve the efficiency of the section, the following are the most notable:

    a. Cash Audit – For the first time since Hurricane Katrina, a complete audit of the money stored in the facility was conducted. When completed, over $**1.6 million dollars** was audited, scanned and deposited into an authorized bank account established by the City. Now, all money received is scanned and deposited on a weekly basis.

    b. DNA Section – A secure DNA storage area was built within the Central Evidence & Property Section. All DNA evidence was audited, cataloged and entered into the BEAST Inventory Control System.

    c. Z-Annex Audit – Years ago, Central Evidence & Property established a secondary location to store evidence. The location, known as the Z-Annex, was not compromised by Hurricane Katrina's flood waters. However, none of the evidence was listed in BEAST Inventory Control System. With the assistance of Project Innocence, a total of **7,031** cases involving **26,018** exhibits were audited, cataloged and entered into the BEAST Inventory Control System.

- *Project Bloodwork*: In January 2012, the ISB began working DNA cases on burglaries and other property crimes. Keep in mind that in May 2010, the police department had a backlog of over 800 sexual assault kits that had not been tested. In as little as 18 months, the backlog was cleared and the department was now moving into using DNA evidence for property crimes cases. Clear and compelling research evidence authored by the National Institute of Justice and other authorities demonstrate the power of using DNA collected on property crimes (burglary, auto theft, auto burglary, etc.) to tie career criminals into crime and often times more serious crimes against persons. By adopting this strategy, the NOPD is at the forefront of innovative police departments using this type of evidence to build stronger crime fighting and prosecutorial success.

An inventory of all burglary cases where blood evidence was present identified **285** cases. To date, 101 cases have been delivered to the Louisiana State Police Crime Lab. Project Bloodwork detectives received **93** responses, which produced **88** *profiles* and **68** *CODIS* matches (*Note: "Profile" is the distinctive pattern of DNA restriction fragments or PCR products that can be used to identify, with great certainty, any person, biological sample from a person, or organism from the environment; "CODIS" is an acronym for the Combined DNA Index System*). To date, **29** burglary cases linked through DNA profiling have been cleared by detectives. Unquestionably these cases, and those in the future, will hold accountable criminals who never would have expected to be arrested.

The NOPD and the LSP Crime Lab have an agreement in place to allow the NOPD to forward 10 (ten) Project Bloodwork cases each month which continues today after starting the program in December 2011. It should be noted that the advances made with DNA evidence could not have taken place without the full support of the Louisiana State Police Crime Lab. Through a Cooperative Endeavor Agreement with the Louisiana State Police, two DNA Lab Technician hires were approved for NOPD. These technicians' cost will be paid by the New Orleans Police Department and these employees will receive specialized training provided by the LSP Crime Lab. Once these employees complete their training and certification, they will be assigned to handle NOPD specific cases and eventually transfer over to the new NOPD DNA Lab once completed.

- *Digital Forensics:* For the first time in the NOPD a Digital Forensics Unit was formed in August, 2011. Equipment and training for the unit was provided by the Taylor Foundation. The Taylor Foundation Grant provides $364,000 over a 3 year period.

Presently, the unit is staffed by two detectives. The detectives are cross-trained in four disciplines including; video forensics, audio forensics, cell phone forensics and computer forensics. DFU detectives download and enhance video from surveillance equipment, cell phones and various recording devices. DFU detectives also download data from cell phones, data may include, videos, contacts, photos, phone records and internet history.

To date, **108** cell phones have been delivered to DFU for forensic examination. Of those, **60** have been completed with tangible evidence returned to the case detective. Moreover, **15** computers have been delivered to DFU for forensic analysis. Of those, **6** have been completed with evidence returned to the case detectives.

- ***Omega Crime View***: Upon assuming command in May 2010, the Superintendent immediately recognized a need to improve and expand upon the *COMSTAT* model that this agency began using in October 1996. Tremendous advancements in crime mapping have occurred over the previous decade which now provides the means to meld resource deployment, crime fighting, and community policing efforts into one comprehensive analytical approach. Critical funding was identified and the *Omega Crime View* software package was acquired. After completing the extensive development and design that went into this project, NOPD began using *Omega* mapping in late 2011 in support of its new *COMSTAT* model and has expanded use of the *Omega* application to direct enforcement activities with pin-point accuracy on crime hotspots (*see '**Data Driven Policing'**). This has resulted in the crime analyst function required to develop skills, knowledge and abilities to enhance mapping techniques, such as *"Hot Spot"* mapping, and to support *COMSTAT*, community policing and DDACTS/DDVCTS efforts.

The new *COMSTAT* model utilizing the *Omega Crime View* technology has also provided greater accountability in performance measurements for command staff and supervisors, including platoon commanders and Community Coordinating Sergeants (Co-Co's) making them accountable for implementing crime fighting initiatives, community-policing strategies and other community outreach programs.

Additionally, the need for community access to timely crime information being reported in neighborhoods was recognized. The *Omega Crime View* mapping technology, which has been available on the '*nola.gov*' website since May 20, 2011, allows this agency to offer a broad range of current crime analysis data to the public and provides a sophisticated search capability that allows the user the option to narrow the focus of their inquiry to a specific address or neighborhood. It was a critical step forward in the NOPD's advancement of transparency to utilize the Crime View software so that citizens of New Orleans could have timely and reliable data. This was a third step in enhanced transparency, the first two being the opening of Departmental Comstat and District Based Comstat meetings to the public in June of 2010.

- *Data-Driven Policing ("DDACTS & DDVCTS Models"):* With the advanced mapping and crime analytic capabilities offered by *Omega Crime View*, NOPD now has the unparalleled ability to use laser-like focus to fight both major and minor crimes within our community. Instead of using manpower over broad areas of random coverage, we now have the computer intelligence and knowledge to narrowly spotlight street level targets, often no larger than four to five square blocks.

At the heart of this approach are two somewhat related, yet, distinctively different methodologies. First, *Data-Driven Approaches to Crime and Traffic Safety* (*DDACTS*) is a law enforcement operational model supported by a partnership among the Department of Transportation's National Highway Traffic Safety Administration and two agencies of the Department of Justice: the Bureau of Justice Assistance and the National Institute of Justice.

DDACTS integrates location-based crime and traffic crash data to assist in determining the most effective methods for deploying law enforcement and other resources, as well as holding District Commands accountable for their actions. Unlike previous iterations of the NOPD *COMSTAT* model that only used the Uniform Crime Report Part I Index crimes (murder, rape, aggravated assault, burglary, theft and auto theft), the new *DDACTS* strategy incorporates numerous UCR Part II crimes (drugs, trespassing, disorder crimes, etc.) so that the NOPD is now focusing on ALL crime, disorder and traffic related issues in a neighborhood. This more broad understanding of crime and disorder is a key component of the NOPD's commitment to community policing as stated in the 65 point plan preamble, "The New Orleans Police Department will no longer tell neighborhoods what their problems are; instead, the NOPD will listen, collaborate and respond proactively." *DDACTS* embodies this philosophic belief by adding to our crime analysis and response strategies all the crimes that occur in a neighborhood, and NOT only those crimes thought critical by the NOPD's old way of analyzing crime focusing on UCR Part I crimes exclusively. Drawing on the deterrent value of highly visible traffic enforcement and the knowledge that crimes often involve motor vehicles, the goal of *DDACTS* is to reduce crime, crashes, and traffic violations across the city. There is a growing body of evidence that "place based" policing is the most likely success strategy for many reasons, not the least of which is decreasing capacity of cities and towns to employee the number of officers desired.

1St District DDACTS

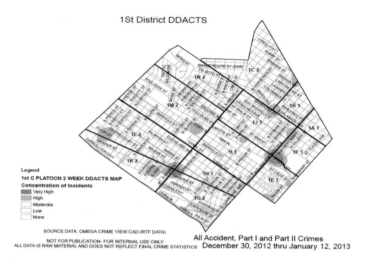

Legend
1st C PLATOON 2 WEEK DDACTS MAP
Concentration of Incidents
- Very High
- High
- Moderate
- Low
- None

SOURCE DATA: OMEGA CRIME VIEW CAD (RTF DATA)
NOT FOR PUBLICATION- FOR INTERNAL USE ONLY
ALL DATA IS RAW MATERIAL AND DOES NOT REFLECT FINAL CRIME STATISTICS

All Accident, Part I and Part II Crimes
December 30, 2012 thru January 12, 2013

The second method of advanced geo-based crime plotting and analysis involves *Data-Driven Violent Crime Trend Strategy*, or **DDVCTS** mapping. In this approach, developed internally by the NOPD crime analysis team, offenses involving homicides, shootings, drugs and gun arrests are carefully charted and linked through analysis allowing for proactive policing efforts to be laser focused in addressing violent crime. *DDVCTS* mapping defines specific geographic areas that are linked in time and place by the events themselves and, as with the traffic safety model, *DDVCTS* maps are updated and published every two weeks to provide managers with reliable information to optimize use of police resources.

5th District D.D.V.C.T.

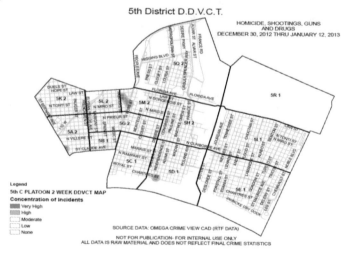

HOMICIDE, SHOOTINGS, GUNS
AND DRUGS
DECEMBER 30, 2012 THRU JANUARY 12, 2013

Legend
5th C PLATOON 2 WEEK DDVCT MAP
Concentration of Incidents
- Very High
- High
- Moderate
- Low
- None

SOURCE DATA: OMEGA CRIME VIEW CAD (RTF DATA)
NOT FOR PUBLICATION- FOR INTERNAL USE ONLY
ALL DATA IS RAW MATERIAL AND DOES NOT REFLECT FINAL CRIME STATISTICS

Cities that have added these new concepts into their arsenal of crime fighting tactics have seen a reduction in the number of crimes committed. The Metropolitan Nashville Police Department was one of the first major police agencies to embrace this innovative data-driven policing approach. After employing *DDACTS* strategies, the communities served by this agency saw not only a decrease in the number of total crashes occurring, but also witnessed a decline in the number of burglaries, robberies, and auto thefts being reported. The *DDACTS* strategy employed by the Nashville police has been credited in assisting in reducing crime over many years in that community.

Here in New Orleans, 2012 was the first full year of deploying *DDACTS* and *DDVCTS* as part of the weekly *COMSTAT* accountability meeting. After the first full year, 2012, the NOPD recorded a 3% reduction in murders, a 16% reduction in rapes, an 8% reduction in armed robbery, an 11% reduction in burglaries and a nearly 13% reduction in auto thefts compared to 2011. As is expected in using *DDACTS* and *DDVCTS*, it is specifically the more efficient use of advanced technologies with the relentless follow up of *COMSTAT* that allows for declining crime while simultaneously sustaining a net loss of 86 police officers in 2012.

In November 2012, a Multi-Agency Gang Unit ("*MAGU*") was formed between NOPD and its local, State and Federal criminal justice partners. *DDVCTS* maps are a key instrument being used by this task force to focus in on violent crime, which we believe was partially responsible for the decrease in the number of serious offenses recorded during the latter part of 2012.

Use of the *DDACTS* and *DDVCTS* models have not only provided the ability to better align our deployment strategies, but have also offered a means to monitor, measure and verify the results of our enforcement efforts. This narrowly focused 'hot spot' approach affords this agency the opportunity to better manage our limited resources and provide a police presence in those areas of the City needing it most.

- **Computerized Case Management System**: The New Orleans Police Department's Computerized Case Management System was implemented in 2010. It is designed to deploy a core criminal investigation case management tool allowing detectives to generate cases, manage case assignments, and track cases within a comprehensive and consolidated solution. It allows for data sharing with appropriate permissions. For arrest cases, it also provides for a more concise and organized reporting venue to the District Attorney's Office, i.e. "*Zip & Ship*" resulting in an increase in successful prosecutions and conviction rates.

13

COMMUNITY OUTREACH & TRANSPARENCY

- *Community Coordinating Sergeants ("CoCo's"):* One of the most notable projects included under the Superintendent's '*65 Point Plan'* was the establishment of Community Coordinating Sergeants (CoCo) in August of 2010. These supervisors are responsible for developing and maintaining extended relationships between citizens, businesses, neighborhood associations and the spiritual community. As these CoCo's educate, communicate and interact with the community, they become an integral part of reducing crime and elevating the overall quality of life. Thanks to a partnership created with Loyola University Professor Dr. Michael Cowan, CoCo Sergeants have received in monthly meetings best practice training in Problem Oriented Policing, Crime Analysis and Crime Prevention through Environmental Design and Neighborhood Watch development helping them to advance their ability to effectively serve.

  Since their inception, CoCo Sergeants have now led over **2,500** meetings throughout the City with over **45,000** persons in attendance. In addition, CoCo Sergeants have played an integral role in successful summer crime initiatives addressing over **14,000** New Orleanians on safety and crime prevention.

  The *CrimeStoppers* program has continued to experience an increase in tips received, with 2012 up more than **25%** over 2011, and 2011 totals up **11%** over 2010. It is likely that one of the reasons behind these significant increases is related to the efforts being made by CoCo Sergeants in fostering community relationships which have resulted in a renewed sense of confidence between citizens and police.

- *Police-Community Advisory Board ("PCAB"):* In February 2011, a proposal was submitted to the Mayor's Office for consideration to create a Police-Community Advisory Board composed of a cross section of community members, advocacy groups and religious leaders to liaison with NOPD. The Police-Community Advisory Board concept and protocol was developed in cooperation with the Department of Justice's Community Relation Service. The purpose of PCAB is to provide input and assist the department with identifying and resolving community issues or concerns. The goal of the NOPD proposal was to create and bring together a diverse group of community and neighborhood representatives that could educate and inform the department about the challenging issues and concerns within specific areas of the City. Police-Community Advisory Boards have now been formed across all of this agency's eight police districts.

- ***El Protector Program:*** In recognition of the City's growing and vibrant Latino and Vietnamese communities, the El Protector Program was introduced to the New Orleans Police Department on January 5, 2011. The program is specifically geared towards improving and enhancing the relationship between the New Orleans Police Department and these limited English proficient (*"LEP"*) communities. Of particular concern was establishing a basis of trust so that these community members felt comfortable reporting crime and utilizing the services of the NOPD. This task is accomplished in a number of ways, including having an official on-call police interpreter, developing Neighborhood Watch Programs with direct participation of both Spanish and Vietnamese speaking officers, and various other outreach programs to targeting these communities. An additional benefit to this program has been the opportunity it has provided towards educating NOPD members about the Latino and Vietnamese cultures.

- ***Office of the Independent Police Monitor:*** In 2010, a cooperative effort between the New Orleans Police Department and the Office of the Independent Police Monitor culminated with the historic signing of the first ever *'Memorandum of Understanding'* between these two agencies. This unprecedented agreement provided independent open access and oversight to the inner workings behind NOPD's internal disciplinary process.

- ***Corona Deploy:*** Also in 2010, a need to restructure the deployment of police resources in concert with community needs and crime trends was recognized. The decades old approach of manpower deployment to the eight patrol districts City-wide was not an efficient or effective utilization of agency resources. Funding was secured to purchase Corona Deploy, a *state-of-the-art* software program which provides for scientific and data based deployment of police officers.

  This software allows users to accurately mine millions of pieces of data and then analyze current use and performance of patrol resources in order to achieve the most efficient and effective match of patrol resources to a known and predicable demand. Resource deployment based on this analysis provides patrol officers across all districts a balanced workload and ensures that citizens City-wide receive an equal distribution of available resources based on demonstrated need.

  After complete analysis of three years of data, and combined with limited changes in patrol district boundaries, in January 2012, patrol resources were redeployed to achieve the balanced and equal workload as identified by the new software. Within each district, officers were assigned to particular shifts based on a time of need analysis provided by the software and within each shift the number of officers allowed off each day was also based a day of week analysis of identified workload. This also allows for better supervision and evaluation of officers because it eliminates disparity in expected workload.

This software was also used to estimate what the desired NOPD personnel strength level ideally would be. After analyzing over 30 million pieces of data, considering the demands of our tourist center(s), detectives, and required support personnel, for the first time the NOPD was able to document and support a minimal ideal staffing level of 1,575 commissioned (police officer through superintendent) officer positions.

- **Bicycle Patrols:** In late 2011 and into 2012, forty-five (45) police bicycles were purchased to enhance the New Orleans Police Departments community policing strategy. Bicycle patrols remove the officer from vehicles and place them in direct contact with the community. They have proven to be very successful as a fundamental practice of building community relations and fostering positive partnerships with residents and businesses.

- **Mounted Patrols:** Effective July 2010, Special Operations Division Mounted Patrol Officers were assigned under the 8th District Commander to streamline and make accountable this resource to the area of the City where it has historically performed the majority of its duties. In addition, the remaining Commanders were afforded the flexibility of cross training officers under their command for mounted patrols which could be deployed at their discretion during '*Mission II*' assignments in Police Districts across the City. Like bicycle patrols, these Mounted Officers provide our Commanders with a valuable resource that provides high visibility and close contact with the community.

- **Alternative Police Response Unit ("APRU"):** The Alternative Police Response Unit was created in December of 2012. The units function is to enhance the level of emergency police services available in the community by handling low priority calls, not requiring the physical presence of an officer, by telephone. By processing these calls in such a manner, the department will be able to increase officer and citizen safety by utilizing field resources to handle higher priority "emergency" and "immediate action" calls.

  Additionally, the APR Unit is tasked with calling complainants on calls holding for more than thirty minutes (when possible). This provides the most up-to-date information about the call, along with letting the citizen know their call is being monitored while waiting for a police response.

INTEGRITY & ACCOUNTABILITY

- *New Leadership:* In 2010, Deputy Superintendent Arlinda P. Westbrook Esq. was selected by Superintendent Serpas to serve as the first civilian director of the Public Integrity Bureau (i.e., Internal Affairs). Since that time, the Public Integrity Bureau has been reengineered and refocused with emphasis on increasing the efficiency and effectiveness of the Bureau's ability to receive, classify, investigate, and track incoming complaints. In addition, the Bureau has increased its ability to effectively supervise and manage the behaviors of officers, including applying new thresholds for identifying and responding to problematic behaviors as early as possible.

- *Disciplinary Reform:* In September 2010, the Superintendent imposed the strict penalty of presumptive termination, without progressive discipline, for sustained complaints against any officer found lying to investigators; or for knowingly filing a false or inaccurate report. To date, nine (**9**) members of the department have been terminated for untruthfulness. Additionally, a new 'Failure to Report Misconduct' policy was implemented requiring department employees who observe or become aware of any act of misconduct by another employee to report the incident to an immediate supervisor. Disciplinary controls were also tightened for interfering with any administrative or criminal investigation.

  PIB was subsequently charged with the renewed focus and aggressiveness for conducting timely investigations into allegations of administrative and criminal wrongdoing made against NOPD members. At the urging of the Superintendent, two Special Agents from the New Orleans FBI Field Office were assigned to PIB for the purpose of assisting our investigators in their targeted effort to root out corruption as well as identify and investigate any civil rights violations by members of the NOPD. Over the past thirty-two months, targeted investigations into administrative and criminal misconduct have yielded the following:

  - ➤ **29** arrests – May to December 2010
  - ➤ **11** arrests – January to December 2011
  - ➤ **12** arrests – January to December 2012

  52 *Total Arrests*

17

Additionally, PIB investigations have yielded a total of **458** disciplinary actions from May 2010 through December 2012 ranging from officers receiving a letter of reprimand to termination.

> ➤ *Year 2010* **– 132 Total Disciplinary Actions**
>   **94** – Suspensions
>   **34** – Letters of Reprimand
>   **4** – Dismissals

> ➤ *Year 2011* **– 205 Total Disciplinary Actions**
>   **149** – Suspensions
>   **44** – Letters of Reprimand
>   **12** – Dismissals

> ➤ *Year 2012* **– 121 Total Disciplinary Actions**
>   **90** – Suspensions
>   **21** – Letters of Reprimand
>   **10** – Dismissals

Since May 2010, the Public Integrity Bureau has reported a steady decrease in the number of citizen and rank initiated complaints against NOPD officers. This downward trend seems encouraging given that the Independent Police Monitor is also structured to accept and forward to PIB complaints of misconduct involving NOPD officers, as well as other governmental agencies (DA's Office, US Attorney, FBI, etc.). In comparing full year 2011 to 2010, overall complaints of employee misconduct were down **13.8%**. In comparing full year 2012 to 2011, overall complaints of employee misconduct were down **16.1%**. This steady decrease, we feel, is directly attributable to a combination of integrity checks and an increase in training related to professionalism (e.g., annual In-Service Training, PPEP training, Leadership in Police Organization training, etc.). The reduction in complaints and disciplinary actions allows additional resources to focus on more serious allegations of misconduct.

• ***Complaint Intake***: PIB's in-house directives regarding complaint intake and classification have been revised in a direct effort to provide more efficient and effective service to the community. Complaint classification protocols have been implemented that are allegation driven rather than anticipated outcome based in determining how a complaint is to be investigated. As a result, PIB has been able to more efficiently triage and route complaints from the intake phase to an investigatory phase.

- **Force Investigation Team:** In February 2012, the New Orleans Police Department formally created and staffed the Force Investigation Team within the Public Integrity Bureau. This team is staffed by (1) lieutenant, (5) sergeants, and (1) officer, all experienced veterans from within the department with extensive investigative experience. In 2012, Captain Chris Pitcher, a FIT specialist with the Los Angeles Police Department, provided a 40-hour specialized training course to NOPD FIT investigators with specific emphasis placed on the handling of officer involved shootings. FIT's investigative responsibilities currently include:

  a. Firearm discharges by law enforcement officer(s) in Orleans Parish resulting in injury or death to a suspect, civilian, or the injury or death of a law enforcement officer(s) while acting under "Color Of Law" while on duty or off duty;

  b. "Custodial Deaths" - any death while in the immediate custody of any member of the NOPD, to include death resulting from a Taser deployment;

  c. Use of physical force exhibited by an officer that results in the suspect receiving great bodily harm and is hospitalized, and;

  d. Firearm discharges whether injury or death does not result.

  In addition to the above, FIT is also responsible for ensuring use of force incidents involving police personnel are consistent with departmental policy and procedures, as well as in compliance with State and Federal laws.

- **Early Warning System:** PIB has developed an increased use of technology, such as the IAPro Internal Affairs database and other back up technology, to track and maintain data to identify and manage potential problematic officer behaviors which require intervention. The IAPro database allows the department to streamline data collection and provide timely statistical reports regarding assigned cases and officer behavior patterns. Officers who exhibit certain behavior patterns are flagged and selected for active intervention including training and job performance improvement planning. PIB had dedicated a full time sergeant and police officer to serve as program coordinator and information technology specialist, respectively, to facilitate any statistical reports necessary in these areas.

The IAPro[1] system is now used to electronically manage and track all complaints received. The system calculates the amount of complaints by an officer using a pre-determined formula. Once a threshold is reached, warning flags are raised indicating an officer may be exhibiting problematic performance.

To address behavioral issues involving its members, the department conducted a comprehensive analysis of the NOPD's existing but infrequently used Professional Performance Enhancement Program ("PPEP"). In May 2011, a panel under the direction of Deputy Superintendent Westbrook, consisting of a psychiatrist, physiologist, university professors, academy staff members, attorneys, and subject matter experts met to develop new training curriculum and lesson plans for PPEP. Originally, officers with professionalism complaints were required to attend one 8-hour Professionalism and Courtesy Training Session. However, based on this panel's recommendation, professionalism and courtesy training was expanded to a more comprehensive 40 hour training program designed to focus on the specific deficiencies of individual officers selected for the PPEP program. The revised program includes training on the following topics: complaint avoidance; cultural diversity; ethics; citizen complaint procedures; Federal & State laws; police policies & procedures; racial profiling/bias-free policing; and stress management. Following a summary of PPEP classes conducted since program redevelopment:

> **2011**: Two 40-hour sessions   / **23** officers required to participate
> **2012**: Seven 40-hour sessions   / **96** officers required to participate

- *Integrity Assurance Controls – Sting Audits*: Prior to 2010, the PIB's Special Investigation Section focused on routine quality assurance checks to monitor an officer's performance in accordance with policy. However, after May of 2010, the Superintendent directed that the efforts of the Special Investigation Section be redirected to root out high level corruption within the department.

The Special Investigation Section began conducting directed sting audits (integrity checks), utilizing confidential informants, and special surveillance equipment, with emphasis on checks that were complaint and intelligence based, as well as, sting operations targeting officers and districts where complaints and misconduct trends, such as theft, excessive force, sick abuse, and Workman's Compensation fraud had been alleged or identified. Many of directed sting audits spawned administrative and criminal investigations which resulted disciplinary action.

---

[1] The IAPro software package was purchased by the New Orleans Inspector General and donated to the NOPD as well as coordinated with the Independent Police Monitor. The IAPro software assist in managing case loads and fundamental assessment of early warning items to assist in identifying officers who may need additional supervision, training or discipline.

Furthering their efforts, the Special Investigation Section was enhanced with additional staff and outside investigative support increasing resources and investigative capabilities. Investigative resources, which include confidential informants and specialized surveillance equipment, are now routinely being used by investigators. Since May of 2010, the Special Investigation Section has performed nearly **500** integrity checks. This focus on integrity has also allowed the unit to promptly address anonymous allegations of misconduct where immediate surveillance is required. Following is a breakdown of sting audits conducted over the past 32 months:

> ➢ **2010 - 13** Audits Conducted
> ➢ **2011 - 243** Audits Conducted
> ➢ **2012 - 240** Audits Conducted

- ***Technology & Accountability:*** Since May of 2010, the NOPD began expanding its use of Mobile Video Units ("MVU's") to document officer/citizen interaction, especially during traffic incidents and pedestrian contacts. All previously installed MVU's have been upgraded to 2nd generation software & hardware to advance latest equipment capabilities. Over 200 marked patrol units and task force vehicles have now been outfitted with MVU's with plans to expand use of this equipment to include marked and unmarked vehicles assigned to the Special Operations Division, all Canine Units and prisoners transport wagons. By repurposing old grants, and requesting new grants, much if not all of the cost for these upgrades have been supported by grant funds.

   Also in the summer of 2010, NOPD began using Automatic Vehicle Locator ("AVL's") technology in its patrol fleet. This feature captures the locations of patrol vehicles and provides supervisors with an important tool needed for ensuring accountability related to most effective and efficient use of our patrol resource. For the first time the NOPD utilized the "historical" data collection feature of the AVL software so that when necessary investigators can review past records of vehicle usage and locations of patrol.

- **Compliance Measures:** Faced with concerns about accuracy of crime reports, particularly '*UCR Part 1*' major crimes, the Superintendent implemented controls designed to measure the effectiveness and accuracy of police services being provided to the community. In June 2010, the **Superintendent's Office of Compliance** began conducting random telephone (recorded) surveys to gauge the citizen satisfaction with police service. The procedure was expanded later this same year to include involvement of NOPD's **Integrity Control Officers** using a similar approach. The survey procedure is based on random selection[2] of '*UCR Part 1 & Part II*' crimes and consists of seven questions, beginning with the accuracy of the report narrative, if there is any additional information the complainant would like added to the case, followed by questions regarding the reporting officer's courtesy, professionalism, knowledge, and ends with a question regarding a rating of the service provided by the NOPD. In each of these audit checks, supervisors check that the report was classified appropriately after confirming the accuracy of the complainant's statement to the report filed by the officer(s). If there is error, these supervisors immediately take steps to correct the reports as required.

In September of 2010, an additional component to measure compliance accuracy was incorporated into this plan requiring **District Platoon Lieutenants** to conduct on-site visits to measure officer performance and accountability in services being provided by our members.

Between June 13, 2010 through December 29, 2012, **1,712** random Citizen Satisfaction Surveys have completed by the Superintendent's Office of Compliance, with victims reporting a **99.8 %** accuracy of the report narrative. Additionally, **91.4 %** of the surveyed victims have responded positively regarding the officer's behavior, appearance knowledge, courtesy and overall satisfaction with service provided. Similar results have been recorded in surveys performed by our Integrity Control Officers. Results of the surveys are regularly reported back to the officers, and their supervisors, whose reports were the subject of the survey to provide necessary feedback.

In addition to these steps, the Office of Compliance has also randomly reviewed, between June 2010 and December 2012, a total of **6,971** reports of all types to ensure accuracy and compliance with NOPD Policy. Taken together, the NOPD has audited **8,683** police actions since the summer of 2010. The following pages provide a snapshot of survey and on-site visits results of over **6,500** follow ups conducted by the Superintendent's Office of Compliance, Integrity Control Officers and Platoon Lieutenants that began in 2010:

---

[2] The NOPD sought advice on creating this random sample method from the Office of Inspector General

OFFICE OF COMPLIANCE Citizen Call Back Survey Results - (06.13.2010 -12.29.2012)

	Q1	Q1a	Q2	Q3	Q4	Q5	Q6	Q7	Response Comparison
Yes	1,709	365		Question 1 -Yes		99%	Question 1a -Yes		23%
No	3	1,230		Question 1 -No		1%	Question 1a -No		77%
Strongly Agree			785	785	759	697	551		42%
Agree			790	798	816	848	719		46%
Neutral			120	115	119	155	233		9%
Disagree			13	11	10	12	183		3%
Strongly Disagree			4	1	2	2	35		1%
Very Satisfactory								704	41%
Satisfactory								760	44%
Neutral								181	11%
Unsatisfactory								45	3%
Very Unsatisfactory								23	1%
Totals	1,712	1,595	1,712	1,712	1,712	1,712	1,712	1,712	

Below is the procedure and questions for conducting an ICO Citizen Telephone Survey.

Q1. The interviewer will review the statement verbatim in the narrative of the report and solicit a response from the Victim as to whether or not the statement describes what occurred. **Yes / No**

Q1a. "Thank you for your answer. After hearing what your statement was recorded as, is there any further information you want to add at this time?" **Yes /No**

Q2. The responding officer(s) was courteous.
Strongly Agree / Agree / Neutral / Disagree / Strongly Disagree

Q3. The responding officer(s) appeared professional.
Strongly Agree / Agree / Neutral / Disagree / Strongly Disagree

Q4. The responding officer(s) conducted his / her duties in a professional manner.
Strongly Agree / Agree / Neutral / Disagree / Strongly Disagree

Q5. The officer(s) appeared knowledgeable about law enforcement.
Strongly Agree / Agree / Neutral / Disagree / Strongly Disagree

Q6. I am satisfied with the follow-up assistance provided to me by the NOPD regarding this incident.
Strongly Agree / Agree / Neutral / Disagree / Strongly Disagree

Q7. I would rate the quality of service provided to me by NOPD as:
Very Satisfactory / Satisfactory / Neutral / Unsatisfactory / Very Unsatisfactory

OFFICE OF COMPLIANCE CITIZEN TELEPHONE SURVEY PERCENTAGE COMPARISON

	Q1	Q1a	Q2	Q3	Q4	Q5	Q6	Q7
Yes	99.82%	22.88%						
No	0.18%	77.12%						
Strongly Agree			45.85%	45.85%	44.33%	40.17%	32.18%	
Agree			46.14%	46.61%	47.66%	49.53%	42.00%	
Neutral			7.01%	6.72%	6.95%	9.05%	13.61%	
Disagree			0.76%	0.64%	0.93%	0.70%	10.69%	
Strongly Disagree			0.23%	0.06%	0.12%	0.12%	2.04%	
Very Satisfactory								41.12%
Satisfactory								44.39%
Neutral								10.57%
Unsatisfactory								2.63%
Very Unsatisfactory								1.34%
TOTAL FEEDBACK RESPONSE (Q-2,3,4,5,7)	POSITIVE 90.44%			NEUTRAL 8.06%			NEGATIVE 1.51%	

23

ICO Citizen Call Back Survey Results - (09.01.2010 -12.31.2012)

	Q1	Q1a	Q2	Q3	Q4	Q5	Q6	Q7	Response Comparison
Yes	390	135		Question 1 -Yes		96%	Question 1a -Yes		33%
No	18	270		Question 1 -No		4%	Question 1a -No		67%
Strongly Agree			294	292	293	266	190		65%
Agree			100	100	119	119	103		26%
Neutral			4	4	13	13	91		6%
Disagree			7	7	3	3	14		2%
Strongly Disagree			1	1	2	2	4		0%
Very Satisfactory								263	65%
Satisfactory								116	29%
Neutral								13	3%
Unsatisfactory								8	2%
Very Unsatisfactory								3	1%
Totals	408	405	406	404	430	403	402	403	

Below is the procedure and questions for conducting an ICO Citizen Telephone Survey.

Q1. The interviewer will review the statement verbatim in the narrative of the report and solicit a response from the Victim as to whether or not the statement describes what occurred. **Yes / No**

Q1a. "Thank you for your answer. After hearing what your statement was recorded as, is there any further information you want to add at this time?" **Yes /No**

Q2. The responding officer(s) was courteous.
Strongly Agree / Agree / Neutral / Disagree / Strongly Disagree

Q3. The responding officer(s) appeared professional.
Strongly Agree / Agree / Neutral / Disagree / Strongly Disagree

Q4. The responding officer(s) conducted his / her duties in a professional manner.
Strongly Agree / Agree / Neutral / Disagree / Strongly Disagree

Q5. The officer(s) appeared knowledgeable about law enforcement.
Strongly Agree / Agree / Neutral / Disagree / Strongly Disagree

Q6. I am satisfied with the follow-up assistance provided to me by the NOPD regarding this incident.
Strongly Agree / Agree / Neutral / Disagree / Strongly Disagree

Q7. I would rate the quality of service provided to me by NOPD as:
Very Satisfactory / Satisfactory / Neutral / Unsatisfactory / Very Unsatisfactory

ICO CITIZEN TELEPHONE SURVEY PERCENTAGE COMPARISON

	Q1	Q1a	Q2	Q3	Q4	Q5	Q6	Q7	
Yes	95.59%	33.33%							
No	4.41%	66.67%							
Strongly Agree			72.41%	72.28%	68.14%	66.00%	47.26%		
Agree			24.63%	24.75%	27.67%	29.53%	25.62%		
Neutral			0.99%	0.99%	3.02%	3.23%	22.64%		
Disagree			1.72%	1.73%	0.70%	0.74%	3.48%		
Strongly Disagree			0.25%	0.25%	0.47%	0.50%	1.00%		
Very Satisfactory								65.26%	
Satisfactory								28.78%	
Neutral								3.23%	
Unsatisfactory								1.99%	
Very Unsatisfactory								0.74%	
TOTAL FEEDBACK RESPONSE (Q-2,3,4,5,7)		POSITIVE 95.89%			NEUTRAL 2.30%		NEGATIVE 1.81%		

Platoon Lieutenant Scene Visits - (09.01.2010 -12.31.2012)

	Q1	Q2	Q3	Q4	Q5	Incident Assessment	Response Comparison
Strongly Agree	1,852	1,851	2,811	2,604			57%
Agree	2,092	2,111	1,144	1,220			41%
Neutral	39	37	45	137			2%
Disagree	39	22	30	25			1%
Strongly Disagree	5	7	10	5			0%
Very Satisfactory					2,744		68%
Satisfactory					1,096		27%
Neutral					82		2%
Unsatisfactory					51		1%
Very Unsatisfactory					68		2%
Totals	4,028	4,028	4,040	3.991	4.041		

INCIDENT ASSESSMENT: *Was the incident marked up correctly?*		
Yes	4,372	99%
No	36	1%
Totals	4,408	

Below are the questions for conducting a Platoon Lieutenant Scene Visit:

Q1. The responding officer(s) was courteous.
Strongly Agree / Agree / Neutral / Disagree / Strongly Disagree

Q2. The responding officer(s) appeared professional.
Strongly Agree / Agree / Neutral / Disagree / Strongly Disagree

Q3. The responding officer(s) conducted his / her duties in a professional manner.
Strongly Agree / Agree / Neutral / Disagree / Strongly Disagree

Q4. The officer(s) appeared knowledgeable about law enforcement.
Strongly Agree / Agree / Neutral / Disagree / Strongly Disagree

Q5. I would rate the quality of service provided to me by NOPD as:
Very Satisfactory / Satisfactory / Neutral / Unsatisfactory / Very Unsatisfactory

INCIDENT ASSESSMENT: Was the incident marked up correctly?
Yes / No

PLATOON LIEUTENANT SCENE VISITS PERCENTAGE COMPARISON

	Q1	Q2	Q3	Q4	Q5	
Strongly Agree	46.00%	45.95%	69.58%	65.25%		
Agree	51.94%	52.41%	28.32%	30.57%		
Neutral	0.97%	0.92%	1.11%	3.43%		
Disagree	0.97%	0.55%	0.74%	0.63%		
Strongly Disagree	0.12%	0.17%	0.25%	0.13%		
Very Satisfactory					67.90%	
Satisfactory					27.12%	
Neutral					2.03%	
Unsatisfactory					1.26%	
Very Unsatisfactory					1.68%	
		POSITIVE 96.25%		NEUTRAL 2.19%	NEGATIVE 1.57%	

HIRING, TRAINING & LABOR RELATIONS

- **Hiring Standards:** Working collaboratively with Civil Service, hiring standards for Recruit candidates was raised in the fall of 2010 requiring a minimum 60 college credit hours and/or consideration based on prior military service. The hiring of new officers is one of the most critical actions of a police department. This raising of hiring standards was a significant step forward in NOPD efforts to aggressively seek out only the very best applicants, and only offer employment to those candidates that meet the highest standards of education, experience and potential success as a Police Officer.

  Training Reforms: In May 2010, the need to increase training was immediately recognized and addressed. One of the Superintendent's first initiatives was to reinstate a minimum 40-hour annual requirement of in-service training for all officers beginning in 2011.

  Additionally, the Academy Staff was tasked with the challenge of increasing professional training to NOPD members through outside resources, such as the type of support which has now been provided by the International Association of Chiefs of Police ("*IACP*"). In 2012, the IACP's '*Leadership in Police Organizations*' training, which is a 120-hour course of instruction that is designed to provide supervisors and managers the advanced skills necessary to become a successful leader was delivered. This training, which utilizes many of the ideas used by the U.S. Military's West Point Academy, has now been provided to **100** NOPD supervisors from the rank of Sergeant and above. The NOPD will identify 14 "train the trainer" candidates from this pool of 100 leaders so that the NOPD can deliver the LPO training to the remaining 200 NOPD leaders, and eventually to all police officers within the department. In 2010, additional supervisory training was presented through support received from the Louisiana Army National Guard ("*LANG*"). LANG provided **258** NOPD supervisors with a 40-hour course of instruction in both '*Basic Leadership*' and '*Advanced Leadership*' techniques. Another focus of supervisory instruction completed in 2010 involved two separate law enforcement training courses *(Recognizing Racial Profiling and Mediation Skills)* presented by the DOJ Community Relations Service. In total, over **180** NOPD mid to upper level managers participated in almost 1,700 hours of this targeted profiling and mediation training.

  Other sources of outside training assistance have been expanded to include the involvement of the DOJ COPS Office, the U.S. Attorney's Office, the Orleans Parish District Attorney's Office and the Louisiana Commission on Law Enforcement.

As evidenced by the following diagram, the increase to the total hours of training provided to NOPD personnel since May 2010 has been dramatic:

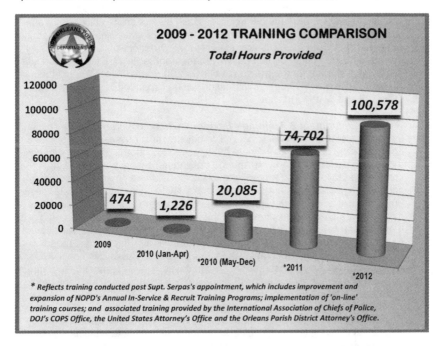

2009 - 2012 TRAINING COMPARISON
Total Hours Provided

* *Reflects training conducted post Supt. Serpas's appointment, which includes improvement and expansion of NOPD's Annual In-Service & Recruit Training Programs; implementation of 'on-line' training courses; and associated training provided by the International Association of Chiefs of Police, DOJ's COPS Office, the United States Attorney's Office and the Orleans Parish District Attorney's Office.*

- **Recruit Training Program:** In May 2011, the Department of Justice's Office of Community Oriented Policing Services ("*COPS*") accepted an invitation by the Superintendent to conduct an on-site review of the NOPD Recruit Training Program. The COPS Technical Assistance Team's review was designed to provide a comprehensive assessment of 'best practices' training standards in support of Academy services. Several of recommendations made by COPS related to the number of hours of training being provided under specific course topic areas have been incorporated into the NOPD Recruit Training Program.

- **In-Service Training Program:** Prior to 2011, NOPD annual In Service Training was 20-25 hours annual, with some of those hours being voluntary. Beginning in January 2011, In-Service Training became a mandatory 40 hour program, and the curriculum is set annually by a group of NOPD training experts. In January 2012, the NOPD's annual In-Service Training Program was, for the first time, divided into two separate tracks of training, one targeting police officers and second addressing supervisors. Curricula and lesson plans were revised to match the unique differences between those performing routine police functions and those responsible for managing outcome and performance.

- ***Police Officer II, III & IV Training:*** The NOPD had not promoted any Police Officer II, III or IV candidates since December 2009. This in-rank training and promotional system (with a 5% pay raise for each step) is a critical tool to advance officers knowledge and morale. Each rank of police officer requires successfully completing a 40 hour specific training program and having a positive work record. Working closely with the Fraternal Order of Police, the NOPD for the first time created an on-line delivery format for the Police Officer II curricula in 2012 which allowed for the promotion of over 200 Police Officer II candidates in November. In the 2013 year, this training will be expanded to include Police Officer III and IV opportunities.

- ***Policy Development & Training - Lexipol:*** In order to deliver quality service to the citizens of this community, our police officers must possess a clear understanding of the tasks they are being asked to perform, guidance on how they are to perform those tasks and the training necessary to succeed in completing those tasks. Recognizing this, a decision was made to conduct a comprehensive analysis of the existing policy NOPD manual and update these procedures in accordance with 'best practice' standards. In order to complete this project, funding was secured and the professional policy development firm 'Lexipol' was selected to assist. In January 2012, NOPD began its transition of its entire Operations and Policy manual to the Lexipol policy manual model with the project scheduled for completion in July of 2013. The revision of NOPD's operations manual will ensures that our employees have the most up to date and current policies at their fingertips to advance their professionalism, confidence, morale and service.

An added benefit to the Lexipol model includes a 21st century electronic policy manual delivery system that uses adult learning principles to educate employees versus memorization. A critical element of the process is the Daily Training Bulletin ("DTB") and testing feature, which provides six minute per day DTB's with a corresponding test that all officers must successfully pass. These training bulletins cover critical policies and reinforce understanding of how to apply those policies. Because the DTB process is timely and dynamic, the DTB's can be tailored to address specific issues as needed. Additionally, the Lexipol service provides for monitoring compliance with the DTB schedule and keeps electronic files of employee participation in DTB and copies of every version of the NOPD operations manual.

Effective August 2012, all commissioned officers as well as active reserve officers have been required to participate and successfully complete 20 DTB's each month. This new training and testing process provides an additional 24 hours of training for each officer each year.

- **Labor Initiatives:** In 2010, the Superintendent and Deputy Superintendents began holding regularly meetings with the leaders from the Fraternal Order of Police (FOP), Black Organization of Police (BOP) and Police Association of New Orleans (PANO). Working together with labor allows for the on-going assessment and requisite realignment of resources and directives, which enhances policy and procedure.

  In addition to meeting with the leaders of the main labor organizations, the Superintendent has expanded contact with other rank and file members through a program referred to as '*Coffee with the Chief.*' On a regular basis, members of the department are randomly selected to meet with the Superintendent and are encouraged to openly discuss any concerns they have regarding departmental operations. Maintaining this open dialogue approach has provided tremendous insight into day to day issues effecting the men and women of the NOPD.

  Another effort designed to seek input from rank and file members of the department was the establishment of an "In Touch" anonymous communication system which began in the summer of 2010. This system allows employees to communicate directly with the Superintendent. To date, more than **900** messages have been received via 'TELLNOPD@getintouch.com' service. This modern day "suggestion" box provides an outstanding opportunity to communicate messages, ideas, etc. This system is designed for use by NOPD employees only. InTouch system messages are routed directly to the Superintendent and are completely anonymous.

- **Evaluation Reform & Performance Initiatives:** Improving performance requires effective analysis. To that end, the Superintendent continues to be a leading proponent of Civil Service and employee evaluation reform and has worked closely with City officials, Civil Service and NOPD's rank and file members in an effort to overhaul the department's outdated employee assessment system. A proposed new system would provide a new focus on customer service (internally and externally to the department), community policing and general employee behaviors. A new feature that will be added is a 360-degree evaluation process in which feedback between the employee and his/her supervisor includes assessments from both the employee's peers and also the employee's subordinates. The purpose of the new Performance Appraisal System, including the 360-degree evaluations, is designed to provide a holistic model for improving individual performance and improving the overall functioning of the New Orleans Police Department.

  On September 12, 2010, a written policy describing NOPD's Job Performance Improvement Plan was implemented. This managerial tool is designed to assist an employee with improving their performance and defines clear criteria and expectations of employee behavior. The plan offers clear objectives and establishes a timeline for improvement. Failure of an employee to successfully complete the terms and conditions of JPIP will be grounds for corrective and/or disciplinary action.

In December 2010, the Superintendent implemented a new written transfer/selection process procedure based on '*knowledge, skills and ability*' criteria. A predetermined set of measures provides a detailed list of objective criteria to be used in the selection process. Available openings are sent out to all employees and a list of openings is also published on the NOPD website with information on how to apply. Applicants are then evaluated and selected through a committee process. The standards are defined so an applicant knows what the assessment panel may consider in their review of the applicant.

CONTINUING THE REFORM MOVEMENT

The 65 point plan released by the Superintendent in August 2010 was appropriately labeled as *'the first steps'* for rebuilding the New Orleans Police Department. The recommendations listed under this plan were the initial reform measures needed to begin our journey in restoring integrity to the department and regaining public confidence.

On March 16th, 2011, the DOJ released an investigative *'Findings Report'* into NOPD operations. That same day, the City's Mayor and its Police Superintendent began plans to target each of the **16** global policy reform recommendations contained in the DOJ study. Within these recommendations were **147** action items which needed to be individually addressed. Since that time, we have not relented in our efforts to tackle the requirements listed at the end of this report and, by June 2012, the City and NOPD had implemented measures addressing over **40%** of these items.

	Global Reform Recommendations:	Total # of Action Items:	Completed	In-Progress	Pending	Disagree	$ Funding
1	Use of Force	20	4	16	0	0	0
2	Stops, Searches, and Arrests	6	0	6	0	0	1
3	Discriminatory Policing on the Basis of Race, Ethnicity, and LGBT Status	5	3	2	0	0	0
4	Services for Limited English Proficient Communities	4	1	2	1	0	0
5	Sexual Assault Investigations	9	7	1	0	1	0
6	Domestic Violence Investigations	5	4	1	0	0	1
7	Recruitment	9	6	1	1	1	1
8	Training	19	9	8	2	0	2
9	Supervision	9	4	5	0	0	1
10	Paid Details	6	6	0	0	0	0
11	Performance Evaluations and Promotions	7	1	6	0	0	0
12	Misconduct Complaint Intake, Investigation, and Adjudication	20	3	16	0	1	0
13	Community Policing	10	5	5	0	0	0
14	Officer Assistance and Support	4	1	3	0	0	0
15	Interrogations	10	3	7	0	0	0
16	Community Oversight	4	3	1	0	0	0
	TOTALS =	147	60	80	4	3	

$ Funding Required = 6

With the submission of the Consent Decree in July 2012, the matrix listed above has been discontinued and expanded to now include the specific 400 plus action items the NOPD will undertake. This matrix served as a guideline pending the submission of the Consent Decree itself. The Consent Decree released in July 2012 offers a broad range of remedies designed to produce sustainable reform within the New Orleans Police Department. These remedies are addressed under seventeen primary categories, which include: 1) Policies & Training; 2) Use of Force; 3) Crisis Intervention; 4) Stops, Searches & Arrests; 5) Custodial Interrogations; 6) Photographic Line-Ups; 7) Bias-Free Policing; 8) Policing Free of Gender Bias; 9) Community Engagement; 10) Recruitment; 11) Academy & In-Service Training; 12) Officer Assistance & Support; 13) Performance Evaluations & Promotions; 14) Supervision; 15) Secondary Employment; 16) Misconduct Complaint Intake, Investigation & Adjudication; and 17) Transparency & Oversight. As evidence throughout this Reform Status Report, many of the reforms initiated in 2010 parallel and predate the same key issues that were addressed in both the DOJ Findings Report and the final Consent Decree.

While issues affecting a proposed Consent Decree between the City of New Orleans and the U.S. Department of Justice remain in question, Mayor Landrieu and Superintendent Serpas are dedicated, and have demonstrated the commitment as noted in this report, to moving forward with all of the reform measures specified under this Agreement. Regularly monthly meetings are now being held between the Mayor and top administration officials to strategically plan for the full implementation of lasting reforms designed to guarantee constitutional policing to all citizens of this community.

Appendix C

324 Second Street, SE
Washington, DC 20003
405.286.6500
www.wparesearch.com

NOCC_CITIZEN SATISFACTION SURVEY_SPRING 2014_MQ_140321.DOCX
ADULTS
MARCH 18-20, 2014

SAMPLE:
n=600 Adults (n=75 per district)
NO CODE/ASK ALL QUESTIONS/NOTE DIFFERENCES IN QUESTION BY SAMPLE SPECIFICATION

INTRODUCTION: Good evening. My name is _____ and I'm calling from Wilson Perkins Allen Opinion
Research, a national public opinion firm. This evening we're conducting a short scientific survey about issues facing
the City of New Orleans and we'd like to get your opinions. All of your responses will remain completely confidential
and you will not be identified by name or by telephone number in any reports of this information. DO NOT PAUSE

1. First, are you or any member of your immediate family, such as your spouse, parents or children, a member
    of the news media, or a Public Relations company, a police officer, or an employee of the City of New
    Orleans?

    IF YES, ASK:
    Are you an employee of the City of New Orleans?

    1. Yes, not New Orleans employee.. TERMINATE
    2. Yes, New Orleans employee 8%
    3. No/All other 92%

2. And in what year were you born? TERMINATE IF UNDER 18, RECODE INTO AGE CATEGORIES

    1. Under 18 ask for member of household over 18................................GO TO Q1
    2. 18-24 ....16%
    3. 25-34 ....20%
    4. 35-44 ....16%
    5. 45-54 ....19%
    6. 55-64 ....15%
    7. 65-74 ....8%
    8. 75+..7%
    9. DK / Refused..TERMINATE

3. And have you ever been convicted of a felony or been imprisoned for committing a felony?

    1. Yes .... TERMINATE
    2. No/All other 100%

298   *Appendix C*

4.   Now, thinking about the police department here in New Orleans, would you say that you are ROTATE
     satisfied or unsatisfied END ROTATION with the New Orleans Police Department overall?

IF SATISFIED/UNSATISFIED, ASK:
And would you say you are VERY (satisfied/unsatisfied) or just SOMEWHAT (satisfied/unsatisfied)?

		Aug '09	Aug '10	Feb '11	Aug '11	Feb '12	Aug '12	March '13	Aug '13	March '14
	TOTAL SATISFIED	33%	50%	60%	47%	61%	56%	58%	58%	60%
	TOTAL UNSATISFIED	60%	42%	34%	46%	33%	35%	33%	36%	30%
1.	Very Satisfied	9%	16%	18%	14%	21%	17%	23%	21%	22%
2.	Somewhat Satisfied	24%	34%	42%	32%	40%	39%	35%	36%	38%
3.	Neither Satisfied nor Unsatisfied DNR	5%	4%	6%	6%	5%	9%	8%	4%	8%
4.	Somewhat Unsatisfied	28%	15%	14%	19%	15%	17%	16%	15%	15%
5.	Very Unsatisfied	32%	27%	20%	27%	18%	18%	18%	22%	15%
6.	Don't Know/Refused DNR	2%	3%	<1%	2%	1%	<1%	1%	2%	2%

5.   And thinking about police performance in your neighborhood, would you say that you are ROTATE satisfied or
     unsatisfied END ROTATION with police performance in your neighborhood overall?

IF SATISFIED/UNSATISFIED, ASK:
And would you say you are VERY (satisfied/unsatisfied) or just SOMEWHAT (satisfied/unsatisfied)?

		March '13	Aug '13	March '14
	TOTAL SATISFIED	66%	74%	72%
	TOTAL UNSATISFIED	26%	20%	21%
1.	Very Satisfied	34%	34%	33%
2.	Somewhat Satisfied	32%	39%	39%
3.	Neither Satisfied nor Unsatisfied DNR	6%	4%	5%
4.	Somewhat Unsatisfied	10%	8%	9%
5.	Very Unsatisfied	15%	12%	13%
6.	Don't Know/Refused DNR	--	2%	1%

New Orleans Crime Coalition/Adults/3543/13344 Page 3 of 13

Next I am going to read you some specific aspects of the New Orleans Police Department's job. For each one please tell me whether you are ROTATE satisfied or unsatisfied END ROTATION with the New Orleans Police Department in that area.

IF SATISFIED/UNSATISFIED, ASK:
And, would you say are VERY (satisfied/unsatisfied) or just SOMEWHAT?

The (first/next) one is...RANDOMIZE

		Total Sat	Very Sat 1.	Smwt Sat 2.	Neither Sat nor Unsat DNR 3.	Smwt Unsat 4.	Very Unsat 5.	Total Unsat	DK/ Ref DNR 6.
	Aug '09	33%	7%	26%	2%	26%	37%	63%	1%
	Aug '10	40%	14%	26%	4%	19%	34%	52%	4%
	Feb '11	47%	14%	34%	6%	17%	28%	45%	2%
6. Efforts to address violent crime	Aug '11	50%	12%	38%	3%	16%	28%	44%	3%
	Feb '12	56%	22%	34%	5%	16%	22%	37%	1%
	Aug '12	46%	17%	29%	3%	18%	30%	47%	4%
	March '13	55%	19%	35%	5%	17%	22%	39%	1%
	Aug '13	60%	25%	35%	3%	14%	21%	35%	2%
	March '14	56%	19%	38%	8%	14%	17%	31%	5%
	Aug '09	39%	7%	32%	3%	25%	30%	56%	3%
	Aug '10	51%	17%	34%	8%	14%	24%	38%	3%
	Feb '11	56%	15%	41%	7%	16%	17%	33%	4%
7. Efforts to address crimes against property, like homes and businesses.	Aug '11	52%	17%	35%	6%	17%	22%	39%	3%
	Feb '12	58%	23%	35%	7%	14%	18%	32%	3%
	Aug '12	55%	22%	33%	5%	15%	19%	35%	5%
	March '13	59%	23%	36%	6%	14%	16%	30%	4%
	Aug '13	59%	21%	38%	7%	13%	16%	29%	5%
	March '14	60%	22%	38%	4%	18%	12%	30%	6%
	Aug '09	19%	5%	14%	3%	20%	55%	75%	3%
	Aug '10	27%	9%	18%	6%	16%	47%	63%	5%
	Feb '11	31%	9%	23%	5%	20%	40%	61%	3%
8. Getting drugs off the streets	Aug '11	29%	10%	19%	5%	20%	42%	62%	4%
	Feb '12	33%	11%	22%	8%	17%	37%	54%	5%
	Aug '12	38%	14%	24%	5%	13%	42%	55%	3%
	March '13	42%	18%	24%	4%	18%	34%	52%	2%
	Aug '13	42%	16%	26%	5%	15%	37%	52%	2%
	March '14	44%	11%	33%	5%	13%	35%	48%	4%

300

Appendix C

		Total Sat	Very Sat 1.	Smwt Sat 2.	Neither Sat nor Unsat DNR 3.	Smwt Unsat 4.	Very Unsat 5.	Total Unsat	DK/ Ref DNR 6.
	Aug '09	55%	18%	38%	7%	15%	20%	35%	3%
	Aug '10	56%	22%	34%	7%	13%	21%	34%	3%
	Feb '11	62%	24%	38%	5%	15%	16%	31%	2%
	Aug '11	57%	24%	33%	3%	16%	20%	37%	4%
9. Enforcing traffic laws	Feb '12	63%	29%	34%	6%	13%	16%	28%	2%
	Aug '12	60%	28%	32%	6%	11%	20%	31%	4%
	March '13	57%	27%	30%	6%	17%	16%	34%	3%
	Aug '13	65%	28%	37%	5%	13%	16%	28%	2%
	March '14	64%	27%	37%	5%	12%	16%	28%	2%
	Aug '09	41%	10%	31%	5%	25%	27%	52%	2%
	Aug '10	50%	19%	31%	7%	14%	26%	40%	3%
	Feb '11	65%	22%	43%	4%	13%	14%	28%	3%
10. Cooperating with the public to address their concerns	Aug '11	55%	17%	38%	5%	19%	19%	38%	3%
	Feb '12	61%	26%	35%	6%	13%	17%	30%	3%
	Aug '12	62%	22%	40%	6%	12%	18%	30%	2%
	March '13	63%	25%	38%	8%	11%	17%	28%	1%
	Aug '13	61%	23%	38%	7%	14%	15%	29%	3%
	March '14	65%	21%	44%	5%	14%	15%	28%	2%
	Aug '09	40%	7%	33%	6%	24%	25%	49%	5%
	Aug '10	37%	12%	25%	8%	17%	34%	51%	3%
	Feb '11	45%	12%	33%	7%	24%	22%	46%	2%
11. The honesty and integrity of New Orleans Police officers	Aug '11	37%	11%	26%	5%	24%	32%	56%	3%
	Feb '12	49%	18%	31%	7%	18%	23%	41%	3%
	Aug '12	52%	18%	34%	5%	16%	24%	40%	3%
	March '13	51%	20%	31%	7%	17%	23%	39%	2%
	Aug '13	56%	20%	36%	6%	12%	22%	34%	4%
	March '14	60%	18%	42%	6%	13%	17%	30%	3%

New Orleans Crime Coalition/Adults/3543/13344   Page 5 of 13

		Total Sat	Very Sat 1.	Smwt Sat 2.	Neither Sat nor Unsat DNR 3.	Smwt Unsat 4.	Very Unsat 5.	Total Unsat	DK/ Ref DNR 6.
	Aug '09	49%	10%	39%	5%	22%	21%	44%	3%
	Aug '10	48%	18%	30%	6%	16%	26%	42%	3%
	Feb '11	56%	18%	38%	7%	20%	16%	36%	1%
12. The professionalism of New Orleans Police officers	Aug '11	51%	17%	35%	3%	20%	24%	44%	2%
	Feb '12	61%	24%	37%	5%	16%	16%	32%	2%
	Aug '12	60%	26%	34%	3%	15%	20%	34%	3%
	March '13	61%	23%	39%	9%	11%	17%	28%	1%
	Aug '13	66%	26%	40%	3%	13%	16%	29%	2%
	March '14	68%	24%	43%	7%	10%	14%	24%	2%
	Aug '09	50%	11%	38%	6%	21%	20%	41%	3%
	Aug '10	45%	15%	30%	8%	15%	29%	44%	3%
	Feb '11	58%	17%	41%	6%	16%	17%	33%	3%
13. The general attitude and behavior of officers toward citizens	Aug '11	51%	16%	35%	4%	19%	24%	43%	3%
	Feb '12	57%	21%	36%	5%	15%	19%	34%	4%
	Aug '12	55%	24%	31%	5%	16%	19%	35%	4%
	March '13	58%	22%	36%	10%	15%	17%	32%	1%
	Aug '13	61%	23%	38%	8%	11%	18%	29%	2%
	March '14	60%	23%	36%	9%	13%	14%	26%	5%
	Aug '09	43%	8%	34%	5%	30%	19%	49%	3%
	Aug '10	46%	15%	32%	5%	17%	28%	46%	3%
	Feb '11	54%	14%	40%	6%	22%	17%	39%	1%
14. The overall competence of the New Orleans Police Department	Aug '11	45%	10%	35%	5%	22%	24%	47%	3%
	Feb '12	57%	20%	37%	11%	11%	19%	30%	2%
	Aug '12	55%	21%	34%	4%	17%	22%	38%	2%
	March '13	60%	23%	37%	7%	13%	17%	30%	3%
	Aug '13	60%	20%	40%	6%	13%	17%	30%	3%
	March '14	66%	20%	46%	5%	14%	13%	27%	2%

Now, thinking about your personal safety...

Please tell me if you ROTATE agree or disagree END ROTATION with each of the following statements:

IF AGREE/DISAGREE, ASK:
And, would you say STRONGLY (agree/disagree) or just SOMEWHAT?

The (first/next) one is...RANDOMIZE

			Total Agree	Strongly Agree 1.	Somewhat Agree 2.	Neither Agree / Disagree DNR 3.	Somewhat Disagree 4.	Strongly Disagree 5.	Total Disagree	DK/ Ref DNR 6.
		Aug '09	69%	31%	38%	2%	15%	14%	29%	0%
		Aug '10	76%	49%	27%	1%	8%	15%	23%	<1%
		Feb '11	74%	37%	37%	1%	12%	12%	25%	<1%
		Aug '11	77%	46%	32%	3%	10%	10%	20%	0%
15.	I feel safe in my own neighborhood	Feb '12	81%	53%	29%	1%	6%	11%	17%	<1%
		Aug '12	79%	47%	31%	1%	7%	13%	21%	0%
		March '13	79%	54%	25%	1%	8%	11%	19%	1%
		Aug '13	85%	54%	31%	<1%	9%	5%	14%	0%
		March '14	81%	55%	25%	2%	7%	11%	18%	0%
		Aug '09	34%	6%	28%	7%	29%	29%	58%	1%
		Aug '10	44%	20%	24%	6%	19%	28%	47%	3%
		Feb '11	45%	14%	31%	6%	21%	26%	48%	1%
16.	I feel safe visiting other areas in New Orleans, outside of my own neighborhood	Aug '11	42%	11%	31%	5%	22%	28%	50%	3%
		Feb '12	39%	14%	25%	4%	18%	36%	54%	3%
		Aug '12	51%	15%	36%	5%	18%	25%	44%	1%
		March '13	45%	19%	26%	7%	20%	28%	48%	<1%
		Aug '13	52%	17%	35%	3%	21%	23%	44%	2%
		March '14	42%	17%	25%	5%	25%	27%	51%	2%

17.   Have you or any member of your household been the victim of a crime during the past twelve months?

		Aug '09	Aug '10	Feb '11	Aug '11	Feb '12	Aug '12	March '13	Aug '13	March '14
1.	Yes	14%	12%	11%	14%	12%	12%	10%	9%	10%
2.	No	86%	87%	89%	85%	88%	88%	90%	91%	89%
3.	Don't Know/Refused DNR	<1%	<1%	0%	1%	<1%	0%	<1%	0%	<1%

New Orleans Crime Coalition/Adults/3543/13344   Page 7 of 13

IF Q17:1 ASK:
N=62
18.   Please tell me, specifically, what the crime was. VERBATIM RESPONSES CODED BELOW

		Aug '10	Feb '11	Aug '11	Feb '12	Aug '12	March '13	Aug '13	March '14
	TOTAL VIOLENT CRIME	19%	17%	24%	9%	13%	23%	7%	1%
	TOTAL PROPERTY CRIME	69%	66%	60%	58%	73%	66%	87%	69%
1.	Rape / Sexual assault	0%	1%	0%	0%	0%	0%	34%	0%
2.	Robbery	12%	11%	14%	8%	10%	18%	22%	11%
3.	Aggravated assault	1%	6%	1%	0%	0%	7%	14%	0%
4.	Simple assault	6%	9%	10%	1%	3%	2%	12%	1%
5.	Burglary	14%	11%	17%	18%	41%	36%	7%	26%
6.	Motor vehicle theft	23%	22%	24%	24%	24%	16%	5%	22%
7.	Theft / Larceny	29%	22%	16%	14%	4%	18%	0%	12%
8.	Vandalism	3%	11%	2%	2%	7%	4%	0%	2%
9.	All other crime (specify_____)	5%	5%	11%	28%	11%	10%	5%	27%
10.	DK/ Refused DNR	6%	3%	5%	6%	0%	7%	4%	4%

IF Q17:1 ASK:
N=62
19.   Did the crime occur in New Orleans or Orleans Parish or somewhere else?

		Aug '10	Feb '11	Aug '11	Feb '12	Aug '12	March '13	Aug '13	March '14
1.	New Orleans / Orleans Parish	100%	87%	93%	90%	97%	91%	97%	89%
2.	Somewhere else	0%	13%	7%	10%	3%	9%	1%	7%
3.	DK/ Refused DNR	0%	0%	0%	0%	0%	0%	2%	3%

IF Q19:1 ASK:
N=55
20.   Did the crime occur in your neighborhood?

		March '13	Aug '13	March '14
1.	Yes	78%	78%	91%
2.	No	22%	22%	9%
3.	DK/ Refused DNR	0%	1%	0%

IF Q19:1, ASK:
N=55
21.   And did you report the crime to the New Orleans Police Department?

		Aug '10	Feb '11	Aug '11	Feb '12	Aug '12	March '13	Aug '13	March '14
1.	Yes	79%	82%	84%	78%	92%	75%	87%	91%
2.	No	20%	15%	14%	13%	7%	22%	13%	7%
3.	Don't Know/Refused DNR	2%	0%	2%	8%	0%	3%	0%	1%

New Orleans Crime Coalition/Adults/3543/13344　　　　　Page 8 of 13　　　　　　　　　　WPA

22. Have you had any contact with officers of the New Orleans Police Department in the past 12 months?

		Aug '09	Aug '10	Feb '11	Aug '11	Feb '12	Aug '12	March '13	Aug '13	March '14
1.	Yes	43%	41%	39%	39%	31%	34%	25%	29%	28%
2.	No	57%	59%	60%	61%	69%	66%	75%	71%	71%
3.	Don't Know/Refused DNR	<1%	<1%	<1%	<1%	<1%	0%	<1%	1%	1%

IF Q22:1, ASK
N=170
23. Was this contact initiated by you or by the police officer?

		Aug '09	Aug '10	Feb '11	Aug '11	Feb '12	Aug '12	March '13	Aug '13	March '14
1.	Respondent	55%	54%	52%	58%	57%	56%	52%	65%	65%
2.	Police officer	26%	25%	27%	24%	17%	30%	28%	21%	18%
3.	Both DNR	9%	14%	12%	12%	13%	8%	9%	9%	4%
4.	Neither DNR	9%	6%	5%	6%	10%	5%	9%	3%	6%
5.	Don't Know/Refused DNR	2%	1%	3%	<1%	3%	1%	1%	2%	7%

IF Q22:1, ASK
N=170
24. And what was the immediate result of your contact with the New Orleans Police Officer? RANDOMIZE

		March '13	Aug '13	March '14
1.	Officer wrote a ticket	6%	12%	7%
2.	Officer issued a summons to appear in court	5%	5%	1%
4.	Officer issued a warning	4%	4%	3%
3.	Officer made an arrest	3%	1%	4%
5.	Nothing DNR	63%	63%	65%
6.	Don't Know/Refused DNR	19%	16%	20%

IF Q22:1, ASK
N=170
25. How clearly did the police officer explain the reason for the contact or interaction? Would you say it was explained ROTATE TOP-TO-BOTTOM, BOTTOM-TO-TOP very clearly, somewhat clearly, not that clearly, or not at all clearly?

		March '13	Aug '13	March '14
	TOTAL CLEARLY	61%	70%	51%
	TOTAL NOT CLEARLY	19%	19%	25%
1.	Very Clearly	47%	48%	37%
2.	Somewhat Clearly	15%	22%	14%
3.	Don't Know/Refused DNR	19%	11%	25%
4.	Not that Clearly	6%	2%	15%
5.	Not at all Clearly	14%	17%	10%

IF Q22:1, ASK
N=170

26.   And did the officer explain to you what you had to do once the contact was over?

		March '13	Aug '13	March '14
1.	Yes	55%	66%	54%
2.	No	21%	26%	27%
3.	Don't Know/Refused DNR	24%	8%	20%

IF Q22:1, ASK
N=170

27.   Overall, would you say that you are ROTATE satisfied or unsatisfied END ROTATION with the way the police officer handled your situation?

IF SATISFIED/UNSATISFIED, ASK:
And would you say you are VERY (satisfied/unsatisfied) or just SOMEWHAT (satisfied/unsatisfied)?

		March '13	Aug '13	March '14
	TOTAL SATISFIED	72%	63%	60%
	TOTAL UNSATISFIED	21%	31%	32%
1.	Very Satisfied	45%	42%	46%
2.	Somewhat Satisfied	27%	21%	14%
3.	Neither Satisfied nor Unsatisfied DNR	5%	2%	3%
4.	Somewhat Unsatisfied	6%	8%	4%
5.	Very Unsatisfied	15%	23%	28%
6.	Don't Know/Refused DNR	3%	4%	6%

28.   Have you called or visited any New Orleans City Police Station in the past 12 months?

		Aug '09	Aug '10	Feb '11	Aug '11	Feb '12	Aug '12	March '13	Aug '13	March '14
1.	Yes	22%	21%	17%	16%	13%	13%	12%	8%	8%
2.	No	78%	79%	83%	84%	87%	87%	88%	92%	92%
3.	Don't Know/Refused DNR	<1%	0%	<1%	<1%	0%	0%	<1%	<1%	0%

IF Q28:1 ASK:
N=47
29.   Was the police station in your neighborhood?

		March '13	Aug '13	March '14
1.	Yes	51%	54%	78%
2.	No	39%	27%	22%
3.	DK/ Refused DNR	10%	20%	0%

IF YES ON Q17, 22, OR 28, READ INTRO AND THEN ASK Q30-31 AS APPROPRIATE
Now, thinking some more about the contact you have had with the New Orleans police department recently, I am going to read you each of the ways you said you have been in contact with the department one at a time. For each one I would like you to tell me about the attitude and courtesy of the New Orleans police Department employee you had contact with.

As I read each one, please tell me if you recall that New Orleans police department employee as being ROTATE pleasant and courteous or rude and unpleasant END ROTATION.

IF PLEASANT/UNPLEASANT, ASK:
And would you say that person was VERY (pleasant and courteous/rude and unpleasant) or just SOMEWHAT?

The (first/next) one is...RANDOMIZE

		Total Pleasant	Very Pleasant 1.	Somewhat Pleasant 2.	Neither /Neutral DNR 3.	Somewhat Unpleasant 4.	Very Unpleasant 5.	Total Unpleasant	DK/ Ref DNR 6.
	Aug '09	53%	27%	26%	15%	9%	16%	25%	7%
	Aug '10	75%	52%	24%	6%	6%	9%	15%	3%
IF Q17:1 OR 22:1, ASK N=196	Feb '11	77%	44%	32%	4%	7%	8%	15%	4%
30. Officers of the New Orleans Police Department you met outside of a police station	Aug '11	77%	48%	29%	6%	4%	9%	13%	4%
	Feb '12	71%	46%	25%	9%	4%	9%	14%	5%
	Aug '12	80%	51%	30%	6%	4%	4%	8%	6%
	March '13	74%	51%	24%	11%	2%	6%	8%	6%
	Aug '13	72%	41%	31%	6%	7%	11%	18%	4%
	March '14	68%	44%	24%	10%	12%	3%	15%	7%
	Aug '09	77%	41%	36%	8%	9%	2%	11%	4%
	Aug '10	51%	28%	23%	20%	8%	12%	20%	8%
IF Q28:1, ASK N=47	Feb '11	71%	38%	33%	5%	6%	7%	13%	11%
31. Employees at New Orleans Police Stations	Aug '11	72%	46%	25%	6%	7%	5%	13%	10%
	Feb '12	57%	38%	19%	19%	6%	8%	13%	10%
	Aug '12	59%	42%	17%	12%	9%	6%	15%	14%
	March '13	62%	43%	20%	12%	5%	15%	19%	6%
	Aug '13	80%	52%	28%	11%	2%	2%	4%	6%
	March '14	63%	39%	24%	5%	11%	10%	22%	10%

Now, thinking about a local crime-reducing effort...

32.　Would you say you are ROTATE familiar or unfamiliar END ROTATION with Crimestoppers, the citizen-run anonymous tip line that offers cash rewards for information about felony crimes?

IF FAMILIAR/UNFAMILIAR, ASK:
And would you say you are VERY (familiar/unfamiliar) or just SOMEWHAT (familiar/unfamiliar)?

		Aug '12	March '13	Aug '13	March '14
	TOTAL FAMILIAR	88%	79%	84%	85%
	TOTAL UNFAMILIAR	10%	17%	14%	13%
1.	Very Familiar	45%	47%	44%	39%
2.	Somewhat Familiar	42%	32%	39%	45%
3.	Never Heard of DNR	2%	3%	2%	1%
4.	DK/Refused DNR	0%	1%	1%	1%
5.	Somewhat Unfamiliar	6%	8%	6%	4%
6.	Very Unfamiliar	5%	9%	8%	9%

IF Q32=1-2, ASK:
N=507
33.　If you had information about a felony crime, would you call Crimestoppers to anonymously share what you knew with law enforcement?

IF YES/ NO, ASK:
And, would you say you DEFINITELY (would/would not) call or PROBABLY (would/would not) call Crimestoppers?

		Aug '12	March '13	Aug '13	March '14
	TOTAL WOULD	90%	90%	91%	88%
	TOTAL WOULD NOT	6%	7%	4%	10%
1.	Definitely Would	82%	79%	74%	73%
2.	Probably Would	8%	10%	17%	15%
3.	DK/Refused DNR	4%	4%	4%	2%
4.	Probably Would Not	2%	4%	4%	7%
5.	Definitely Would Not	4%	3%	1%	3%

308

Now, just a few more questions for statistical purposes...

34. What is the highest level of formal education you have completed?

1.	Less than high school graduate	11%
2.	High school graduate	30%
3.	Some College	28%
4.	College graduate	19%
5.	Post graduate	11%
6.	DK/Refused DNR	2%

35. What is your race?

1.	White	34%
2.	Hispanic, Mexican, Latino, Spanish	5%
3.	African-American	56%
4.	Asian	3%
5.	Other (specify) _____	1%
6.	Refused DNR	1%

36. How long have you been a resident of New Orleans?

1.	Less than 1 year	<1%
2.	1 to 4 years	4%
3.	5 to 9 years	3%
4.	10 to 15 years	10%
5.	More than 15 years	80%
6.	DK/ Refused DNR	3%

37. Do you own or manage a business in New Orleans?   IF YES SPECIFY OWN/MANAGE

1.	Yes, own	11%
2.	Yes, manage	4%
3.	DK / Refused DNR	1%
4.	No	83%

38.   Sex: BY OBSERVATION

    1.   Male   48%

    2.   Female   52%

39.   Police District: PRE-CODE

    1.   District 1   9%

    2.   District 2   19%

    3.   District 3   17%

    4.   District 4   15%

    5.   District 5   8%

    6.   District 6   11%

    7.   District 7   16%

    8.   District 8   4%

Index